ALSO BY ROBERT H. PATTON

The Pattons: A Personal History of an American Family

Up, Down & Sideways

Life Between Wars

Patriot Pirates

Patriot Pirates

THE PRIVATEER WAR FOR FREEDOM AND FORTUNE IN THE AMERICAN REVOLUTION

ROBERT H. PATTON

PANTHEON BOOKS · NEW YORK

Pantheon Books and colophon are registered trademarks
of Random House, Inc.

Library of Congress Cataloging-in-Publication Data
Patton, Robert H. (Robert Holbrook), [date]
Patriot pirates : the privateer war for freedom and fortune
in the American Revolution / Robert H. Patton.
p.   cm.
Includes bibliographical references and index.
ISBN: 978-0-375-42284-3
1. United States—History—Revolution, 1775–1783—Naval
operations.   2. Privateering—United States—History—18th century
3. Franklin, Benjamin, 1706–1790.   4. United States—Foreign
relations—France.   5. France—Foreign relations—United
States.   I. Title
E271.P27 2008
973.3'5—dc22   2007033612

www.pantheonbooks.com
Printed in the United States of America
First Edition
2 4 6 8 9 7 5 3 1

for Vicki, of course

and for the memory of my father,
George S. Patton IV

The New Englanders are fitting out light vessels of war, by which it is hoped we shall not only clear the seas and bays here of everything below the size of a ship of war, but that they will visit the coasts of Europe and distress the British trade in every part of the world. The adventurous genius and intrepidity of those people is amazing.

—Thomas Jefferson, July 1775

It is prudent not to put virtue to too serious a test. I would use American virtue as sparingly as possible lest we wear it out.

—John Adams, in support of Congressional approval of independent privateers, October 1775

Contents

Illustrations

Beset by a sudden squall in April 1775, a small British sloop, "very much torn to pieces by the gale of wind," ducked into the sheltered bay off Beverly, Massachusetts, sometime after dark. It proved a false refuge, for the next morning two fishermen armed with pistols rowed out from the town wharf and claimed the beleaguered vessel as a war prize. After its crew of five men and two women surrendered without protest, the event went down as Beverly's first capture of enemy loot—a single barrel each of flour, tobacco, rum, and pork.

Citizens excitedly kept watch on the bay in anticipation of more prey. Their vigilance was rewarded when His Majesty's ship *Nautilus* ran aground while pursuing *Hannah*, an armed schooner recently commissioned by George Washington to hijack enemy transports supplying British troops in Boston, twenty-five miles south.

People flocked to the beach and began shooting at the stranded warship "very badly many times" with household muskets and a motley battery of antiquated cannon. "'Tis luck they fired so high," *Nautilus*'s captain wrote afterward. Even so, one of his seamen lost a leg in the barrage and another was killed before the vessel rose off the sand on the incoming tide and fled to open water. Ashore, men had body parts "blowed off" by misfires of gunpowder and by accidentally shooting one another.

The mad fervor of the region's saltwater colonials was well known to British authorities. There'd been incidents of government supply crews abandoning ship down one side as marauders in converted fishing boats clambered up the other side wielding clubs and cutlasses. In response, the Royal Navy's commander in Boston, Admiral Samuel Graves, had directed his captains to "burn, sink, and destroy" suspicious vessels and to "lay waste and destroy every town or place from whence pirates are fitted out."

The spiraling violence made everyone cry foul. Americans cursed "Graves and his harpies." The British retorted that "a thief might with as much truth and reason complain of the cruelty of a man who should knock him down for robbing him!"

British leaders told themselves "those vermin" would be easily crushed, "especially when their loose discipline is considered." But an unsigned letter from a naval officer stationed in Boston and published that winter in a London newspaper gave a darker assessment. "They are bold enough to dare and do anything," he wrote of the American sea raiders. "Whatever other vices they may have, cowardice is not one of them."

INTRODUCTION

The American Revolution never impressed me. For one thing, it seemed far surpassed by the Civil War in terms of drama and palpable grit, Currier & Ives compared with Mathew Brady, powdered wigs and tricorner hats compared with the sprawled bodies and forever-young faces of the dead in that road at Antietam.

One of my colonial ancestors, General Hugh Mercer, was mortally wounded at the battle of Princeton in 1777. A famous painting by the Revolutionary War artist John Trumbull depicts Mercer sprawled on the ground parrying a British redcoat's bayonet, yet the work's heroic appeal pales beside the letter composed by my great-great-uncle at a Gettysburg field hospital where he lay dying after Pickett's charge; or beside the chunk of Yankee cannonball that killed his brother, Colonel George S. Patton, at Winchester one year later. Retrieved by a surgeon from Patton's gut, the shrapnel is crescent-shaped and rusted red at its edges, and lies heavy in your hand when you hold it.

Ken Burns's 1990 television documentary, *The Civil War*, blended scholarship and artful detail to make its subject powerfully immediate to millions of viewers, creating through music, images, and lyrical voiceovers a video equivalent of the poignant artifacts passed down from my doomed Rebel forebears. A steady outpour of histories and novels keeps the Civil War current today, as do perennial pageants of battle reenactment, lucrative speculation in its memorabilia, and the war's fundamental relation to African American history and the struggle for civil rights. Small wonder the Revolution can't compete.

The great figures of American independence remain intriguing, of course. Enduring popular interest in the Founding Fathers confirms our desire to view them as human and accessible—as people like us, and yet not. But the proverbial search for an era's characteristic specimens is a tall order when prospecting among such singular men. Put another way, can George Washington possibly have been anything like anyone we know? In photographs of Abraham Lincoln's gaunt face we glimpse the terrible toll of prosecuting a war that took hundreds of thousands of lives. Of Washington, however, we praise his wisdom, vigilance, and modesty, but on a personal level generally recall him as dour and toothless.

The Revolution suffers in the same way. Bunker Hill and Valley Forge seem mere milestones in the march of progress rather than fateful occasions of risk and peril. Joseph Ellis observes, "No event in American history which was so improbable at the time has seemed so inevitable in retrospect as the American Revolution." Conversely, the Union's triumph over the Confederacy never comes across as a foregone conclusion; that sense of precariousness gives its memory lasting vitality. Yorktown occurred almost a century before Appomattox. The added distance dulls the suspense and thus the humanity of the Revolution, allowing us to see it as myth, which is to say, scarcely to see it at all.

This book looks at the Revolution in a way that has brought the subject to new life for me. Maritime privateering—legalized piracy in the shortest of shorthand—engaged multiple areas of Revolutionary life that, examined together, present a colorful and surprisingly broad portrait of the era. Washington, his army stymied in its siege of Boston in 1775, initiated the enterprise offhandedly. "Finding we were not likely to do much in the land way, I fitted out several privateers, or rather armed vessels, in behalf of the Continent."

Offering a percentage of spoils as inducement, the call for citizen sailors to raid British shipping tapped the same vein of self-interest and comradeship that had led the colonies to seek independence in the first place. It attracted a slew of waterfront denizens as varied in seamanship as in motive and whose balance of greed and patriotism tilted from case to case. The emergence from that hodgepodge of some of the most intrepid mariners in American history highlights the strategic element of Revolutionary privateering, for they would spearhead what became a massive seaborne insurgency involving thousands of privately owned warships whose ravages on the enemy dwarfed those of the fledgling United States Navy.

The industry of privateering proved a boon to the battered wartime economy. It supported shipbuilders, service workers, and a complex network of agents and legal officials to adjudicate captured prizes. It sparked wild speculation in purchased shares in privateer ventures, gave sailors a chance to make more money in a month, through crewmen's shares of the loot, than they might otherwise earn in a year, and enabled investors who bankrolled successful voyages to create fortunes that survive to this day.

The financial fluctuation of privateering and other wartime commerce was a social obsession. Suspicious of all centralized authority, whether a king or legislature, the colonists took a similar view of wealthy capitalists, acknowledging their stature while embracing rumors of ill dealing with righteous zeal. Ostentatious success drew particular skepticism, but with inflation soaring due to Congress's reckless printing of money to fund the war, businessmen had little choice but to spend as fast as they could lest their profits depreciate to nothing. It made sense to build mansions, buy fancy goods, and invest in myriad ventures, though doing so frequently prompted, whether whispered in town or declaimed in the halls of Congress, allegations of corruption and treachery.

The vicissitudes of any commercial market were exaggerated in privateering with its violence and uncertainty. The savviest entrepreneurs made it merely one part of their investment portfolio. Some who bet on it heavily wound up among the wealthiest men in America. Others came to regret participating after losing their shirts or their public honor.

It's often overlooked that in the years leading up to 1775 rising anger over Britain's restrictive trade policies coincided with an economic surge in the colonies. Americans were the most prosperous people in the world, and also the lowest taxed. In fiscal terms rebellion was inspired by ambition rather than hardship, by a desire not for financial freedom but for *more* financial freedom. This push for opportunity spurred people's envy of success, their scorn for failure, and their increasingly dubious view of their compatriots' integrity.

The Declaration of Independence may have been an audacious leap of political optimism, but the society from which it sprung was steeped in cynicism. "This corrupt age" was a widespread sentiment echoed by General Nathanael Greene in a 1778 letter urging a cousin to get into trade "on an extensive scale." His reasoning was pragmatic. "Without wealth a man will be of no consequence. Mark my words for it—patriotism and every sacrifice will soon be forgotten." It was ironic advice given Greene's misgivings about the many outside ventures he pursued during the war, including the one that cost him most dearly, "a gamester's hope" as he ruefully put it—privateering.

Its inherent risks, financial and mortal, drastically steepened once the Royal Navy recognized the magnitude of the threat and moved to destroy it. Adapting tactics as ruthless and crafty as those of the colonists, Britain dispatched dozens of warships after the privateers and their partners in nautical daring, the blockade-runners who smuggled arms and contraband across the Atlantic. American losses were huge, but sailors and businessmen deemed the potential payday worth the risk. "One arrival will pay for two, three, or four losses," wrote the Philadelphia financier Robert Morris. "Therefore it's best to keep doing something constantly."

Their aggressive spirit set privateers apart from the Continental Army, which never did much "in the land way" except hold out long enough for France to make up its mind to formalize an alliance with America. Washington, ever the realist, acknowledged early on that his best strategy was "to sink Britain under the disgrace and expense" of slogging through to victory. Simply surviving against the vaunted British military was an amazing feat involving countless small- and large-scale offensive operations to keep the enemy off balance, under strain, and demoralized. But essentially the Continentals won by not losing; or, in the manner of modern guerrilla insurrections, by making the cost of victory too high to seem worth it to a complacent, superior foe. Privateers, on the other hand, carried the war to Britain. Many were plain bandits; some were genuine patriots. Yet whatever their motivation, they panicked the British public, intimidated the merchants, and humiliated the crown.

Privateering had a longstanding tradition. For centuries, governments at war had authority under international law to license independent operators to plunder the shipping of a declared foe. The Continental Congress, in permitting civilians "to cruise on the enemies of these United Colonies," was exercising what it presumed to be its sovereign right. But deeming Congress and thus its edicts to be illegitimate, Parliament passed a "Pirate Act" in 1777 that, in denying privateersmen the legal rights typically granted to prisoners of war, allowed them to be held without trial or prospect of exchange. The controversial bill divided British lawmakers and citizens, many of whom believed it unconstitutional and bound "not only to destroy the liberty of America, but this country likewise." It motivated humanitarian groups in the cause of prison reform and sharpened the split between Britain's hawks and doves, undermining the war effort to the advantage of the American underdogs.

The plight of its captives turned privateering into a political phenomenon as well as a naval and economic one. The issue particularly absorbed Benjamin Franklin. Dispatched to France in 1776 to negotiate a treaty of alliance, he sent aid to jailed privateersmen and arranged for many to escape with the help of sympathetic Britons. But his primary interest was more cunning than altruistic. With Britain and France still outwardly at peace, he encouraged American skippers to sell their British prizes in French ports, a breach of neutrality he knew would infuriate Britain.

The French foreign ministry rebuked Franklin and Silas Deane, a fellow diplomat with many shadowy ties to privateering, for overstepping their authority. But the continued collusion between privateers and French merchants was like a stick beneath a scab, aggravating Britain's relations with its fellow superpower across the Channel. America desperately needed France's military partnership in order to induce Britain to capitulate. Franklin and Deane, concluding that "some accident may probably bring on a war sooner than is desired by either party," used privateering to get the ball rolling.

The Continental Navy, notwithstanding the exploits of John Paul Jones, was a non-factor in determining the war's outcome; much to Jones's outrage, competition from privateering robbed it of the ships and manpower needed to become a decisive force. Privateering's contribution to the eventual victory, though far greater in statistical terms, is difficult to assess, for Britain was a massive sea power able to absorb considerable damage without losing its dominance. But the psychological impact was major.

Newspapers on both sides of the Atlantic carried running accounts of privateer actions that readers followed like standings in a pennant race. The details were lurid, the facts often wrong, but the up-and-down tally of ocean kills and captures generally uplifted Americans and unsettled Britons, who couldn't understand why their naval Goliath couldn't crush those pesky Davids.

In both countries, popular support for the war hinged on perceptions of its progress, and one consistent perception was that the privateers—"rebel pirates" in the British view, "our little cruisers" in the American—were swarming the seas at will. The descriptive term of choice for their depredations was "insult," which in its eighteenth-century usage connoted physical assault as well as social effrontery, the kick in the shin and the thumbing of the nose.

Privateering's undersung role in defeating Britain is one thrust of this book. Close-quarter engagements among little boats on a wide ocean are its central feature; so numerous were these, our capacity for astonishment at the bravery and brutality risks becoming exhausted, like seeing too many cathedrals or beautiful sunsets. But beyond the sea battles, Revolutionary privateering represents a rare historical instance in which the experiences of its participants perfectly coincide with its role in the broader society, for the impetus behind privateering's growth from a New England fad to a transatlantic phenomenon, from small-time to big business, was the same for its lowliest seamen and richest investors: to make money and whip the British besides. That combination of impulses, fortuitous for American independence if not for every American, is my larger subject.

"There is a time for understanding the particular," writes Gordon S. Wood in *The Radicalism of the American Revolution*, "and there is a time for understanding the whole." This book trusts that the particular sometimes reveals the whole. Though no study of Revolutionary privateering could pretend to give a complete picture of that complex era, the enterprise combined service and self-interest in a fluid balance whose shifts and moral accommodations constitute a basic theme of American life both today and in 1776.

As an arm of warfare in a stratified age, many among our most notable patriots considered privateering coarse and demeaning. "No kind of business," one lawmaker complained, "can so effectually tend to the destruction of the morals of people." Its freebooting sailors were praised and scorned in the same breath. Its advocates in Congress were, out of social embarrassment, often ambivalent about their support; and privateering profits, when and if they came, were hushed up by respectable businessmen. Such contradictions are totally recognizable to our modern sensibility and open a window on Revolutionary America, which, for me at least, has long seemed too obscured to care.

Any history that would connect scruffy, illiterate deckhands with such lofty characters as Silas Deane or the talented and naïve General Greene; connect assorted low-level merchants and bureaucrats with such powerful money men as Robert Morris, William Bingham, and the notorious Brown brothers of Providence, Rhode Island; or the urbane Ben Franklin with the cantankerous captains who, despite complaints about prize money and lack of respect, repeatedly took on the Royal Navy as if actually putting the cause before the cash—any history looking to connect such men through the web of privateering ought to take as its starting point an event no less unlikely. So rather than open with an overview of the Revolution's political background or, say, a description of some especially bloody battle, I'll begin in Rhode Island's Narragansett Bay, where His Majesty's eight-gun schooner, *Gaspee*, ran aground on June 9, 1772, eighteen months before the Revolution's most famous act of maritime sabotage, the Boston Tea Party.

The date is interesting because it came twelve years and one day after a passenger ship on a pleasure cruise struck the same sandbar at the same time of evening. Aboard that earlier vessel was twenty-four-year-old John Brown, scion of Providence's wealthiest merchant clan. The incoming tide had lifted Brown's vessel off the shoal seven hours after its grounding, the memory of which, in 1772, would have reminded him that if he wanted to strike the stranded *Gaspee*, the time was now or never.

Patriot Pirates

One

The devil himself has not more cunning than these people.
—*John R. Livingston, New York merchant, on dealing with Rhode Island businessmen in 1776*

Rhode Island deputy governor Darius Sessions might as well have listed John Brown by name when, two months before *Gaspee* ran aground, he warned the governor that "a number of gentlemen of this town" were becoming annoyed with "a schooner which for some time past has cruised in the Narragansett Bay and much disturbed our navigation."

Brown, "a stormy petrel and bold adventurer," was the most prominent of four brothers who'd expanded their late father's Providence-based shipping business into a conglomerate dealing in everything from pig iron to African slaves. Over six feet tall and more than two hundred pounds, his imposing physique was matched by aggressiveness that a year earlier had led him temporarily to quit the family partnership in order to sink all his cash into new ventures, a plan his cautious younger brother, Moses, predicted "will sooner or later lose the whole at one throw."

John's primary venture was, through illicit "navigation," dealing West Indian (Caribbean) molasses to New England rum distillers in defiance of trade laws imposed almost forty years earlier to prevent British sugarcane planters from being undersold by the French and Dutch. Like most Rhode Islanders, he'd never paid heed to the Molasses Act of 1733 or any other of the assorted Navigation Acts restricting, for the benefit of British producers, colonial trade in everything from lumber to wool hats.

Founded as a haven for religious tolerance, the colony had "a reputation for contraband, quirkiness, and eccentricity." Geography abetted its notoriety as a smugglers' paradise. A wedge of coastline without a resource-rich hinterland, its towns dotted like hideouts among the islands and inlets of Narragansett Bay, Rhode Island played a hustler's role in the larger New England economy. Many of its most successful entrepreneurs were middlemen, conveying goods from producer to seller, profiting through markups and by keeping costs, namely customs duties, low. Nothing riled them more than government vigilance in limiting trade.

In neighboring Massachusetts, political protest, though rooted in issues of taxation and government intrusiveness, maintained a veneer of high-toned philosophical argument with Britain's distant rule. Samuel Adams, Boston's most influential revolutionary polemicist at the time, admitted, "I get out of my line when I touch upon commerce." Not so John Brown, whose sense of persecution always centered on money. He'd rarely complained about the Navigation Acts as long as he could dodge them. But after *Gaspee* proved too diligent in its patrol of local waters, Brown and his fellow "gentlemen of this town" petitioned the governor for relief.

Anger over *Gaspee*'s activities was just one example of the rising and often unreasonable antipathy Americans felt for Britain. Everyone knew Rhode Islanders had been sneaking contraband through Narragansett Bay at a ferocious clip for decades; in some years as much as 80 percent of rum exports from the colony's more than thirty distilleries derived from illicit molasses. *Gaspee* was merely fulfilling its duty of putting teeth into long-standing trade laws, but that didn't stop locals from harassing its crewmen when they were in port or from calling its zealous young skipper, Lieutenant William Dudingston, "a hogstealer and a chickenthief."

The problem was, authorities long had turned a blind eye to smuggling rather than disturb the healthy percolation of a colonial economy that was employing half the English merchant fleet in the import of huge quantities of English manufactures, especially high-profit luxury goods such as linen, lace, and housewares (called "conveniences" by increasingly flush American consumers). The "salutary neglect" with which Britain had treated the colonies was defined by this tacit indulgence of unrestrained commerce. Naval interdiction was minimal. Customs officials were absent, corrupt, or powerless. And judicial procedures were so tangled with red tape and tilted with hometown bias as to make prosecution of scofflaws all but impossible.

But the rules had begun to change in 1763 when Britain's national debt soared after the Seven Years' War (called the French and Indian War by Americans). Strapped for money and deeming the bustling colonies as due to start paying their share of the postwar tax burden, the government revamped its trade laws to more effectively extract revenue from America. In the case of the Sugar Act of 1764, the approach was carrot-and-stick. As an incentive toward compliance the duty on foreign molasses was halved; at the same time, customs offices were reopened, the use of search warrants was expanded, and warships were dispatched to monitor coastal approaches.

It was too late. Increasingly regarding themselves as Americans rather than dutiful British subjects, people were loath to give up the commercial freedom their government's former indifference had encouraged. Tariffs that in Parliament's viewpoint were fair and indeed rather mild given America's prosperity were greeted by the colonists as tantamount to demanding that each family's firstborn be consigned to the royal treasury.

Relations turned rancid between merchants and customs officials. Ship seizures doubled between 1771 and 1772. One, *Fortune*, belonged to Jacob Greene & Company of Coventry, Rhode Island. *Gaspee* took it in a typically rough shakedown capped with *Fortune*'s skipper, twenty-three-year-old Rufus Greene, a family cousin, getting his skull cracked under a companionway hatch when he resisted.

Nathanael Greene, Jacob's brother and business partner, railed at the loss of their cargo of rum and sugar. "I have devoted almost the whole of time in devising and carrying into execution measures for the recovery of my property and punishing the offender." He vowed to sue Lieutenant Dudingston; not surprisingly, Rhode Island law accorded merchants extraordinary protections against government overreach. But others in the local business community contemplated a more drastic course.

The seizure of *Fortune* sparked an escalating flurry of charges and countercharges. The first salvo was the mildest. "I have done nothing but what was my duty," responded Dudingston to the accusation that his conduct was, in the words of Rhode Island governor Joseph Wanton, "illegal and unwarrantable." Rhode Island's royal charter conferred autonomy on its General Assembly and its elected governor, surpassing any other American colony. Consequently Wanton's loyalty to the king was by no means a sure thing, a fact known to Admiral John Montagu, commander of the Royal Navy's North American station.

Montagu called the governor's complaint against the lieutenant "insolent" and threatened to hang "as pirates" anyone who obstructed his mission. Wanton retorted that the lieutenant "was a pirate himself," whereupon each referred the matter to his higher-up, Montagu to the secretary of state, Wanton to the General Assembly. There, between the plod of diplomatic communication and a mutual desire to avoid further confrontation, it might have languished until the Greenes sued to regain their property. But two actions by the British brought tensions to a flashpoint.

First, Dudingston sent *Fortune* and its cargo up the coast to the admiralty court in Boston—a violation of Parliamentary law, held dear throughout the colonies, dictating that customs seizures be tried under local (hence favorable) jurisdiction. Dudingston, aware of Rhode Island's rigged legal system, assured the admiral that "the inhabitants of this government" would gladly sacrifice the captured rum "as bait" if guarding it through the course of a long trial kept *Gaspee* in Newport harbor rather than out on patrol. But the move was perfect fodder for political firebrands such as Samuel Adams in their fierce denunciation of Britain's "violent infringement of our rights." Montagu supported his lieutenant, however, and in such rude style it was a personal slap at Rhode Island's proudest men.

He was known to be coarse. (John Adams, shocked by the admiral's public assertion that Mrs. Montagu's backside was "so broad that she and I can't sit in a chariot together," called him, "brutal, hoggish.") Still, the General Assembly was dismayed to read, in letters presented by Wanton, the admiral's utter rejection of any civil authority over his officers. "You have no business with them, and be assured it is not their duty to show you any part of my orders or instructions to them." He warned against sending "the sheriff" on any such "ridiculous errands" as trying to arrest Dudingston. The sheriff he had in mind (Rhode Island had one for every county) was John Brown, elected in 1771.

A few days later a Brown-owned packet (mail) boat heading up the bay defied *Gaspee*'s signal to lower its sails and submit to inspection. The vessel, *Hannah*, tacked across a submerged sandbar to make its getaway (the same one Brown had hit twelve years earlier), traversing shoals that moments later snagged its pursuer. The jubilant crew then mooned the British goodbye, "their faces to the opposite point of the compass from those with whom they were parting." When *Hannah*'s skipper docked at Providence that evening and told his boss about trapping *Gaspee*, Brown launched phase two of his answer to Montagu.

Seven hundred of Providence's four thousand inhabitants were men above age sixteen. They resided with their families in close-set houses or in rooms above their shops along the town waterfront. Drumming a call to arms outside a popular tavern, Brown quickly mustered a band of sixty compatriots to strike a blow against His Majesty's taxman. Eight longboats pushed off shortly after 10 p.m. to row the seven miles to where *Gaspee* lay aground. Two and a half hours later, they closed on their target.

The schooner was seventy feet long with a crew of nineteen, its armament an array of fixed cannon bored for a six-pound ball and small swivel guns used to rake the topsides of enemy vessels with antipersonnel shot. Its low freeboard above the waterline made the vessel vulnerable to boarding, and British lookouts hailed the longboats and warned them to stand off.

Dudingston appeared on deck "in his shirt" carrying a pistol and sword. His demand that the intruders declare themselves was met with a shout. "I am the sheriff of the county of Kent, goddamn you. I have a warrant to apprehend you." Brown was the sheriff of Bristol County. One of his shipmasters, Abraham Whipple, was the sheriff of Kent under whose jurisdiction *Gaspee* now lay. Witnesses later differed as to who gave the shout, though certainly it fit Brown's character to claim authority, valid or not, personally to clap Dudingston in irons.

The longboats pulled fore and aft of the schooner where its carriage guns couldn't aim. The lieutenant discharged his pistol down into the dark before receiving a musket ball in the groin fired by someone below. Raiders swarmed aboard and subdued the crew with barely a fight. Three hours later, Brown, checking around to make sure his men had left behind no evidence of their identity, was nearly struck by spars and rigging that fell to the deck. *Gaspee* had been set afire, probably by tipping over the galley stove and scattering its embers in the hold. Documents had been ransacked, petty valuables stolen, its crew and wounded skipper deposited on shore, where they heard the vessel's powder explode as it burned to the waterline.

The last of the longboats rode the incoming tide northward to Providence, arriving at daybreak. The raiders dispersed, "little conscious of the crime they were committing and the penalty they were incurring." One young man was seen later that day "parading himself with Lieutenant Dudingston's gold laced beaver on his head."

If the raiders were oblivious to the severity of their act, local officials were not. Fearing that Rhode Island's unique freedoms under its charter might be rescinded by a vindictive Parliament, Governor Wanton immediately launched an inquiry involving proclamations, rewards, sworn depositions, and a lot of gaudy outrage at "this daring insult upon authority." At the same time, he and the entire Providence community hindered the process at every turn, converting an obvious case against the attack's ringleaders into a fog of conflicting testimony that implicated many and singled out none.

Like the attack itself, the yearlong inquiry showed how quickly Americans could mobilize into group action in which private interest and anti-British sentiment coincided. After all, these were people who often bitterly feuded. On a broad level, for example, other colonies long had resented Rhode Island's "intent to take an advantage of sister colonies" by violating their collective boycott of certain British goods in protest of the Navigation Acts. In 1770, New York, Philadelphia, and Boston had refused to do business with "parasitical" Rhode Island merchants unless, through compliance, they began sharing the financial hit caused by the boycott. Though these nonimportation agreements eventually broke down due to the colonies' temptation "to turn the self-denial of their neighbors to their own immediate advantage," the mistrust of Rhode Island persisted.

Even so, citizens everywhere were alarmed by rumors that suspects in the *Gaspee* raid might be sent to Britain for trial. In Massachusetts, John Adams decried the inquiry as "the Star Chamber Court, the Court of Inquisition." His cousin Samuel, confronting "such provocation as is now offered to Rhode Island," on the one hand warned of potential "rivers of blood" while on the other urged the colony to do nothing "which may by the invention of our adversaries be construed as even the appearance of acquiescence in so grasping an act of tyranny."

In March 1773 Thomas Jefferson reacted to the ongoing inquiry by calling on the Virginia House of Burgesses to coordinate resistance to British legal encroachment wherever it occurred. "We were all sensible that the most urgent of all measures was that of coming to an understanding with all the other colonies to consider the British claims as a common cause to all, and to produce a unity of action." Committees of correspondence were established throughout the colonies as a result, a major step in the unification of their often contentious constituencies. And all due to actions undertaken by a little-loved colony whose maverick government, a Newport loyalist wrote Montagu one month after the *Gaspee* attack, "bears no resemblance to any other government under the crown of England."

Political disputes within Rhode Island were likewise set aside to present a united front against the *Gaspee* inquiry. In recent years, territorial rivalries had divided the colony as its commercial hub shifted north from Newport at the lower end of Narragansett Bay to Providence, where a sheltered, upriver harbor and proximity to interior Massachusetts and Connecticut had proved a long-term advantage.

The more established Newport featured a blithe, loyalist-leaning aristocracy whose indifference to the anti-British nonimportation agreements had, by association, hurt Providence's reputation in the eyes of other colonies. In 1770, the upstart northern town had scored a coup by outbidding Newport to become the home of Rhode Island College. The move was good for business and, its supporters hoped, would garner "every other public emolument" that accompanies a prestigious place of learning. The political tussle was heated and personal, and tipped in favor of Providence on the basis of "zeal," wrote Moses Brown, expressed in practical terms by construction discounts and free land given the project by his brothers, Nicholas and John.

Yet the Newport–Providence factions joined together to shield the *Gaspee* raiders from justice. The collusion was exemplified by the partnership of Governor Wanton and Lieutenant Governor Sessions, from Newport and Providence respectively, in obstructing the very inquiry they headed. It also figured in the deluge of rebuttal to testimony supplied by Aaron Briggs, an eighteen-year-old indentured servant variously described as "Negro" and "mulatto" who'd been coerced into rowing one of the longboats to the *Gaspee* attack.

Briggs identified John Brown as the shooter of Lieutenant Dudingston. Coupled with statements by British crewmen that the raiders were "well dressed, many of them with ruffled shirts, and appeared as storekeepers, merchants, or masters," the testimony was proof enough for Admiral Montagu. He demanded the arrest of Brown and other "principal inhabitants of the town of Providence."

But then a number of gentlemen, including several from Newport, came forward with sworn assertions of Briggs's "general bad character." This in turn was enough for Wanton, who informed the admiral that on the basis of Briggs's "villainy" his testimony "must wholly be disregarded." In a parting jab disguised as a defense of Sheriffs Brown and Whipple, the governor clucked about British authorities "conspiring in the most horrid manner to charge the officers of state with a crime that the whole world knew they could not possibly be guilty of."

As the inquiry approached its second year, Montagu gave up. His main witness had been labeled a fraud. Multiple townspeople had signed, often with an illiterate X, virtually identical statements claiming "no intimation of an intention to burn the *Gaspee*, nor do I know any person or persons concerned in that transaction, or ever heard who they were." A coordinated, collective amnesia left the Wanton-led investigating commission no choice but to inform royal authorities of "there being no probability of our procuring any further light on the subject."

Admiral Montagu did, however, take pains to help Dudingston survive the fallout of *Gaspee*'s destruction. Undoubtedly harsh in his antismuggling methods, the lieutenant's subsequent travails rather balanced the scale. Forced to plead for his life as he lay bleeding on the deck, he'd offered his bed linens to bind his wound rather than see a colonial surgeon tear his own shirt to make a bandage. When the raiders demanded payment for the seized rum, he promised "whatever reparation law would give" and asked only that his crew not be mistreated.

While recuperating in bed three days later, Dudingston was served legal papers by Sheriff Whipple demanding £300 (roughly $50,000 today) in damages for the Greene family. A local jury convicted him on grounds that his authority to conduct searches pertained only to the "high seas" and not Narragansett Bay. After his lawyer missed the appeal date due to weather "exceeding tempestuous," the order went out for Dudingston's arrest.

In a bit of good fortune, he was in England at the time, facing court-martial for the loss of his ship. Montagu's assertion that he was "a sober, diligent, good officer" helped exonerate the young man, who went on to become an admiral and, as well, the father of a son he named William Montagu Dudingston, in gratitude.

A year before the *Gaspee* raid, a wealthy Newport customs official named Charles Dudley had been beaten by a street mob protesting the arrest of a Connecticut rumrunner. Governor Wanton had investigated the incident and ruled it a random mugging by "drunken sailors and lawless seamen," hence impossible to prosecute. Seeing the *Gaspee* case given an identical whitewash, Dudley sympathized with Dudingston and personally paid the Greenes' £300 award on the lieutenant's behalf.

John Brown, far from exultant over the raid he'd orchestrated, lived in fear of summary arrest throughout the course of the inquiry. Even after it came up empty he kept a low profile, asking his brother Moses to represent the family on Rhode Island's committee of correspondence formed in mid-1773.

Moses possessed little heart for activism. Morose by nature, he tended to question his family's materialistic values whenever tragedy struck one of its members. His wife's death the previous February had seemed a rebuke from heaven, and before the year was out he withdrew from business and politics. Having received comfort during her illness at the meeting house of the Society of Friends, Moses converted from Baptist to Quaker, embracing strictures of nonviolence and neutrality that later clashed with his sympathies for the Revolutionary movement.

No less profoundly for this pillar of Rhode Island mercantilism, his conversion compelled Moses to free his slaves on the basis "that the holding of Negroes in slavery however kindly treated by their masters has a tendency to encourage the iniquitous practice of importing them from their native country and is contrary to that justice, mercy, and humanity enjoined as the duty of every Christian." He set them up with employment, education, land, and money, then lobbied his brothers to abandon the "guinea trade."

Nicholas, the eldest, had lost a fortune bankrolling a voyage several years earlier in which 88 out of 196 slaves had died at sea, most from disease, some at the hands of the crew during an attempted uprising, and the rest from jumping overboard rather than submitting to captivity. Joseph, a technician rather than a speculator, managed the family's iron foundry and spermaceti candle factory, so like Nicholas was content to quit the slave business for practical reasons. Though neither displayed his fervor in the cause of emancipation, Moses wrote that "happily they and I lived to regret" their earlier participation "in that unrighteous traffic." The same couldn't be said of John.

On the contrary, he expanded his participation even after the General Assembly's 1774 ban on bringing slaves into Rhode Island. His way around the law was through the "triangular trade," whereby the proceeds of rum exported to Europe went toward the purchase of African slaves for delivery, via the brutal Middle Passage across the Atlantic, to West Indian markets, where they were exchanged for molasses and sugar to supply distilleries back in New England. It was an efficient, self-perpetuating cycle that required investors to put up money only to fund the initial cargo of rum, and featured a further advantage of keeping actual slaves, with all the squeamish details their traffic involved, far out of sight and mind of Puritan-descended New Englanders.

Moses attributed his brother's slave activities to "love of money and anxiety to acquire it," but they expressed John's philosophy as much as his greed. "As the arch individualist, he was inalterably opposed in principle to any interference by government with so-called free enterprise in business." That same philosophy had motivated his raid on *Gaspee*, though history would judge it much differently.

Chastened by his close brush with the law, John tempered his political passions after 1772 and concentrated on business. But his past caught up with him in April 1775 when he was arrested in Newport by Captain James Wallace of HMS *Rose*, a twenty-four-gun frigate. Popular hatred of Wallace, who was said to erupt in "mad fits" of randomly discharging his cannon into coastal villages, was the best measure of his success against illicit trade, now suppressed to the degree that a majority of Newport businessmen had moved to Providence to pursue prospects further inland. He accused Brown of

John Brown, a hard-nosed businessman, epitomized Rhode Island's reputation for nonconformism and self-interest. His aggressive ventures in cannon-production and private warships furthered the Patriot cause and fattened his wallet, not necessarily in that order. His activities in the African slave trade would fracture his family and forever damage his legacy.

selling flour to colonial militia in Massachusetts. On delivering his prisoner to Admiral Samuel Graves, Montagu's successor at the Royal Navy's Boston headquarters, the charge was expanded to include participation in the *Gaspee* affair.

Moses saved the day. Rushing north to appeal to Graves and the British Army's General Gage, he put his pacifist credentials on the line with a promise that his brother, the renowned rabble-rouser, would personally lobby the Rhode Island government "to adopt a more moderate and conciliatory attitude" toward the crown. In a testament to the commanders' desire to douse further fires of rebellion—three hundred British had fallen in battles at Lexington and Concord a week earlier—Graves and Gage approved John's release on assurances "binding both upon the Browns and the

British officials." And indeed John, who'd wept with dread while in the brig in Boston Harbor, kept his end of the bargain, telling the General Assembly four days later "that it is now in the power of this colony and continent to make such propositions to his Excellency General Gage as will effectively put a stop to any hostilities."

It took him only a month to return to form, however. He filed a court claim for £10,000 against Captain Wallace not on the expectation of winning but rather to counter perceptions that the Browns had gone soft on the British. Moses was furious that the suit violated his promise to military authorities and impugned his reputation for "sincerity and honesty." Unmoved, John shrugged that he was "so clear in opinion that the measures now taking to force America are wrong that it is out of my power to restrain myself from wishing success to the country in which I was born."

His differences with Moses now widened past reconciliation, John renewed ties with his eldest brother. Nicholas combined political gloom ("Divine providence hath left the two countries to be scourges to punish each other for their sins," he wrote) with a cool eye for opportunity. Partnered as Nicholas Brown & Company, the brothers' first project was to supply American troops mustering in Massachusetts.

Beyond arms, uniforms, and blankets, gunpowder was most lacking, its import banned by the British since 1774. On taking command in July 1775, George Washington found the Continental Army, a patchwork of New England militia dug in around 6,500 redcoats in Boston, to be so bereft of powder and lead that "for want of them we really cannot carry on any spirited operation." His infantry had ten shots per man. His artillery feared returning enemy volleys lest it have no ammunition to repel a British breakout.

Advised of the shortages, the recently convened Continental Congress announced an up-front offer of "a generous price" for military goods. Merchants pounced. Beyond imploring them to "not take undue advantage of the distresses of their country so as to exact an unreasonable price," Washington had no choice but to pay what was demanded.

More than 90 percent of the gunpowder used by rebels in the first three years of the war originated abroad. Most of it came through Philadelphia, but with Boston under occupation and New York torn with political strife (two-thirds of its inhabitants were British sympathizers), Providence was in good position to take early advantage. The Browns launched "powder voyages" to Spain, Holland, and France, where suppliers were eager to grab some of the bountiful American trade after decades of control by the mercantile houses of Britain.

The natural dangers of seafaring were compounded by threats of Royal Navy interception. Soon the preference, as in the triangular slave trade, was to make the West Indies the exchange point of American commodities for European munitions. This left the journey's long transatlantic leg to slow, durable, heavy-laden square-riggers rendered immune to British harassment by the sovereign flags they flew and by their neutral destinations, among them Spanish Cuba, St. Eustatius in the Dutch Antilles, and French-owned Martinique. It left the shorter, homeward run to swift American sloops and schooners manned by men with knowledge of coastal waters and the capability, if pressed by British blockaders, of darting into any convenient harbor on the eastern seaboard and hauling their cargoes overland from there.

Military trade was a seller's market in the extreme. Merchants as readily sold "warlike stores" to any other paying customer, usually provincial governments bolstering local defenses or outfitting naval squadrons to patrol their rivers and harbors, as to the Continental Army. Washington's lack of leverage was apparent in one deal with John Brown, whose last-minute retraction of an agreement to deliver fifteen casks of gunpowder was unapologetic. The General Assembly had offered more money, Brown shrugged, hence he "must give them the preference."

The arms business was far from a sure thing, however. Several of the Browns' early voyages "entirely failed," and tactical tips included in their sailing instructions to skippers ("run in by night so as to escape them") clearly came of painful experience. The ability to take risks and absorb losses was a key factor in their company's emergence as an important supplier of powder and weapons.

To ensure its needs took precedence, Congress formed the Secret Committee to begin financing supply expeditions in the fall of 1775. Lacking credit or hard currency, the committee shipped tobacco, indigo, grain, or timber as barter for foreign munitions. Merchants brokered the deals. They used Congress's money to buy export commodities and to hire vessels, captains, and crews. Then they arranged with their foreign contacts to complete the exchange on the other end.

They received commissions on each phase of the transaction—5 percent of the value of the initial cargo, 2.5 percent of its sale price overseas. Congress covered any losses, news of which often came matter-of-factly from merchants with no real stake in the outcome. Reported one firm after spending a $45,000 advance on German arms, "It unfortunately happened that the ship has never been heard of and our agent perished in her. This of course prevented the execution of the contract." The advance wasn't refunded.

It was a lopsided arrangement to say the least. Since merchants worked on commission rather than set fees, there was no incentive to seek cheaper terms; indeed, higher prices meant higher commissions. The availability of items in foreign ports was hard to predict given voyages lasting weeks and months, so dispatching a cargo of tobacco in hopes of converting it to munitions was no assurance that the vessel would return with mortars and firing flints instead of pickles and table linen. And letting merchants, as enticement to participate in the effort, piggyback their private trade aboard vessels bound by contract to make military purchases created an environment vulnerable to manipulation.

Merchants commonly gave their captains shopping lists in which military supplies shared priority with high-demand civilian goods or personal wants such as the "good Florence oil, a chest of claret, and a keg of the best brandy" that Nicholas and John tacked onto a government order for sulphur, guns, and canvas. Initially, no negative stigma attached to these glaring conflicts of interest. It was accepted that capitalism and patriotism went hand in hand. John Brown bragged of unloading on Congress a surplus of candles that had been decaying in storage. He got top price and a commission besides. The army, once the candles were sold in France, got two hundred firearms and three thousand pounds of gunpowder.

But Congress grew impatient with results falling short of promises. Nicholas Brown & Company delivered only nine of thirty-six tons of powder stipulated in contracts worth $44,000, for example. After temporarily forbidding any international ventures not explicitly tied to military procurement, Congress concluded that the economic necessity of open trade outweighed the likelihood of some American goods falling into British hands. Merchants thus were permitted again to make deals in their own interest, meaning munitions, though always desirable, could take second place to whatever foreign products might pull a higher price back home.

"Powder expected to fall soon," ran a typical purchase order. "All kinds of dry goods very high, selling at four times cost in America." The decision? "Would advise you not to be large in powder. Put every shilling you can command in dry goods." The needs of the army, in short, could wait.

Striking liberal arrangements with savvy, experienced businessmen was Congress's best option to supply Washington's troops early in the war. The Secret Committee went on to appoint its own agents to negotiate foreign arms purchases while merchants gladly resumed independent operation. Though government contracts had offered surefire returns, huge markups on private imports were worth the risk of going it alone.

Too, critics had begun to complain about the Secret Committee's operating procedures. A number of its members had received lucrative arms contracts. Willing, Morris & Company, a Philadelphia firm run by the committee chairman, Robert Morris, cleared £12,000 in powder deliveries "without any risk at all," John Adams grumbled. The deal prompted "vitriolic" exchanges among members of Congress "on the general theme of business and patriotism."

As war profits became manifested in business expansion and ever grander lifestyles, resentment increased. Commercial ties to the government invited suspicions of graft and, in a new development, inhibited merchants from obtaining munitions for themselves rather than for their country.

Nicholas Brown & Company began reflecting this altered priority in 1776. The "many accusations" of price gouging ("indecent as well as uncharitable," sniffed John) were followed with charges that when it came to cannon and gunpowder, the company wasn't interested in selling at all, preferring to arm its own vessels rather than supply the army and navy.

The Browns' affronted contention that they were "as deeply engaged in the cause of the United States as any other men on the continent" wasn't the denial it appeared to be. Though still seeking profits through traditional paths, they indeed were withholding munitions in expectation of embarking on an exciting new enterprise. It was the *Gaspee* paradox all over again—in doing for themselves, they were advancing the cause more than anyone could have realized. Begun in Massachusetts and quickly embraced by Providence's wily entrepreneurs, privateering had come to Rhode Island.

1775

Eight weeks after the battles at Lexington and Concord, HMS *Margaretta,* an armed cutter carrying four cannon and 40 crewmen, sailed to Machias, Maine, seeking lumber to fortify the Boston garrison. It was commanded by a Royal Navy midshipman named James Moore. Hoping that news of the recent bloodshed hadn't yet reached this far north, he planned to trade for the lumber with cargo items from two supply ships in convoy with him. Unfortunately villagers had heard rumors of war out of Massachusetts and were disinclined to deal.

To drive home the point they erected in their town green a "liberty pole," a tall pine stripped of all but its top branches that had become a symbol of patriotic solidarity. Moore, a young man clearly on edge, demanded they provide the lumber and chop down the tree or else be shelled by his guns. The strong-arm tactic backfired. Immediately a mob assembled with "fouling pieces, pitchforks, a few scythes, and ten or twelve axes," commandeered one of the British supply ships, *Unity,* and rammed it into *Margaretta.*

Moore shot and killed the first boarder and threw several hand grenades. Hollow shells of cast iron packed with powder and carrying a lighted fuse, they exploded among the Americans "with great effect" but didn't deter the onslaught. Moore and five of his men were hacked to death and *Margaretta* was seized.

The leader of the assault, thirty-one-year-old Jeremiah O'Brien, was awarded *Unity* as a personal prize by the Massachusetts Provincial Congress. He requisitioned *Margaretta*'s guns and set off to hunt supply ships running between Boston and Halifax, Nova Scotia, site of the Royal Navy's North American shipyard. In July he captured an enemy sloop and took it as his next vessel, which he renamed *Machias Liberty*.

He quit the Massachusetts navy to hire out as a civilian skipper in 1777, eventually earning enough money to build a twenty-gun warship in Newburyport. Upon its completion in 1778, he put up a £2,000 bond for a privateer commission (one of more than two hundred issued in Massachusetts that year), recruited a crew of 130, and undertook an expedition to the West Indies. It ended when his bid to pick off a straggler from a convoy en route to New York brought him "within musket shot" of an enemy frigate.

At such close range a privateer had no chance against a frigate's firepower, which could bring a barrage of hurtling metal from up to two dozen twelve-pound cannon mounted along each side. The frigate HMS *Brune*, for instance, once obliterated a twelve-gun privateer with a single broadside. Its captain reported that in trying to treat the many wounded among the American schooner's sixty-one crewmen, his boarding party found the vessel "so much damaged that we hardly had time to get them all on board before she sunk." Similarly, a successful Boston privateer, *Speedwell*, carrying fourteen guns and ninety men, took a frigate's broadside "between wind and water" (the portion of the hull normally below the waterline but exposed to the air if the vessel is heeled over in the wind). The result was that "she immediately foundered, and all her crew (the mate excepted) perished in the accident." O'Brien therefore had little choice but to surrender.

He did time on the prison ship *Jersey* ("dysentery, fever, frenzy, and despair") before being transferred to Britain's Mill Prison. There, according to an account written in 1898, "the special malice of the British government" made him "the object of personal ill-treatment." He escaped two years later, rowed across the English Channel, hopped a French ship to America, and got back to Maine just as hostilities ended. With nothing left of his wartime earnings, he worked as a customs official till his death in 1818.

O'Brien's fame from the Machias attack (which has been called the founding event of the United States Merchant Marine because the ship he rammed into *Margaretta* was an unarmed transport) evidently made him cocky. While still in the Massachusetts service he'd boasted that "I shall not pay any regard" to financial regulations. True to his word, he later was accused of stealing "sundry articles" from captured prizes and docked wages "for that sum as so much unjustly received." Ultimately seizing a dozen prizes as a privateer, he got no complaint from his navy superiors when he jumped to that roguish business. Rather, as a Continental official told John Hancock, "They are glad they've got rid of him."

Two

The first fortunate adventurer will set many more on pushing
their fortunes. Consequences may be very pernicious.
—from notes on the privateering debate in the Maritime
Committee of the Continental Congress, October 1775

B ritish merchants counted on a quick end to the war. Since previous flare-ups and trade interruptions had redounded to their
benefit once relations with America returned to normal, many
began stockpiling desirable European goods in anticipation of
higher prices in the wake of hostilities. Edmund Burke, longtime
Parliamentary critic of George III's colonial policies, noted the dangerous exposure of those "exhausting their capital to the last far-
thing" on the bet of future windfalls, especially if, as he predicted,
the conflict became a protracted struggle whereby the consequences
to Britain "will be gradual and therefore incurable."

The king all but guaranteed that result by opting on a middle
course between reconciling with the rebels and swiftly overwhelming
them. He rejected the eleventh-hour Olive Branch Petition of compromise sent by members of Congress in July 1775, yet he delayed in
mobilizing a decisive military response. Even as battles were fought
and forces added to the American theater, his generals in the field
were told to put out feelers to Revolutionary leaders in search of a
peaceful solution, a tentative approach to warfare that undercut the
resolve of British officers and troops.

Loyalists, standing to lose their homes and livelihoods, were espe-
cially critical of their government's dithering. Fretful editorials in
London newspapers that "the African trade has felt the blow . . . the
West India trade staggers . . . our manufactures begin to feel it . . ."

were mild compared to shrieks of "Where is the boasted navy of our country?" from panicked American Tories.

The panic was shared by officials isolated in colonial ports with only sea routes to supply them. In the summer of 1775 the royal governor of Georgia found that rebel boats had bottled up Savannah harbor with "power to plunder anything that arrives here." He sent an urgent plea to Admiral Graves to send a frigate south to disperse them. The letter was intercepted by colonists who substituted, under the governor's seal, a buoyant fabrication saying that everything was fine. "I now have not any occasion for any vessel of war, and I am clearly of the opinion that His Majesty's service will be better promoted by the absence of any vessels of war in this port."

Not that Graves had any to spare. His fleet was expected to patrol more than a thousand miles of coastline between Canada and Florida with fewer than fifty warships. Ten were assigned to Massachusetts Bay alone, charged with stopping the flow of arms into New England. They were also to escort British transports into Boston, where, hemmed in by the Continental Army, provisions were running critically low; and they were to repel, Graves wrote with irritation, local sea raiders "continually popping out as soon as a merchant ship appears."

Meanwhile the British ground commander, General Gage, demanded that Graves start hijacking colonial trade for foodstuffs of any kind. "The king's troops must be supplied!" Agreeing that "every stratagem must be used," the admiral coerced loyalist ships exporting "bread, beef, peas, oatmeal, and rice" out of New York to change course from Britain to Boston, and he arranged with double-dealing merchants from Newport to "put on the appearance" of seizing their cargoes by force.

Graves was pompous and timid, but even a bold commander couldn't have fulfilled a mission described as "perhaps the most ungracious duty that has ever fallen to the lot of a naval officer." Reports circulated in Britain that "within his own department the admiral is more hated and despised, if possible, than he is by the rebels." He fell into despair as a result. "We are in every way more harassed than if on an enemy's coast. My patience is nearly exhausted."

George Washington monitored Graves's travails through observers posted in whaling dories and from his vantage point on the heights surrounding Boston's central peninsula. Realizing that the redcoats and some one thousand loyalist citizens jammed with their backs to the harbor were "suffering all the calamities of a siege," he was satisfied that they were no more capable of attack than he was. Some guerrilla-style actions were launched—navigation beacons sabotaged, a lighthouse burned, impostors planted among Royal Navy pilots to deliberately run ships on the rocks—but till Washington amassed more powder and cannon there was little else to do.

Impatient to act, he eventually sent a force under Benedict Arnold to British-held Quebec and another under Henry Knox to retrieve fifty artillery pieces captured at Fort Ticonderoga in upper New York the previous spring. But in the fall of 1775 his most promising operations occurred at sea.

Before the war, a huge proportion of Massachusetts men had participated in fishing, shipbuilding, or ocean trade. In the coastal towns, one in six owned or part-owned a trade vessel, and the number of fishing and whaling boats exceeded one thousand, employing thousands of men. Washington consequently was deluged with advice about how best to deploy the region's maritime clout. Not all of it was selfless, however. One gentleman offered a plan to torch Royal Navy vessels where they lay at anchor, though not "without an advantage in proportion to the service I may do." To discuss his fee, he could be contacted at a local coffeehouse "care of Mr. Hugh James, the barkeeper."

Congress had specified in its rather nervous appointment of Washington as commander in chief that he be circumspect and receptive to advice. Accordingly he hesitated to make decisions "under the sole guidance of my own judgment and self-will" and instead consulted with officers and political leaders. When seeking some way to break the stalemate of the Boston siege, he "deliberated at intervals of three weeks with Massachusetts lawmakers and Congressional delegates." Their counsel invigorated his efforts to make real what had seemed mere fancy when he first surveyed the bustle of enemy vessels in Boston Harbor. "A fortunate capture of an ordnance ship would give new life to the camp, and an immediate turn to the issue of this campaign."

It wasn't a new notion. Massachusetts skippers, armed with neither legal authority nor heavy weapons, had been converting their fishing and cargo boats to bare-bones warships for several months now. On June 20, 1775, the colony's Provincial Congress had resolved to outfit its own navy to counter British "piracies." One week later, Nicholas Cooke, a Rhode Island distiller soon to become governor when revolution fever deemed Joseph Wanton insufficiently pro-war, called for other colonies to follow suit as "a great means of protecting our trade and also of picking up many provision vessels."

Not waiting for outside approval, the Rhode Island Assembly had chartered two sloops under the command of John Brown's *Gaspee* cohort, Abraham Whipple, whose first capture was one of the small tenders accompanying HMS *Rose*, the frigate that earlier had brought Brown in irons to Boston. *Rose*'s captain, James Wallace, vowed to hang Whipple "at the yard arm" for his thievery, to which the latter taunted, "Always catch a man before you hang him."

When Rhode Island formally urged Congress to finance "an American fleet" on August 15, debate commenced full tilt. Many members thought the idea of taking on the Royal Navy insane. Still hoping for "a speedy reconciliation," they feared that mobilizing Continental warships would incite enemy blockades of the Delaware and Chesapeake bays, strangling commerce in Philadelphia, Baltimore, and Virginia. John Adams and two others, Silas Deane of Connecticut and John Langdon of New Hampshire, were assigned to review the matter and make a recommendation to Congress.

Merchants by profession, Deane and Langdon favored an aggressive buildup. (Deane proposed New London, Connecticut, as the future navy's home base—a nice central location, plus he had business interests there.) Adams conceived the Continental fleet as strictly defensive, keeping "our harbors and rivers" as safe havens for vessels of the foreign trade so crucial to America's survival. Leave the perils of open ocean to private adventurers, he cautioned. "To talk of coping suddenly with Great Britain at sea would be quixoticism indeed."

While Congress debated launching any navy at all, the issue in Massachusetts, where commerce raiders had enjoyed just enough success to whet visions of big gains to come, was whether to follow through on the proposed provincial navy or turn loose the citizenry's "pecuniary zeal" by legalizing privateering. The second course promised an instant navy at no cost to the government. Two points argued against it. If privateering flourished, fewer sailors would sign up for government service. And it had the potential, in the minds of some, to encourage social unruliness. Advocates sneered. In the face of British aggression, they said, "The delicacy is absurd surely."

Discussion in Philadelphia and Massachusetts followed parallel tracks for much of that fall. Congress moved to establish a Marine Committee to oversee the production of thirteen frigates of twenty-four to thirty-two guns. Massachusetts lawmakers reiterated their support for a provincial fleet and considered petitions for privateer licenses as well. Expected to play a harassing role at best, privateers were envisioned as the third element of a nautical triple threat featuring Continental warships for ocean combat and midsized provincial vessels for coastal defense.

The Massachusetts General Court officially endorsed privateers in November with "An Act for Encouraging the Fixing out of Armed Vessels." The act, termed "a political curiosity" when it was reprinted in London soon thereafter, permitted citizens to "equip any vessel to sail on the seas, attack, take and bring into any port in this colony all vessels offending or employed by the enemy." It outlined procedures for obtaining commissions and laid the groundwork for establishing prize courts to assess and apportion the booty.

Men who'd pushed hardest for the act's passage were first in line with applications. Many shared qualities that primed them for this new venture. In their twenties and early thirties, sons of merchants and ship captains, natives of ports outside Boston unhampered by British occupation, they leaped to the twin call of freedom and enterprise. Elbridge Gerry of Marblehead, vowing to make privateers "swarm," had challenged hesitant lawmakers in October, "can we doubt the propriety of encouraging individuals by giving them the advantage resulting from their reprisals?" Ten months later he signed the Declaration of Independence at age thirty-two.

One of Gerry's business partners was twenty-four-year-old Nathaniel Tracy, whose access to gritty mariners from his town of Newburyport made Tracy one of privateering's first high-fliers. Just south, in Beverly and Salem, the Cabot and Derby shipping clans set about refashioning their trade vessels into warships, cutting gunports through the bulwarks and clearing holds to make room for extra crewmen needed to take possession of prizes and sail them home for trial. Only difficulties in acquiring weapons slowed the rush to get into the game. Once those became available, Elias Hasket Derby predicted, "There will be not less than one hundred sail of privateers out from the continent."

In early 1776 Elias's brother Richard Jr. was put in charge of outfitting warships for the Massachusetts House of Representatives. Such insider connections were essential in what became a frenzied scramble for cannon and powder, and helped Elias turn his prediction into a massive understatement.

On October 5, 1775, John Hancock, president of Congress, excitedly forwarded to Washington spy reports out of London of a convoy on the way bearing huge loads of military ordnance. The general had been readying armed schooners on his own authority since the previous summer and was well along in commissioning "vessels to be armed and manned to intercept transports daily arriving at Boston." The vessels were leased, their crews comprised of soldiers whose pay was to be supplemented by shares of any prizes. As commander in chief he could dip into his thin supply of munitions as needed, but that was his only advantage in what proved a frustrating process.

Critical of men "so basely sordid" as to temper their patriotic commitment "for the sake of a little gain," Washington deemed one-third of a prize's value to be sufficient for his sailors; that is, their shares would derive from one-third of the total (the captain getting the largest piece of that, then the surgeon, the lieutenants, on down to the privates and cabin boys), with the remaining two-thirds going to the government. Congress later increased the crew's allotment to half the prize, but it hardly countered the conflict ahead, for privateers, once authorized by law, were entitled to the whole thing. The ramifications are obvious in retrospect—higher rewards make for greater appeal—but for Washington they were a lesson yet to be learned.

A stranger to the region, he depended on local officials to help equip and man his vessels. Crews were drawn from a regiment of former Marblehead watermen commanded by Colonel John Glover, a fisherman and wharf owner in Beverly. Glover was tough and dedicated. His regiment, expert in boating, later ferried the Continental Army under fire from Long Island to the New York mainland in August 1776, and would make history transporting 2,400 troops across the wintry Delaware River in Washington's famous Christmas crossing. But his supervision of Washington's schooners, though instrumental in getting them to sea, bore the same conflicts of interest and recriminations that soured other business-patriotic endeavors.

Glover leased his own *Hannah*, a sixty-foot vessel named after his wife, to the government at premium rates. He installed his son as the ship's first officer and his brother-in-law as its sailing master. For captain he proposed a friend, Nicholson Broughton, who brought his son-in-law aboard as second lieutenant. Messages from headquarters grew tense. "The price you mention for bread is monstrous . . . cannot but think a desire to secure particular friends or particular interests does mingle in the management of these vessels . . . the General is much dissatisfied."

In Glover's defense, dealing with workers and suppliers required endless haggling and "hearty damns." Shipyard carpenters were "the idlest scoundrels in nature, and such religious rascals are they, that we could not prevail on them to work on the Sabbath." Aggravations aside, Glover realized that serving as an official maritime agent would be a plum job in the long run, good for the cause and also the pocket thanks to the 2.5 percent commission on all expenditures and proceeds. He named his brother Jonathan as Marblehead's agent and another friend, William Bartlett, as Beverly's. Diligent and savvy, the two struck a side deal soon after their appointment in which they agreed to split commissions on "all prizes that are and shall be hereafter sent into Marblehead, Salem, and Beverly."

If Washington was annoyed by his project's delays and cost overruns, the performance of Captain Broughton almost caused him to abandon it altogether. It took several months to reach a breaking point; the general's unfamiliarity with naval matters led him to show inordinate patience with those seemingly more informed. But Broughton was a mess from the start.

All too pleased to avoid battle with the Royal Navy, the fifty-one-year-old skipper ignored Washington's other mandates of kind treatment of captives and respect for non-enemy vessels. Fearing to stray far from port, Broughton preyed on ships cruising near shore between New Hampshire and points south—the same routes favored by area merchants, many of whose ships he seized in triumph, including one whose American captain Broughton deemed "too polite" and thus certainly a traitor.

With prize courts yet to be formed, Washington handled each case, mucking through details he'd expected would sort themselves out under "rules which take place among private ships of war." Broughton's first capture showed how complicated those rules could get. *Unity*, a colonial transport, had been seized by the British and diverted to Boston when *Hannah* intercepted it. *Unity* belonged to John Langdon of the Continental Congress, and Washington directed that vessel and cargo be returned to him at once.

Recaptured prizes were common to privateering through the ages. There were legal criteria—how long the prize was in enemy hands, how difficult was its recapture—on which to base prize awards and paybacks from owners to those who'd recaptured their lost property. It's understandable that Broughton's men resented losing out on *Unity*'s spoils, but when thirty-six of them mutinied Washington wasn't sympathetic. He had Langdon compensate *Hannah*'s officers $130, but on the mutineers he bestowed "a reward of a different kind," thirty-nine lashes for the ringleader and reassignment to the trenches for the rest.

His headaches didn't end there. Each of *Hannah*'s next seven captures had to be restored to its American owner with damages paid out of Continental coffers for goods pilfered by the crew. The schooner's deployment ended when Broughton was chased into Beverly by HMS *Nautilus*. He beached his boat in panic and damaged the keel, incidentally winding up as the expedition's sole casualty when he caught a cold leading an all-hands retreat through waist-deep October seawater.

Inexplicably promoted to "acting commodore," Broughton next sailed north to Nova Scotia at the head of two newly outfitted schooners in search of the convoy John Hancock had reported. His scorecard improved insofar as only four of the seven prizes he captured had to be returned to their proper owners. But even his legitimate booty was lackluster—fish and firewood, mostly—so in frustration he anchored at Charlottetown on Prince Edward Island and began a two-day looting binge.

He took captive the mayor and justice of the peace and set off for Beverly laden with shoes, woolens, household silver, and forty tubs of butter. Expecting a glorious reception upon his return in December, he learned that most of the prizes he'd sent back earlier had been rejected as unlawful.

Orders came for Broughton and his second-in-command, John Selman, to report at once to Washington, who received them just after releasing the Canadian hostages with apologies for their mistreatment. "He met us on the steps of the door," Selman wrote. "He appeared not pleased." They were fired on the spot.

Broughton's jaunt netted Congress a £500 loss once reparations to aggrieved merchants were tabulated (not counting a £2,000 damage claim from the Charlottetown mayor). Conceding that he was "not a competent judge" of these matters and "had no time to attend them," Washington gave up trying to manage schooner operations. His plea to Congress to accelerate the creation of prize courts signified his frustration with finances and a fresh pragmatism about their importance: sailors needed to know they'd get their prize money.

Clearly no expedition led by such "indolent and inactive souls" as Broughton and Selman could succeed. This applied also to the general's land commanders, most of whom had been appointed for political reasons of "sectional balancing" and who in their inexperience were as inept as they were overconfident. Till battle distinguished the true fighters, reputation and bluster were the main credentials recommending officers for leadership positions. Two men who possessed these qualities in excess helmed a pair of ships out of Plymouth that fall.

Rhode Islander Sion Martindale, a rumored participant in the *Gaspee* raid, complained about his boat from the start. More than 120 feet long with ten cannon and ten swivel guns, *Washington* was the biggest of the Continental schooners. Already far over budget, Martindale requested more firepower, a top surgeon, a fife-and-drum crew, and a last-minute refit of the ship from schooner to brigantine. Brigs carried square sails, schooners wedge-shaped sails in a fore-and-aft rig; brigantines combined the two for a square-rigger's speed before a favorable wind and a schooner's maneuverability in contrary winds.

Washington wondered if these demands meant Martindale intended to take on enemy warships rather than stick to the mission of seizing unarmed transports. He needn't have worried. Launched late in November after weeks of delay, *Washington* compiled a record of disputed captures, a brief refusal of the crew to sail until warmer clothing was issued, and much grumbling from its officers about payment for their one legitimate prize of a load of hay, all in a mere eight days of service that ended in capture by a British frigate a few miles outside Plymouth harbor.

Newspaper accounts of the battle were glorious. Readers took pride that *Washington* had been "attacked by a twenty gun ship which boarded them several times and was beat off" and that its heroic crew had succumbed to British attackers only when "overpowered by their great force but not before they had every officer on board killed and all the men to eighteen out of seventy-five." The truth was less thrilling, however. Washington's chief supply officer, Stephen Moylan, assessed the vessel's legacy bluntly. "She was fitted out at enormous expense, did nothing, and struck without firing a gun."

Chased down by HMS *Fowey*, Martindale had surrendered at once. It's perhaps unfair to blame him. When his ship later was inspected for possible use by the Royal Navy, it was condemned as "totally unserviceable . . . unfit for war . . . not fit for sea."

Martindale and his crew went to Britain as prisoners of war. There, the captain laid out Congress's plans for a naval force and heartened his captors with testimony that his men had joined the rebellion only because they "would have been hanged as traitors to America for daring to refuse."

He reappeared in Massachusetts the following June seeking nine months' back pay and reimbursement for £80 in personal expenses. Most of his men wound up serving on British vessels, though whether under threat or by choice is uncertain. At least one accused Martindale of trading them for his own release, promising they'd serve the king "voluntarily, which was false and by that he was sent home to America again."

Those left in Britain were eventually incarcerated at Forton Prison, not far from the Royal Navy dockyard at Portsmouth, or at Mill Prison in Plymouth. The facilities weren't hellholes. The climate was tolerable, the townspeople generous with food and clothing. But American mariners would be jailed there by the thousands in the coming years, many already ill from prolonged confinement below deck on whatever ship had captured them. Overcrowding, neglect, mismanagement, and corruption led to shortfalls in rations and medical care that rapidly turned perilous.

And then there was an ominous letter from William Howe, the new British Army commander in Boston, written in December to a colleague back home. "Uncertainty about the fate of the crew of the *Washington* would deter others from privateering. Besides," he continued, "I could wish a distinction to be made between prisoners taken on shore and on sea, which last mode of war will hurt us more effectually than anything they can do by land during our stay at this place."

Fifteen months later, Prime Minister Frederick North would fulfill Howe's wish by introducing before a lightly attended session of the House of Commons a bill empowering the king "to secure and detain persons charged with, or suspected of, the crime of high treason committed in North America, or on the high seas, or the crime of piracy."

This was the controversial Pirate Act, denying due process and prisoner exchange to captives charged with committing "piracy upon the ships and goods of His Majesty's subjects." Its passage in March 1777 would ignite "a fatal quarrel" between Britain's pro- and antiwar factions over its potential to legitimize "oppression and tyranny through every part of the realm." It also left the American inmates at Forton and Mill with only escape, death, or consenting to join the Royal Navy as their means of getting out.

William Coit was the second of Washington's Plymouth skippers. Called "a humorous genius" by one contemporary, he joked that his ship's cannon dated back to the Pilgrim era, "and never fired since." Shooting more than one at a time "would split her open from her gunwale to her keel," he said. With no lack of courage he engaged British warships on several occasions and tried to hijack a supply ship anchored in Boston Harbor in range of enemy shore batteries. He also ran aground his first day at sea and bagged a slew of prizes belonging to patriot merchants.

Dismayed by the rapacity of Coit's men "in stripping the prizes of every little thing they could lay their hands upon," Washington sacked the captain after a few weeks. "The plague, trouble, and vexation I have had with the crews of all the armed vessels is inexpressible. I do believe there is not on earth a more disorderly set."

It was a bleak time. Short-term enlistments were due to expire at the end of the year. Continental soldiers were packing for home in alarming numbers. Washington criticized "the deficiency of public spirit," but from their perspective the lack of arms promised a winter of only tedium. He'd hoped success at sea might encourage reenlistment, but his schooners' performance so far was a bust.

The gloom lifted slightly when Hancock's British convoy reached Boston missing its largest transport. Word went out that finding the straggler "would be the most fortunate circumstance that could happen for the public good as well as the captors."

Three days later, *Lee*, a recently launched schooner of four guns and 50 crewmen, was hailed at sea by a lone British ship four times its size. Battered and disoriented after a stormy crossing, the ship's crew thought *Lee* was a Royal Navy pilot craft come to guide them into Boston. Seized without resistance, the defenseless *Nancy* carried tons of ammunition, thousands of muskets and uniforms, and a three-thousand-pound mortar pronounced "the noblest piece of ordnance ever landed in America" when later deployed by the Continental artillery.

Washington's manpower woes were far from solved; before long he increased enlistment bonuses and began admitting free African Americans into the ranks. But the *Nancy* windfall gave the campaign a much-needed shot of good news. "Surely nothing ever came more apropos," he wrote. On delivery of the arms, "universal joy ran through the camp, as if each one grasped victory in his own hands."

The surge of optimism was reflected a week later in one officer's mockery of news that the loyalists in Boston had established a theater to entertain themselves during the bleak occupation. "They have opened with a tragedy. It's very probable they may conclude with one."

Meanwhile *Nancy*'s inventory was published under banner headlines throughout the colonies. Rumors of its value swelled from £10,000 to Thomas Jefferson's giddy estimate of £30,000 two weeks later. Businessmen and mariners applauded *Lee*'s coup. "The men on board have made their fortunes in this adventure." This was premature, however. Prize settlement was still a chaotic free-for-all in which everyone angled for a piece of the pie and few were satisfied.

The crew's award was to come out of the net proceeds from the sale of the captured ship and cargo after all expenses were paid. Expenses on the front end of an expedition included fit-up, supply, and, in the case of Washington's schooners, the initial government outlay to lease and arm the vessel. On the back end, bills were submitted from every quarter for services large and small relating to settling the prize: hauling and storing cargo; housing passengers from the seized transports; doing their laundry (2 pounds, 3 shillings); making crutches (3 pounds, 12 shillings); digging graves (6 shillings).

In the absence of prize courts, it fell to the government-appointed agents to reconcile the books. But since they too participated in the process, taking commissions and often loaning, at interest, their own money to resolve disputes and expedite voyages, they had trouble asserting authority over mistrustful merchants and sailors. Beverly agent William Bartlett, careening between exasperation at his job and dread he might lose it, begged Washington's support "with regard to such vessels, for if I have no power to make such demands I make myself appear ridiculous to the eye of the world." Neither he nor his Marblehead counterpart, Jonathan Glover, cleared a cent their first year. The wait was worth it, however. When Congress settled their accounts in 1777, payments totaled $70,000—more than $1 million in today's terms.

The army's dire need for *Nancy*'s supplies left no time for an orderly appraisal before they were requisitioned and put into use. Bartlett and Glover clamored for funds to placate disgruntled petitioners. Washington had seen enough graft among businessmen and mariners to stipulate that they "make out abstracts for the amount of which warrants will be given them." This red tape requirement was a delaying tactic necessitated by Congress's slowness in directing settlement procedures and issuing payment. It also reflected the general's shifting focus back to ground operations.

Powder voyages undertaken by American merchants had improved his army's combat capability. In late January Henry Knox's artillery pieces began arriving from Fort Ticonderoga, enabling Washington at last to threaten Boston with serious bombardment. By March, when the British conceded their untenable position and evacuated, his involvement with his little squadron of schooners had dwindled to rote communications of reprimand and encouragement.

Matters languished further with the appointment of Artemas Ward as Boston commander after the Continental Army marched south. Confronted with the backlog of prize claims, Ward threw up his hands on the excuse of "having received no instruction on this point." Washington wrote from his new headquarters in New York that accounts must be settled and that warrants would no longer suffice. "They will have cash for the goods." But five months had passed since *Nancy* was taken. Its cargo was long gone, and still no court had convened to apportion its value retroactively. "This procrastination is attended with very bad consequences," Washington wrote.

He'd learned from experience with his armed schooners that patriotism carried only so far. Everywhere entrepreneurs were paying top dollar for weapons and offering big signing bonuses to Continental officers and crewmen as incentive to join privateers once their service terms expired. With any more delay in paying out prize money "it will be impossible to get our vessels manned," he warned.

In this environment of growing discontent among Continental crews and the dynamic promise of civilian privateers, the continued aggressiveness of certain naval captains was remarkable. First among these was John Manley, *Lee*'s forty-two-year-old skipper. He'd captured *Nancy* out of pure luck; the 250-ton transport, after hailing them to approach, had surrendered to eight marines in a longboat. But luck played no part in Manley's dogged pursuit of other prey despite pay delays and mutinous threats from his crew. On learning of Sion Martindale's surrender, for example, he'd rushed his vessel to sea lest his men hear the news and lose heart.

A mysterious figure, the British-born Manley had changed his surname from Russell upon settling in America, and probably gained his skill in navigation and gunnery while serving in the Royal Navy. He captured nine supply ships in his first two months of operation aboard *Lee*. Two were larger than *Nancy*, though laden with food for the British garrison rather than arms. Another, *Concord*, carried a packet of official letters each of which, Washington informed Congress, "breathes nothing but enmity to this country."

The discovery led to a significant change in policy regarding lawful captures. A stickler for diplomatic decorum, Washington had forbidden taking British ships not specifically engaged in military support. However, the inclusion of virulent government directives in an otherwise benign shipment of clothing and coal prompted his vow that whether *Concord*'s supplies were "made a prize or not, we must have them."

Congress agreed. Deeming "any goods, wares, or merchandize" to be potential "necessaries" for the enemy, it ruled that British vessels and cargo "of what kind so ever shall be liable to seizure." The edict greatly expanded the target list of prizes in American waters, a further incentive to sailors and merchants contemplating a move to privateering.

Manley's success increased to thirteen the number of Continental prizes awaiting settlement; a like number of privateer captures had also yet to be tried. Unable to manage the process from Philadelphia, Congress finally tossed it to Massachusetts lawmakers, decreeing that all captures past and future be "libeled in the courts of admiralty erected in said colony." Three prize districts were created, with the most active Middle District, comprised of Boston and the North Shore ports, under the jurisdiction of the Salem court.

Beginning in the spring of 1776, when the courts at last got underway, settlements of Continental and privateer captures were adjudicated together without distinction, a step welcomed by everyone involved in the still embryonic enterprise. Not least of these were the maritime agents in Salem, Beverly, Gloucester, Plymouth, and Portsmouth, New Hampshire.

Taking their cue from Congress's legal melding of Continental and civilian prize claims, agents began soliciting outside business to supplement their official duties. In exchange for commissions or partnership shares they helped outfit private warships, represented owners and investors during the settlement process, and kept accounts for mariners still at sea when their prizes arrived home for trial. And in the consideration, as one privateersman put it before embarking, of "the uncertainty of my life being continued and the chance of being captivated by the enemy," agents also saw that a client's family received his prize money should he be killed or captured.

Competitive rivalries grew. Jonathan Glover tried to poach a successful skipper out of Beverly, William Bartlett's territory. "I am informed that Captain Waters has not employed any person as agent for him and his officers," he wrote a mutual friend. "As I am agent for Captain Manley, I should be glad to serve them likewise." Such tactics were a natural consequence of privateering's rising stakes. In time they became cutthroat.

Nancy's capture mortified Britons. Of the challenge of supplying a distant army by sea, a London newspaper conceded, "Providence militates for the Americans." Publicly dismissing the loss as "a mere misfortune," the admiralty quietly ordered transports to sail in armed convoys from now on and moved to replace Admiral Graves with the former governor of Newfoundland, Molyneux Shuldham.

Loyalists in America applauded the move. "What excuse can be found for a British admiral who tamely and supinely looks on and sees fishing schooners, whaleboats and canoes riding triumphant under the muzzles of his guns and carrying off every supply destined for your relief?"

Skeptical members of Parliament claimed Graves was a scapegoat for the navy's administrative failings. They accused the Earl of Sandwich, whose inept leadership of the admiralty would benefit the American cause throughout the war, of giving orders so "artfully discretional" that any setbacks could be "laid upon the admiral."

Graves maintained that his performance had been exemplary, that Shuldham, a vice rather than full admiral, lacked the stature for the job, and that his dismissal was unjust. Graves's wife, on the other hand, welcomed their return to Britain, claiming that the pressures of foreign command had "rendered him good for nothing."

Shuldham directed the naval evacuation of Boston and, in July, the one-hundred-vessel armada that landed the British Army at Staten Island, New York. With Boston no longer a British stronghold, much of the war's maritime activity shifted south. Rebel merchants had been swapping commodities for European munitions at neutral islands in the West Indies for more than a year. Now Britain began funneling troop supplies to America through its colonies at Jamaica, the Bahamas, and primarily Antigua, where it maintained a shipyard and an admiralty court.

Waters from Trinidad to Canada teemed with warships and transports under opposing flags chasing or fleeing one another. Captured British prizes were sailed to Massachusetts for trial, American prizes to Antigua or Halifax. On the way, all were vulnerable to recapture and redirection to an enemy port; and all, quite commonly given the great distances involved, might be recaptured yet again, requiring courts to balance claims and counterclaims in order fairly to distribute prize money.

George III's midwinter decree that any American vessel seized "during the continuance of the rebellion" would bring rewards to its captors further crowded the scene, invigorating Royal Navy crews and eventually tempting British sympathizers in New York and the West Indies to launch privateers of their own. The aggressiveness paid off. A loyalist crowed that rebel shipping was being decimated. "There is not one in ten that escapes, coming or going." A patriot merchant concurred. "More than half the American vessels that have sailed since the middle of February are taken."

Congress's Robert Morris, a marine administrator and major arms merchant, was unfazed. "We must expect many more losses and think ourselves happy if a sufficient number does but return to keep the Continent supplied." Meanwhile Massachusetts lawmakers continued to receive applications for privateer commissions and for "Letters of Marque and Reprisal," the latter a permit for trade ships to mount heavy weapons in order to snap up any British transports encountered under sail. One man generously informed the General Court that he was preparing a fishing trip "for the good of the country and especially for the poor" but would appreciate a letter of marque and "eight swivel guns" just in case.

Joseph Reed, George Washington's secretary, advised his boss that most American commerce raiders and the investors behind them remained confident in the wake of the king's decree, but some were having second thoughts due to "old prejudices and new fears." The prejudice stemmed from privateering's seedy reputation, the fear from its newly manifest danger.

Forty-five American vessels fell to Shuldham's North American squadron between January and April 1776. The admiral praised his men's performance through "this long and severe winter" but warned his superiors that "however numerous our cruisers may be, it has been found impossible to prevent some of our ordnance and other valuable stores in small vessels falling into the hands of the rebels." His candor wasn't appreciated, and in June he was replaced by Richard Howe, brother of the army's commander.

Admiral Howe was sympathetic to the colonists and as interested in conducting peace talks as in controlling the seas. The peace commission he immediately undertook with his brother lacked authority to speak for the crown and ultimately was spurned by Congress, but the combination of his diplomatic distractions and the continued shift of maritime activity to the south brought another commander, Vice Admiral James Young of Antigua, to the forefront of the Royal Navy's interdiction efforts.

In a testament to the importance of Dutch and French islands as magnets for American powder voyages, Admiral Young's mere eight warships captured thirty-one blockade runners in two months of operation that spring. The admiral perceived better than anyone the scale on which those supposedly neutral governments were tacitly allowing the sale of strategic supplies to the rebels. In March he presented French officials with detailed intelligence, including names and cargo lists, of multiple American vessels that had loaded up with munitions at the port of Saint-Pierre on Martinique.

Young challenged the island governor, "I cannot suppose a person of your high rank and equitable way of thinking would act with duplicity in a matter of such consequence." The governor, "astonished" by the allegation, assured Young that Martinique merchants dealt in "grain, flour, and vegetables," and that any suggestion of illicit arms sales could only have reached the admiral "through means which I flatter myself to believe that his delicacy would not permit him to make use of," that is, by the vulgar tactic of spying. This exchange of archly polite charges about violations that were blatantly obvious to all sides would continue for two years.

On March 23, 1776, Congress issued a proclamation formally targeting "all vessels" belonging to Britain as fair game for civilian and Continental warships. After months of deliberation during which time New Englanders had leaped into privateering, leaders in Philadelphia finally embraced the enterprise in a big way, going so far as to distribute preprinted, preauthorized commission forms complete with blank spaces where names of ships, captains, and owners could be inserted with minimal fuss. John Adams was jubilant. "It was always a measure that my heart was much engaged in."

This latest shot in the ongoing tit-for-tat signaled open season on British shipping. From Antigua, Admiral Young entreated his superiors for reinforcements, stressing the threat indicated by "intelligence from America that ships of force are arming there which are said to be intended to intercept the homeward bound West India ships both from these islands and Jamaica."

His point, dismissed by the admiralty, was that rebel mariners no longer would limit themselves to powder voyages and hijacking inbound supplies to British forces in America. With the entire ocean now in play, they would prowl the European coast and the mid-Atlantic for British vessels bearing goods from anywhere in the world, further pressuring a British economy already squeezed by the loss of its American market.

In response to Young's plea came a single armed sloop which carried word from London that no others were forthcoming. Blind to the impending onslaught, the admiralty informed him that that HMS *Shark* would be sufficient "to reinforce your squadron, intercept the ships and vessels belonging to the North American colonies in rebellion, and also to give proper protection to the homeward bound trade."

By the time these orders arrived in May, more than a hundred privateers had launched from New England and set course for the West Indies. Young's squadron had only four vessels on active duty due to maintenance breakdowns caused by heavy service. *Shark* brought that number to five.

His orders concluded with a stern warning to steer clear of "foreign islands" so as not to give "just cause of complaint" to France or the Netherlands, a condition the admiral can only have found exasperating given his knowledge of their flourishing trade in munitions meant expressly to spill British blood. But with its empire strained and its military overstretched, the crown chose to balance strategic and diplomatic priorities with the result that it fell short in both. Young in his Antiguan outpost sensed this early on. So did British merchants abroad and at home.

The potential trade loss due to the war was estimated at £6 million annually. Little wonder, then, that the merchants' response to their government's rosy posturing was cynical and shrill. They peppered newspapers and politicians with dire alarms that "the precarious and defenseless situation of His Majesty's servants will entirely ruin the people and trade of this government." And despite admiralty claims of the rebels' maritime impotence, they began collecting "private surveys and attestations" of rampant enemy privateers to absolve them from liability should their cargoes start disappearing at sea.

The Royal Navy captains "on cruising station" in North America privately shared the same foreboding about the enemy's spreading ocean insurgency. "Time is drawing fast," one of them wrote a colleague in August 1776, "that requires our presence in the English Channel."

1776

His capture of *Nancy* in November 1775 made John Manley famous throughout Massachusetts. "As many towns contend for the honor of his birth as there did for that of Homer's," wrote one fan. A Salem pub was named after him, and he was the subject of a popular drinking song with the refrain, "And a'privateering we will go." Washington gave Manley the honorary title of commodore so that it "could inspire," he wrote, "the captains of the other armed schooners."

The first to fulfill that hope was James Mugford, a twenty-six-year-old Marblehead seaman. In the final days of the British occupation of Boston he'd been pressed into service aboard HMS *Lively*, gaining release after his wife persuaded the captain that the newlywed couple should be reunited. He then talked his way into command of a Continental schooner, *Franklin*, on the basis of having overheard his captors discussing late-arriving British supply ships that were unaware of Boston's recent evacuation.

Royal Navy frigates still patrolled Massachusetts Bay. Within sight of their anchorage just south of Boston's main channel, Mugford intercepted *Hope*, a three-hundred-ton transport, and brought it into the harbor after threatening to execute its crewmen if they didn't sail where he directed them. Its cargo of a thousand muskets, ten cannon, and seventy-five tons of powder made it the richest prize of the Revolution.

British frigates had been unable to prevent *Hope*'s capture due to "the wind being easterly." Their commanders therefore were "intolerably vexed and chagrined that the above ship should be taken and unloaded in their open view" and were ready when *Franklin* and its crew of 16 returned to sea two days later.

Hugging the shore in order to elude capture, the schooner ran aground at the north end of the harbor. Five longboats carrying one hundred armed soldiers bore down from two frigates hovering in deeper water. According to the *Boston Gazette*, Mugford surprised "our base and unnatural enemies" by cutting his anchor cable to let the current swing his vessel perpendicular to their approach. He got off a broadside of grapeshot at point-blank range with "two boatloads killed" as a result. His men hacked with cutlasses as boarders climbed over the rail, strewing the deck with severed fingers and hands. Mugford himself was seen "righteously dealing death and destruction" to five redcoats with his pike.

Night fell. A small privateer, *Lady Washington*, joined the fight, in the darkness confusing the British into thinking they were outnumbered and prompting their retreat. The Americans claimed "fifty or sixty" enemy killed. British officers listed seven in their logbooks. Aboard *Franklin*, Mugford and one crewman lay dead. He received a grand burial in Marblehead complete with muffled drums and poetic elegies. "Don't give up the vessel, you will be able to beat them off," went down in local lore as the dying words of a fallen hero.

John Skimmer was *Franklin*'s next skipper. In 1777 he was upgraded to a fourteen-gun Continental brig called *General Gates* in honor of the victor at Saratoga. The last of his many sea battles was against *Montague*, a loyalist privateer.

Prowling the sea without international license, the loyalists feared that capture meant a pirate's noose. Consequently, they fought "with ferocity rather than bravery" through three hours of beam-to-beam volleys. When *Montague* ran out of ammunition, its gunners jammed every available piece of metal down their cannon barrels, "including jackknives, crowbars, and even the captain's speaking tube." A double-headed shot (used to shred an opponent's rigging) that had torn through its main

CAPT! JAMES MUGFORD,
of the
SCHR. FRANKLIN CONTINENTAL CRUISER 1776.

James Mugford captured the supply ship, Hope, *from under the guns of Royal Navy frigates. His gallantry in defending his schooner made him a local hero. But the cutthroat maneuvering by maritime agents to profit from* Hope's *sale would bring scorn from the privateering community.*

cabin was retrieved, loaded, and fired back at *General Gates.* The shell struck a swivel gun and sent its shattered pieces through Skimmer's skull, the happy sight of which inspired the loyalists to fight for two more hours until the last of them surrendered.

Skimmer had seized twenty-two prizes in his career, yet few had paid out due to muddled prize procedures, leaving his widow and eleven children destitute. Their plight came to the attention of Robert Morris, who demanded of his congressional colleagues that "something must be done for poor Captain Skimmer's family."

In September the captain's survivors were awarded an annual pension of $400, a generous sum. Wartime inflation would cut its value by more than 90 percent by the time the pension, for budgetary reasons, was terminated three years later.

Three

Those who have been engaged in privateering are making large fortunes in a most rapid manner. I have not meddled in this business which I confess does not square with my principles.

—*Robert Morris to Silas Deane, September 1776*

I propose this privateer to be one third on your account, one third on account of Mr. Prejent and one third on my account. I have not imparted my concern in this plan to any person and therefore request you will never mention the matter.

—*Robert Morris to William Bingham, December 1776*

The patriot expedition against Fort Ticonderoga in May 1775, which secured the artillery pieces instrumental in driving the British from Boston a year later, had been financed with £300 surreptitiously drawn from the Connecticut treasury by Silas Deane, the colony's thirty-seven-year-old representative in Congress. He left promissory notes for the money that later were honored, and any fallout from his disregard of proper accounting procedures vanished in the euphoria of the expedition's success. But as an episode in which a desirable end justified dubious means, the affair exemplified Deane's lifelong penchant for improvisation and hustle.

His Yale education had brought into tantalizing reach the advantages of status and wealth not always available to the sons of blacksmiths. Left sole guardian to six siblings while still in his early twenties, he added an *e* to the Dean name to distance the family from its middling roots. He engaged in constant legal disputes with relatives and business partners, and ascended in society via two "brilliant marriages" to women from prominent families. His first wife, with whom he had a son, died in their fourth year of marriage, his second while he was abroad in 1777.

Deane liked luxury and stylish company, and wasn't one to cut his personal spending even when money was tight. He called it "a peculiar fatality" that he bounced from "one scheme and adventure after another," but his expensive tastes and the expediency of many of his dealings made his fate by and large his own fault.

In early 1776 Deane was chosen to be Congress's undercover emissary to Paris. He got the job through the influence of Robert Morris of the Secret Committee for trade and the Committee of Secret Correspondence, the latter a foreign relations group seeking to establish a formal alliance with France. Like Deane, Morris had no patience for bureaucracy. "How tedious and troublesome it is," he wrote the new emissary, "to obtain decisive orders on any point wherein public expense is to be incurred."

In observing that war's chaos and devastation "are circumstances by no means favorable to finance," Morris meant public finance. On a personal level he thrived, ascending from "a leading young merchant from Philadelphia" in 1775 to the so-called "financier of the Revolution" by war's end. Early on he helped equip Washington's army through his business contacts in Europe. Later as Superintendent of Finances he would keep the American economy afloat by stabilizing its worthless currency through a juggling act of monetary austerity, foreign trade, hat-in-hand international borrowing, and cash infusions from his own holdings.

In an era of widespread belief that all procurement officials speculated with government money and manipulated prices to increase commissions, Morris's critics took little regard of his contributions. John Adams weighed his "vast designs in the mercantile way" against a "masterly understanding, an open temper, and an honest heart." But others placed him among a supposed cabal of merchant-dignitaries whose public service disguised, in the ominous insinuation of Virginia-born diplomat Arthur Lee, "some deep design against our independence at the bottom. Many of the faction are, I know, actuated by the desire of getting or retaining the public plunder." Such suspicions were fostered by the fiscal contrivances of men like Morris and Deane no matter the benefit they often rendered the cause.

Deane sailed for Europe in March. Three months later, Morris sent a second protégé abroad, this time to Martinique in the West Indies. The island was France's gateway to New World trade and a booming hub of international commerce. Its inhabitants' eagerness to sell weapons to the rebels under the protection of French neutrality was a magnet to the Secret Committee and a thorn to Great Britain.

Morris's appointee, William Bingham, presented himself on Martinique as a private businessman. Born to wealth, Bingham was well educated and worldly, possessed a composed efficiency belying his twenty-four years, and displayed none of Deane's compulsive personal and financial turmoil. He quickly secured military wares for shipment home on Congress's account, disseminated American propaganda and upbeat war reports to French officials, and began monitoring activities of the French fleet in the West Indies "and whether they mean to act for or against America." On Congress's recommendation, he partnered with local merchants to promote his entrepreneurial cover and solicited "private adventurers" of any nationality to raid British shipping for profit.

The triangle formed by Bingham and Deane on each side of the Atlantic and Morris in Philadelphia became a busy backchannel of financial opportunism and patriotic zeal, elements never more entwined than in the men's involvement in privateering. But Congress's embrace of privateering's quintessential "private adventurers" would sour when rumors arose late in the war that Morris, Deane, and Bingham had invested in warships with public money and skimmed the profits for themselves.

By then their circumstances had drastically diverged. Morris was still a financial colossus, though overambition was poised to undo him. Deane was ruined—scorned by his nation and friends. Only Bingham withstood the storm of indignation, for which he thanked the obscurity of Martinique. "If my services had been more conspicuous I might perhaps have had much to fear." He didn't mean fear from the British. It was an American "voice of calumny" that assailed him and his colleagues, "the pursuits," Bingham said, "of the envious."

Yet in Deane's case at least, a cautionary note written before the war suggests he might have blamed himself as well. "I have known very honest men, when unfortunate, to suffer in their character and never retrieve their affairs only because of their being careless." It was a prescient observation, for though Deane's honesty remains debatable, his carelessness and misfortune are certain.

His assignment in France was twofold. First, he was to arrange weapons shipments from French suppliers on the promise of future remittance with American commodities, which is to say on unsecured credit extended to a lone agent who had few funds, no official title, no political power, and no authorization from the full Congress, which had been kept in the dark about his mission. Second, he was to parlay a letter of introduction from Benjamin Franklin, internationally famous for his study of electricity, into face-to-face meetings with French officials in order to gauge their willingness to strike a military and commercial alliance with America.

The obstacles were considerable. Whatever social refinement Deane possessed was superficial and not indicative of a nuanced intellect suited to negotiate, in a language he barely spoke, the maze of indirection and subtext that characterizes all diplomacy, and which was the particular forté of French foreign minister Charles Gravier, Comte de Vergennes, the most powerful and adroit statesman in Europe.

In Deane's favor, however, was France's bitter antipathy toward Britain. Its fall from world dominance resulting from defeat in the Seven Years' War had been a point of national humiliation ever since the Peace of Paris was signed in 1763. The wish to get even in any way possible made Vergennes receptive to Deane's overtures.

The French king, Louis XVI, was only nineteen when he'd assumed the throne in 1774. Cautious in his domestic rule, he was likewise skittish about provoking war and thus disinclined to push the limits of international neutrality agreements, which for many years had balanced the power in Europe between Britain and Portugal on one side and France and Spain on the other.

Vergennes held a bolder view. At fifty-eight, experienced and wily, he manipulated policy toward his objectives and then presented it to the young king as inevitable. There was no disagreement within France that a Britain shorn of its American colonies would be a fine thing. Out of deference to his monarch's sensitivities, however, the foreign minister couldn't yet openly back the American rebellion. But he was prepared, in his words, "to connive at certain things."

Even before meeting Deane he'd approved a loan of 1 million livres (about $10 million) to Roderigue Hortalez & Company, a dummy firm created to funnel covert aid to America. Spain, as eager as France to see Britain beaten, matched the loan, as did a consortium of friends of the company's founder, Pierre-Augustin Caron de Beaumarchais.

A playwright (he later wrote *The Marriage of Figaro* and *The Barber of Seville*) and political gadfly, Beaumarchais had a zest for capitalism, court intrigues, and American liberty. Vergennes designated him Deane's unofficial liaison to local arms dealers, and beginning in the summer of 1776 Beaumarchais and Deane began acquiring military supplies to ship to the Continental Army. They took customary commissions and planned to replenish the Hortalez accounts once Congress's commodity shipments, especially tobacco, began arriving from America.

The company's funds were almost all gone when a letter came in late July from the Secret Committee apologizing "that we have been so unfortunate in our remittances to you." The Royal Navy was raising havoc with American transports and the situation was getting worse. "Hitherto you will think yourself unlucky in these untoward circumstances," the letter warned, adding brightly, "but this must not dispirit us."

Deane panicked. Hortalez was a shell, after all, a fiction necessitated by neutrality agreements among the governments of France, Spain, and Britain. Loans ostensibly made to the company were in reality extended to Congress on the basis of its promise, certified by Deane, to deliver valuable cargoes as repayment. Delay could prove "a mortal stab to my whole proceedings," he wrote. Beaumarchais, having promised Vergennes and others a multifold return on their investment, was no less exposed. In the shadow of disaster their friendship was cemented.

It was a remarkable collaboration of two incorrigible yet idealistic mavericks. Born into the watchmaking Caron family, the forty-four-year-old Frenchman had, like Deane, initiated his social climb by marrying a rich widow; later he added "de Beaumarchais" for noble effect. Along with self-invention he shared Deane's romantic view of the role he might play in American independence. Deane relished his place "on the great stage of Europe" and the boost his supply deals could give the war effort; his initial sales pitch to Vergennes had included a vow that aiding America would bring forth between their countries "the most lasting, extensive, and beneficial commercial intercourse and connection that the world has ever seen."

Beaumarchais was no less expansive in courting America's trust and, he hoped, its exclusive reliance upon him as its arms broker. "Look upon my house," he wrote Congress, "as the chief of all useful operations to you in Europe, and my person as one of the most zealous partisans of your cause."

His characterization of himself as "useful" echoed Deane's desire to be of "the greatest and most extensive usefulness," and for each man the fulfillment of his wish proved a harsh blessing. Though they hoped to get rich through commissions and private ventures stemming from their government work, their devotion to American liberty was real and their belief that they were indispensable to its attainment honest if overblown. The recklessness with which they ran their operation—inflated promises, shoddy accounting—was excusable in their minds as incidental to the integrity of their intentions.

Historians generally rate Deane as little more than a "catspaw" or "venal dupe." His early acquisition of French military aid is judged a minor feat in light of Vergennes's predisposition toward any plan to take Britain down, and the self-interest so much on his mind tends to blight even his nobler moments. Yet during his first months alone in France Deane was a novice gambler at a high-stakes table with very few cards to play, who somehow stayed in the game for the good of his country.

His superiors in Congress were no help. Months went by without a word. "The want of instructions or intelligence or remittances has sunk our credit to nothing," he anxiously wrote after spending millions of borrowed dollars on supplies for twenty-five-thousand troops. His partner, Beaumarchais, was undaunted ("this is depressing, but depression is a long way from discouragement"), but Deane agonized that French officials were getting "extremely uneasy" about the lack of positive news and financial reciprocation from America.

Unaware of the commitments already made in its name, the Secret Committee ordered him in October to entreat the French court for further loans "sufficient to dispatch immediately very considerable quantities of stuff." As exactly how to accomplish this without collateral, "We hope you'll be able to influence them by one means or other."

Forced to find new ways of enticing suppliers, Deane relied less on Franco-American solidarity and instead fell back on his roots in market capitalism, a shift he admitted to Congress. "Politics and my business are almost inseparably connected." His point was that mere salesmanship no longer sufficed. With zero credibility left, he had to provide instant rewards in order to attract money and materiel.

One of his ploys originally had been suggested by Arthur Lee, the Secret Committee's representative in London. Young and ambitious, Lee had met Beaumarchais in 1775 and conceived with him the idea of a commercial front as a means secretly to aid American fighters and get rich to boot, an idea later put into practice (to Lee's furious envy) by Beaumarchais and Deane through Hortalez & Company. Beaumarchais subsequently urged another of Lee's proposals on

Deane—to accept the many petitions of European aristocrats, "especially soldiers of fortune," to become Continental Army officers.

Though most of the applicants were vainglorious ne'er-do-wells seeking high commands to suit their egos, Deane, in taking up the idea, believed much of their braggadocio. A colleague in America sniped that he was "unable to say nay to any Frenchman who called himself count or chevalier." Deane went so far as to affront Congress with a suggestion that placing all its forces under the command of a proven foreigner might "give character and credit to your military, and strike perhaps a greater panic in our enemies." Its military detriment aside, however, his recruitment of foreign officers ingratiated him with influential European families ("the best ones of their class") at a time when he had little else to offer.

Marquis de Lafayette, who joined the Americans through Deane's auspices in 1777, was one success, but by and large the foreigners were dead weight and aroused only annoyance when they appeared at Washington's headquarters waving generals' commissions authorized by an American civilian a world away in Europe. "Harassed to death with applications," Deane signed up almost twenty of these poseurs that fall. He surmised that their reception was chilly but believed his dire situation warranted the inconvenience back home. "I have made one excuse after another until my invention is exhausted." He had to grant favors if he expected to obtain them. Informing Congress of one officer he accepted in November while negotiating a shipment of two hundred brass cannon, he acknowledged bashfully, "I hope the terms I have made with him will not be thought exorbitant, as he was the principal means of engaging the stores."

Privateering posed another way of attracting support. From his earliest days in France, Deane had been beseeched by "persons of the first property" to license private warships to seize British prizes and sell them in America. (Neutrality agreements forbade French ports from receiving prizes.) Against a backdrop of worsening war news—in early fall the Continentals were driven at great loss from Long Island and Manhattan, and by November important bastions at Fort Lee

Silas Deane, shown here at the height of his prestige as a freewheeling diplomat-entrepreneur in Paris, dabbled in politics, privateering, and anti-British terrorism. His compulsive leaps from deal to deal left him with many enemies and few friends when his fortunes took a fall.

and Fort Washington had been overrun by the British, setbacks Deane downplayed in Paris as "skirmish rather than battle"—a bright spot was the success of the privateers. Europeans following the war with intense interest agreed that "what is certain on the side of the Americans is their activity at sea and the ships of the crown they are capturing."

With the same visions of wealth that dazzled the New Englanders, European shipowners offered Deane a piece of their privateering profits in exchange for his signature, but he was reluctant to act on his own authority. In frantic letters to Congress he proposed a series of schemes such as fomenting native revolts in the British West Indies, recruiting disgruntled British fishermen on the Grand Banks, razing the Scottish port of Glasgow "by a single frigate," and sending Deane "curious American productions" such as insect collections or "a few barrels of apples" as gifts for whichever "certain personage" he was trying to woo at the moment; for the French queen he suggested saddle horses since she was "fond of parade, and I believe wishes a war."

His repeated requests for blank privateer commissions came across as another mad notion at first, but he was adamant about their strategic potential and their efficacy in forging partnerships with potentially helpful Europeans. "You may have any number of recruits in Europe for such ships," he wrote his superiors excitedly, "and by sending out commissions have individuals join you in the adventure under your flag." Yet as 1776 wound down, no commissions came.

Frustrated on every front, he appeared powerless and out of touch to his French hosts. Underscoring that impression was the lack of Congressional confirmation, four months after the fact, of the signing of the Declaration of Independence. Rumors of the document had reached Europe in August, yet without a copy in hand he had no basis to refashion his requests for military aid as coming "from the United Independent States of America" rather than an outlaw band of British rebels.

He appreciated the legal significance of the Declaration overseas as Congress did not, for it directly related to his hope of unleashing foreign privateers against Britain. The point had been brought home earlier that fall when a Massachusetts privateer working the eastern Atlantic had entered the Spanish port of Bilbao to put its captives ashore. Britain had immediately demanded the skipper, John Lee of Newburyport, be handed over as a pirate.

Deane had realized at once that an important precedent hung in the balance. A Spanish decision to uphold Lee's commission would implicitly acknowledge American sovereignty. "If the reverse, the only ground on which the determination can go against the captain is that the United States of America or their Congress are not known in Europe otherwise than by common fame in newspapers." Official acknowledgment was key because privateers sailing without a legitimate flag were plain criminals fit for hanging, a fate few mariners cared to risk.

He sought Vergennes's help and again found him sympathetic for reasons purely in France's interest. The foreign minister earlier had praised "the order issued by Congress to its shipowners to chase indiscriminately all English vessels in all parts of the world. The desire to make captures more easily may attract privateers in the European seas where the English are less on their guard." Vergennes knew that Spain's support of Captain Lee would encourage anti-British privateers (of any nationality) to seek shelter in the ports of continental Europe, making evasion from the Royal Navy easier and prosecution by British courts harder. And short of a French declaration of war, anything that undermined Britain's effort to subdue the American uprising was fine by him.

When Spain indeed decided, at Vergennes's behest, to protect Lee from British justice, Deane called it "striking proof of what I have so positively asserted of the good disposition of both these courts." Coupled with the arrival in November of a copy of the Declaration of Independence, the decision led him to predict that local ports would spawn dozens of privateers once Congress supplied the commissions. "Hasten them out I pray you," he implored in a letter of December 3. By then he'd learned enough about Old World treaties to understand their fragility. "This is a capital stroke and must bring on a war." The war he sought was between Britain and France. Mutual mistrust was the tinder to which privateers might apply a spark, especially now that their right to lay up in harbors just across the English Channel had been publicly affirmed.

On the day Deane wrote that letter, Benjamin Franklin landed in France with instructions from Congress to head up the diplomatic mission with Deane and Arthur Lee as his co-commissioners. With a keener sense of the strength of America's negotiating position, Franklin took an artful, more confident approach. He knew that France very much wanted an alliance with America and simply feared committing too soon lest the rebellion fail and Britain, bruised but intact, turn a vengeful eye on those who'd meddled in its affairs. He also knew the French objective of a diminished, defeated rival carried a nightmare alternative of Anglo-American reconciliation and Britain's subsequent rebirth as an invigorated power.

Franklin dropped Deane's hard-sell style and let silence and feigned ambivalence draw France into making a move. In his first meeting with Vergennes, he listed the advantages to France that would result from American independence before dangling the possibility of rapprochement with Britain "unless some powerful aid is given us or some strong diversion is made in our favor." Moreover, France had better act quickly if it wanted to be America's preferred trading partner. "The opportunity of securing all the advantages of that commerce, which in time will be immense, now presents itself. If neglected, it may never return."

Later he played the same angle when it became evident that British spies were passing to London inside information of his activities in Paris. He made no effort to root them out or avoid them, preferring to foster, for French consumption, an impression of collusion and potentially warming relations between the rebel leadership and the crown.

Such subtlety was part of Franklin's character as it emphatically was not of Deane's. At seventy, Franklin was not a man in a hurry. His wry, haphazard style exasperated his colleagues but confounded his foes. His seeming indifference to fashion and fame—all catnip to Deane—enchanted the French public and made him the perfect foil to the sophisticated, crafty Vergennes. "I rise at six, write until seven, dress and breakfast by eight," Deane wrote, then work "until nine, then sup and go to bed by eleven." Franklin would never have tolerated such an arduous schedule. But then, he was integral to American independence and French geopolitical gamesmanship whereas Deane was merely useful.

Franklin would shrewdly manipulate tensions between France and Britain to an eventual breaking point in 1778. His co-commissioner Arthur Lee, disliked by everyone who worked with him in Paris, skulked on the sidelines of the negotiations hatching theories of his colleagues' financial skullduggery that Franklin attributed to Lee's outright insanity, a diagnosis Deane thought "very charitable" given "the malignity of his heart."

Meanwhile Deane concentrated on supply operations and the gathering presence in local waters of privateers emboldened, as Vergennes had foreseen, by Spain's support of Captain Lee. He always had enjoyed socializing with seamen and shipowners. Now he happily immersed himself in maritime matters, which was where the money flowed with its rewards, temptations, and taint.

In May 1776 a transport flying Spanish colors had been boarded by patriots in Delaware Bay and found to carry strongboxes containing $14,000. The Maryland captain informed his colony's leadership that the boxes "are marked W M from whence he thinks they belong to Willing & Morris, and that there may be more money on board."

Willing, Morris & Company was a Philadelphia merchant house named for its founder, Thomas Willing, and for Robert Morris, the Liverpool-born financial wizard Willing had plucked at age twenty from the counting room and made partner in 1754. Concealing its money in the hold of a foreign ship caused no great surprise. The firm was known to engage in extensive trade on behalf of Congress, one-fourth of whose total cash disbursements between 1775 and 1777 went to one company—Willing & Morris. No one expected the breadth of that trade to be limited by the fact that Morris ran Congress's procurement efforts through the Secret Committee, negotiating with himself in many transactions. People might mutter about conflicts of interest, but they accepted them as standard procedure.

Morris's positive dealings with British merchants before the war had dampened his zeal for rebellion. Believing reconciliation still to be worthwhile, he'd voted against the Declaration of Independence but signed it once it was passed, a moment of hesitancy that neither his fellow congressmen nor his Pennsylvania constituents held against him. His political ambivalence later served him well when clear-eyed, unpopular measures were required to counter America's wartime economic tailspin.

Congress, unable to secure large loans from foreign governments or to coerce the thirteen states to contribute significant funds to the national effort, had no way to raise revenue except by issuing more and more currency, a short-term remedy that caused the Continental dollar to lose 97 percent of its value by 1779. Bucking the same clamorous tide for fiscal expansion that had propelled the Revolution from the start, Morris pushed Congress to quit printing paper money, to abandon price controls and laws artificially upholding currency values, to demand that states contribute tax revenues to Congress, and to charter a centralized institution, the Bank of North America, to make loans and manage debt on a stringent, hard-money basis.

But while his pragmatism may have helped him make difficult policy decisions, it left an impression of flexible allegiances that would hurt him in the future. Morris was candid about preferring traditional European mercantilism to the unruly markets of the American democracy. He called common folk "vulgar" and "misguided," and based his political and economic philosophy on belief that "the interests of moneyed men" went "hand in hand" with the public good. And despite personally funding decisive military campaigns at Princeton in 1777 and Yorktown in 1781, he never accepted a government position without first stipulating that it not interfere with his private business.

As for privateering, whose exploding popularity he observed as a member of Congress's Marine Committee, his opinion was mixed only insofar as it pertained to his own involvement. He extolled privateering's strategic and commercial potential while refraining from participating out of loyalty to former business partners. Having enjoyed, he wrote Deane in September 1776, "extensive connections and dealings with many worthy men in England," Morris "could not consent to take any part of their property because the government has seized mine." Instead he made money on private trade and from commissions earned organizing supply voyages for Congress.

The ventures often commingled, as in an order for "linens and other European manufactures" he quietly placed with William Bingham in Martinique. Agreeing to split profits rather than pay him a commission, Morris had Bingham tuck the civilian wares into a cargo of muskets aboard a Continental sloop bound for Philadelphia. With Congress footing the shipping expenses, including if the vessel was sunk or captured, the inside arrangement was advantageous, borderline legal, and typical.

Morris presented such deals to Bingham and to Silas Deane through paired sets of instructions. He outlined government purchases in what he termed "political" letters, while his private purchases came in accompanying "commercial" letters. The high rate of interception at sea required that duplicates be sent on multiple vessels; captains were to throw them overboard in sacks weighted with cannonballs if threatened by enemy patrols.

Most letters to Deane never reached him—another instance of his consistent bad luck, since much of Morris's communication with Bingham and various European merchants got through, a matter of mere chance which nevertheless stirred Deane's paranoia about being ignored by colleagues in America. If he was not the right man "to solicit in your behalf," he complained after an extended silence out of Philadelphia, "let me entreat you to tell me so and relieve me from an anxiety which is become so intolerable that my life is a burden."

Certainly Morris, through letters sent if not received, tried to include Deane in "so fair an opportunity of making a large fortune since I have been conversant in the world." Citing huge markups on "every kind of goods" and also on the ships that delivered them (by 1777 merchants and privateer investors, who sought to convert them to warships, were paying £4,000 for vessels that months earlier had gone for £1,000), he urged Deane's "utmost exertion" in dispatching European cargoes "2/3ds on account of Willing, Morris & Company and 1/3d on your account."

Lest his seriousness be unclear, Morris hinted at big paydays ahead thanks to the power of his position. "I shall be ever mindful of you while I hold a seat in the public councils and ever after in my private capacity."

That tantalizing promise, combined with a growing confidence among European exporters that the profit potential of American markets more than compensated for the high risk of seizure by the Royal Navy, heightened Deane's frustration at being unable fully to participate in the boom. Ever short of personal funds, he proposed a partnership to Morris whereby he would arrange shipments to America entirely on Morris's account; when the cargo arrived, Deane's one-third stake would be deducted from the proceeds before he took his share of the profits. It was a fair deal since, as Deane noted, "I shall have the principal charge of the affair here," and Morris likely would have accepted it but for another lag in transatlantic mail that opened a major rift between them.

The financier had set up his younger brother as Willing & Morris's representative in the French port of Nantes. Contrary to Robert's fond view that his brother was merely "frolicksome," Tom Morris, apart from his financial ineptitude, was known to drink and whore "at least twenty-two hours of every twenty-four." Deane, when Robert requested an honest report of his brother's behavior, was wary that "men in such cases are prone to be offended" by unpleasant truths, in this case the consensus opinion that Tom was one of "the lowest reptiles of human society."

Unfortunately Deane's discreet hint that "pleasure has got too strong hold of him" took six months to reach Philadelphia. In the interim Robert appointed his brother "Superintending Agent" for the Committee of Secret Correspondence, a post empowering him to arrange government arms deals and to supervise privateer prizes once French ports began receiving them. Tom's slide into deeper debauchery soon forced Deane and Franklin to petition for his dismissal, a recommendation Congress adopted in a public pronouncement that left Robert, having not yet received Deane's gentle warning of Tom's decline, shocked and humiliated.

At once he terminated his friendship with Deane on grounds of betrayal and maintained the estrangement through 1777, until testaments of Tom's dissolution poured in from so many quarters that he could no longer deny their truth. Tom died of alcoholism in January 1778. John Paul Jones, in Nantes refitting his Continental sloop, honored him with a thirteen-gun salute. But by then Robert had loudly renounced all ties to his brother ("the worthless wretch") in order to preserve his own reputation. He would do the same with Deane in time.

In late 1777 Deane learned from a months-old newspaper that his wife Elizabeth had died in Connecticut. She was the correspondent to whom he'd expressed his hopes and fears most candidly. Moreover, losing connection to her aristocratic family further spurred his quest for the status wealth confers, a quest driven as well by concerns about supporting his son and by glittery reports from home that his younger brothers Barnabas and Simeon were making fortunes in private trade. As a result he grew more prone than ever to impulsive schemes of moneymaking and war meddling, schemes that in addition to dabbling in privateers included speculation in the London stock market on the basis of war headlines from America and, most bizarrely, backing an attempt to burn down the Royal Navy shipyards in Portsmouth, England.

Deane's cohort in these ventures was a thirty-three-year-old American expatriate named Edward Bancroft. A member of British science's Royal Society, Bancroft was a physician, a botanist of tropical plants specializing in natural poisons, and an expert in the chemistry of dyes. Like Deane's garrulous French partner, Beaumarchais, he enjoyed money and luxury. Unlike Beaumarchais, he was indifferent to American independence, a frame of mind which freed him to play both sides of the conflict with astonishing facility.

Sixty years after the Revolution it would emerge that Bancroft was a British spy. Purely in it for the money (he received a lifetime pension of £500 a year for his services), he tracked the secret negotiations between France and America under the pseudonym "Edward Edwards." He befriended John Paul Jones when the captain was feted in France after his great victory over HMS *Serapis* in 1779, and as Franklin's personal secretary he had access to the old diplomat's correspondence. But Deane was his most valuable asset.

A double agent, Bancroft passed British secrets to the commissioners in Paris almost as often as he passed their secrets to London; much was deliberate misinformation meant to plant mistrust between the Americans and French, but some was accurate and helpful, such as his warnings about Royal Navy deployments outside French ports to intercept supply ships and privateers. His British spymasters regularly opened his mail out of suspicion that he was double-crossing them, and though George III had purchased his allegiance, the king called him "entirely an American" and held that "no other faith can be placed in his intelligence but that it suits his private views." Bancroft's countrymen, on the other hand, trusted him completely. The Committee of Secret Correspondence even had suggested him as a desirable overseas contact in its original orders to Deane.

By coincidence, Deane's first job after college had been to tutor the young man, so their rapport was fast renewed. Bancroft instantly grasped his former teacher's value as a source, and volunteered to be his interpreter in meetings with Beaumarchais and French officials. Thus he learned about the ruse of Hortalez & Company and about Vergennes's clandestine support of America, information he promptly gave the British ambassador to France, David Murray, Lord Stormont.

Vergennes's subsequent denials of collusion to Stormont in the face of detailed evidence gathered by Bancroft mirrored those of French authorities in the West Indies disputing the presence of American ships in their harbors. The denials were patently barefaced and hollow, yet there was little Britain could do beyond issue threats it couldn't carry out.

Before long Deane and Bancroft were addressing one another as "my dear friend." Together they imbibed the Parisian nightlife and chased every type of financial gambit from real estate to privateers in "an indissoluble partnership in infamy launched on a sea of claret." Deane's esteem for his American friend wasn't unreserved, however. "Doctor Bancroft has been of very great service to me," he wrote in December 1776, "but it costs something."

Though he questioned the speed with which Bancroft had culti-vated his trust, their dealings increased as Deane's diplomatic chores were taken over by Franklin and his ties to Morris deteriorated due to distance and misunderstanding. By the end of 1777 Bancroft was his primary confidant and business partner, and any doubts he'd had about the man's integrity had yielded to blind dependency.

Historians have speculated that Franklin knew Bancroft was crooked and that he retained him as secretary on the sly bet that

Edward Bancroft was brilliant, charming, ambitious, and lethal. The expatriate American scientist was Silas Deane's closest confidante in Paris. When Deane wrote in 1776 that Bancroft's friendship "costs something," he had no idea how much.

information leaked to Britain would compel the French foreign ministry to hurry up and tie the knot with America. His word on the subject was typically blithe. "If I was sure, therefore, that my *valet de place* was a spy, as he probably is, I think I should not discharge him for that, if for other reasons, I liked him."

Deane's relationship with Bancroft ran on similar lines: affection trumped suspicion. They were friends, and when Deane's career later collapsed Bancroft alone stood by him, supporting him emotionally and financially in what would seem an anomaly in a spy's usual relationship with his victim but which squares with Bancroft's oddly humane approach to betrayal. Though a cynical manipulator, he cared for Deane even as he exploited him; cared for him even as, evidence suggests, he plotted his murder.

Meanwhile young William Bingham was having a good war on Martinique. A bustling way station for France's Caribbean and South American trade, the island, located three hundred miles north of Venezuela, was a placid backwater compared to the political hotbed of Paris. His official reception there in July 1776 had carried none of the cautious diffidence Vergennes had shown Deane three months earlier. Indeed, the community's support for America was evident even before Bingham's vessel, *Reprisal*, dropped anchor.

Its captain, Lambert Wickes, carried a bitter grudge. A month earlier in Rhode Island, he and his younger brother Richard had helped unload more than a hundred barrels of gunpowder off a stranded American blockade-runner. As British longboats approached, the Americans had abandoned ship after furling fifty pounds of powder inside a canvas sail, creating a time-delay fuse, which they lighted near the vessel's remaining cargo of unloaded ammunition. Redcoats from two of the longboats "soon boarded her; one was close under stern, the others very near. Those on board had given three cheers and fired their arms after our people when the fire took effect on the powder and sent 30 to 40 of them into the air." The transport was blown to bits. Body parts and debris rained down on the water. In horrified rage the British frigate standing offshore fired several volleys after the fleeing Americans. These were ineffectual save for one shot that pierced Richard Wickes "through the arm and body" and killed him instantly. Lambert wrote their family, "I have lost a dear brother and a good officer which I know not how to replace."

He got a chance to settle the score while bringing Bingham into Martinique's port of Saint-Pierre. After a Royal Navy sloop approached to inspect *Reprisal*, Wickes lowered a dory to put Bingham ashore and then wheeled about to bring his guns to bear. "He struck us three or four times," the captain of HMS *Shark* reported, "one of which came through the quarter and wounded a marine with the splinter." People onshore flocked to watch the battle. They cheered when the fort overlooking the harbor opened fire on *Shark* and sent a cannonball through its sails, forcing it to withdraw.

Bingham watched wide-eyed as Wickes was "complimented and caressed beyond measure" by the crowd when *Reprisal* docked. He described his own feelings with the same precision he would bring to his job as congressional agent. "Never did I feel the sensation of joy in a more lively degree." He sent *Reprisal* home with a mixed load of weapons for Congress and housewares for Willing & Morris. The transaction earned him £742 and set him on course to become, on his return to Philadelphia four years later, one of the richest men in America at age twenty-eight.

Success didn't come easy. Bingham was constantly hampered by his government's laxness in sending commodities to exchange for military supplies, repay loans, and cover his expenses. Making matters worse, Congress maintained a head-in-the-sand blindness to the pressure its fiscal irresponsibility placed on its agents, at one point abdicating entirely and telling him to send his overdue bills to the commissioners in France. Since they were strapped themselves, this prompted Franklin's demand that "a stop be put" to Bingham's attempt "to draw upon me at pleasure to support his credit under the idea of its being necessary to do so for the honor of Congress."

Still, the young man enjoyed operational advantages in Martinique that soon gained him a formidable reputation among its merchants and foreign visitors, "treated with as much respect," marveled a London newspaper, "as the British ambassador at Paris."

The island's remote location encouraged the flouting of traditional protocol. Its governor and military commander gleefully snubbed British protests over the firing on HMS *Shark* and went so far as to offer a naval escort to *Reprisal* on its return trip to America, a gesture the foreign ministry rejected as too incendiary. "They were afraid of commencing hostilities," Bingham lamented, "as the French navy is very weak in the West Indies."

He too pushed limits with his superiors. Within days of arriving he sent letters to Philadelphia and Paris laying out strategies of wartime commerce like a veteran magnate. He told Silas Deane to ship goods through him rather than straight to America. It was costlier due to reloading onto smaller, more elusive vessels and paying the middlemen (including Bingham), but it was safer "as by this means the risk may be divided."

To Robert Morris he stressed the need for efficient communication. Rather than ask random captains to carry mail, he proposed a regular schedule of "fast sailing, well appointed" vessels to ply between Martinique and the American mainland. Six months later, the Committee of Secret Correspondence likewise sought to buy two packet boats in France to facilitate contact with its diplomats there, a belated acknowledgment of the mail delays that had so bedeviled Deane.

Martinique's inhabitants were well informed of international events. European ships neutral in the ongoing war brought in mail and newspapers free from Royal Navy harassment. And American ships on powder voyages to Saint-Pierre were numerous and persistent. Many were intercepted, but enough got through with the latest news from their ports of origin to give Bingham a broader sense of current affairs in Europe and America than was available to Congress or the Paris commissioners. His network of procurement agents on other foreign-held islands enhanced his knowledge of world developments and market trends. Before long he was making unilateral purchasing decisions that those awaiting his shipments in America had no choice but to accept.

Morris, with whom he had extensive side deals in addition to their government work, conceded that "none but persons on the spot can have a just idea of the perpetual changes that take place in every branch of business." Congress grumbled, however, forgetting that military supplies were in erratic abundance even on Martinique. If arms were temporarily unavailable, Bingham might substitute molasses or tea that Congress at least could exchange, at values much higher than their original cost, for tobacco, flour, indigo, and other colonial commodities prized by foreign merchants. Such profit-based purchases generated "a ministerial fortune" for him and Morris and should have benefited the government as well, increasing its buying power abroad. But Congress consistently failed to fulfill its end of the commodities-for-weapons arrangement.

Most of the problem in getting shipments to its agents was due to capture by Royal Navy patrols, but much was caused by bureaucratic inattention, shortsightedness, and incompetence. "If Congress means to succeed in this contest," Morris scolded his colleagues, "they must pay good executive men to do their business as it ought to be done, and not lavish millions away with their own mismanagement." But as Deane had quizzically observed in countless letters from Europe, mail and cargoes carried by private vessels enjoyed a higher rate of arrival than those sent by government vessels despite facing similar threats of capture. That the same officials (namely Morris and his business associates) managed both private and public commerce suggests they were more vigilant when out for themselves.

Certainly they were more aggressive in hiring ships and crews and dispatching them nonstop from multiple ports; more daring in sailing in winter weather (when the Royal Navy held closer to port); and more prepared to endure losses on the bet of future success. Still, in the knowledge that "when cargoes arrive either one way or other the profits are ever so great," they clearly took unethical advantage at times.

In October 1776, Morris had Bingham log a government cargo into Willing & Morris's account "as we want to throw funds into your hands." The bookkeeping maneuver may have been part of the common flux of debt that ran between Congress and the era's powerful money men. "It should be said," notes the economic historian E. James Ferguson, "that an officer in Morris's position would, in the normal course of events, sometimes owe the government money and thus have use of public funds to conduct his private trade; and at other times the government might be in debt to him." After the war, however, Morris admitted diverting more than $80,000 to his accounts without returning it. Those funds had undoubtedly supported his business ventures while Congress's in the meantime had floundered.

Unable to tap into government coffers, Bingham used privateering to generate cash and bolster his credit through prolonged periods of nonpayment from Congress. En route to Martinique aboard *Reprisal*, he'd seen Captain Wickes snatch three British cargo ships and send them home for settlement. With an eye for efficiency, Bingham, at his first meeting with the island commander, General

Comte d'Argout, inquired whether American privateers could carry prizes to Saint-Pierre, a destination nearer the hunting ground of Britain's West Indian trade routes. D'Argout's immediate reply, given six months before Deane frantically championed the case of Captain Lee in Spain, could only have come on remote Martinique. "If the American cruisers should bring any prizes into our ports, we will not prevent their selling or disposing of them as they think proper."

Bingham leaped into action with none of Deane's misgivings about licensing privateers on his own authority. He required only a nominal American identity before approving applications. A single crewmember was sufficient; everyone else involved—the captain, the owners—could be foreign. If caught by the Royal Navy in the act of pursuing a British prize, the ship could produce its commission signed by Bingham to assert its status as a legitimate privateer. If detained for routine inspection, it could show French papers and be spared further harassment by virtue of its neutral flag.

When spy reports about "one Bingham, an agent from the rebels" reached Lord Stormont in Paris, he erupted. "What they have hitherto only attempted in Europe they have executed in the West Indies, and in such a manner as calls loudly for redress." That redress came when France, under British pressure, replaced D'Argout with the "more reliable" Marquis de Bouillé. Stormont remained skeptical. "They will continue to play the same game, but it will be played with more decency and address."

Sure enough, he soon was back at the French foreign ministry with a list of Bingham-sponsored privateers still working out of Martinique. With appropriate shock Vergennes exclaimed, "Why, this is a fleet!" Stormont followed with a threat. "If a fire is lighted at the extremities it will soon arrive at the center."

Assuring the ambassador that the matter "should be inquired into," Vergennes instructed the island commander to rein in the American agent, that "distance from the seat of empire" did not excuse the disregard of international treaties. But by then Bingham had preemptively met with Bouille to promote "the harmony and exchange of good offices which have hitherto subsisted uninterruptedly between the government of Martinique and the United States of America."

Stormont knew about the meetings and doubted that matters would improve. Sure enough, at the same time Vergennes was tossing him superficial concessions the foreign minister was privately telling his aides that Britain, despite its attempt at intimidation, had no greater sway over French policy than anyone else. "Whoever can pay the most can be assured of the preference." France had rebuilt its military from the shambles of defeat in the Seven Years' War and increased its naval presence in the West Indies. "Fire at the center" was nothing to fear any longer.

Only minimally constrained by Martinique's new regime, Bingham's privateering activities vaulted him into the financial stratosphere. His involvement was "early and active," he wrote. During his first six months on the island, 250 British ships carrying cargoes worth more than $10 million were waylaid in the West Indies. Saint-Pierre was the privateer destination of choice to settle prizes and refit for the next cruise. Fourteen arrived there in one week alone, with Bingham's take on a single shipload of coffee and sugar exceeding a quarter-million dollars in today's terms.

One afternoon a year after the agent's arrival, British spies counted "eighty-two English ships, some of which were of considerable value," anchored at Saint-Pierre awaiting sale. "Every prize vessel proper to be converted to a privateer is fitted out as one. They all have commissions from Mr. Bingham."

The port was awash in captured goods ranging from Irish linens to African slaves. There was no pretense of legitimacy. "Guinea ships are sold immediately and publicly without condemnation." And since the merchandise was illicit, it could be bought cheaply, with slaves that elsewhere fetched £40 each going for less than £30.

Merchants on the British islands of Bermuda, Grenada, and Antigua came to regard Martinique's privateers as a routine business hazard, regularly journeying to Saint-Pierre to buy back their stolen goods. One spy report noted that a British captain whose slave ship had been hijacked "actually contracted with Mr. Bingham for the schooner and Negroes for a considerable sum of money, though not the full value of them."

Insurance rates on Britain's West Indian trade tripled from prewar levels and import prices in London rose almost 20 percent. Some trading firms dispensed with national pride and committed "the unusual and unholy spectacle" of booking cargoes on French ships to discourage American theft. Though ostensibly authorized by Congress, it was common knowledge that most of the West Indian privateers were foreign-manned surrogates, a further affront that incited British outrage against "the agent Bingham, who commissions all the French pirates."

In December 1776 the Committee of Secret Correspondence, uneasy with the power accruing to Bingham in his faraway post, told the Paris commissioners to quit sharing with him "the business passing between you and us" because "we think him rather too young." Morris ignored the policy, informing committee members, "I have this day written to Mr. Bingham a full state of intelligence to this time."

Bingham's specialty was commerce, not diplomacy, yet Morris understood that the agent's international contacts made him indispensable to the war effort regardless of his low security clearance. He also was indispensable to Morris, who'd sent him to Martinique on orders, Morris confided to Silas Deane, "to procure some arms for the government and with another view that I need not mention." Beyond their private trade collaborations, Bingham had become, through letters exchanged that fall, the older man's sounding board in resolving his personal qualms about privateering.

Those qualms had centered on loyalty. The Royal Navy's seizure of Morris's cargoes had seemed, in the early months of the war, insufficient cause to justify the turnabout of seizing cargoes belonging to his former friends in Britain. He had his limits, however, and by December, "having had several vessels taken from me and otherwise lost a great deal of my property by this war, I conceive myself perfectly justifiable in the eyes of God or man to seek what I have lost from those that have plundered me."

Bingham, an expert in the field by that time, recommended a number of capable captains with whom they could jointly venture. One of the first was an Acadian-born skipper named Coctiny de Prejent. Demanding confidentiality, Morris proposed that the three of them buy "a stout privateer" to cruise "amongst the outward bound West India men." He'd use Willing & Morris's funds to furnish his stake in the project even though his partner, Thomas Willing, "objects positively" to privateering, and he vowed to repay the debt out of the vessel's earnings should the cruise be successful. "If not, I will repay them the amount here."

To expedite prize payouts, Morris advised Bingham to sell, "without formal condemnation," slaves, commodities, and dry goods on Martinique, but to send "cargoes as are suited to the Continent [that is, arms and gunpowder]" directly to America for sale. He closed with a reminder to make sure the ship's crew obeyed the rules of humane conduct mandated by its commission. The nervous tone of his letter bespoke a traditional gentleman's uneasy view of privateering. Lest anyone say he'd come to it out of mere greed, he offered *Retaliation* as the warship's new name to symbolize that his motives were righteous.

Morris's misgivings soon evaporated. By the spring of 1777 he was pestering Bingham "to increase the number of my engagements in that way." Moreover, "it matters not who knows my concern." Yet their blossoming partnership had the unexpected consequence of tilting the power between them toward Bingham. He was where the action was; he hired the boats and managed the prizes. Eventually Morris, in his rush to participate in the Martinique boom, ran up more than half a million dollars in personal debt to the young man, an obligation that "sits heavy with me." His early bossiness toward Bingham ("If you cannot attend closely you had better get some other to do the business or hire an excellent clerk to assist you") turned petulant and plaintive. "It is not necessary to be so pressing with me about remittances . . ."

Upon first appointing him, Morris had feared Bingham was "fanciful" and wondered if "experience could cure him of this." But as "your affectionate friend" congealed to "dear Sir" in his letters, it was

Robert Morris, the so-called "financier of the Revolution," had a hand in funding most every significant strategic and logistical initiative undertaken by Congress during the war. His sense of propriety kept the Philadelphian from investing wholeheartedly in privateers—for a while.

clear the financier found it hard to accept that his protégé had become his master.

Before he was dismissed under British diplomatic pressure, the commander at Martinique, General D'Argout, sent a letter to his superiors describing "exactly the real state of affairs" in America. It was December 23, 1776, and as he rightly observed, "the situation is almost desperate."

Congress's ill-planned operations in Canada had failed when the expected welcome by Canadians eager to become America's fourteenth colony never materialized. A British naval force had seized Newport in early December. Congress had packed up and fled to Baltimore as British troops advanced through New Jersey. And Washington's army, its retreat into Pennsylvania capped with the mass expiration of enlistment terms in November, had shrunk to less than three thousand men, a number soon to be halved when December enlistments expired. While Thomas Paine challenged "the summer soldier and the sunshine patriot" to persevere despite the hard times, Washington was confiding to his brother, "I think the game is pretty near up."

In D'Argout's opinion, the general's "only resort" was to "gather as many troops as possible in order to fight a pitched battle with decisive results." Three days later Washington did exactly that, crossing the Delaware River back to New Jersey and striking the Hessian garrison at Trenton. Buoyed by the victory, his men agreed to march against General Charles Cornwallis's army at Princeton, ultimately forcing more than eight thousand British regulars to yield most of New Jersey before both armies settled into their winter quarters.

In addition to calling upon their patriotism, Washington personally pledged a new signing bonus to persuade his men to fight on. He begged Morris likewise to "strain his credit upon such an occasion," and the financier spent a frantic night going house to house among his friends borrowing any hard money he could find, from English crowns to Spanish gold dollars.

Sending the money to Washington by horseback, Morris apologized for the delay due to no couriers being awake that early in the morning. He'd been the only member of Congress to stay in Philadelphia rather than flee the approaching British. Lukewarm on rebellion at a time when his peers had howled for it, he noted now that "many of those who were foremost in noise shrink cowardlike from the danger." His commitment carried "a heavy heart" but was absolute. "I shall remain here until the enemy drive me away."

D'Argout had contended in his letter to Paris that the Continental Army's earlier defeats in New York and New Jersey were "far more injurious in their effects than they are in themselves." The same was true of the victories at Trenton and Princeton. Their greater significance was psychological rather than tactical, providing a boost of optimism to carry America into another year of fighting. They brought an opposite reaction in Britain.

Edward Bancroft, in London in February when news of the two battles arrived, notified Deane that it "very much depressed the spirits of administration here." He saw a chance to short-sell stocks on the London market in order to profit from their decline, an investment strategy enhanced by any tips on further bad news that Deane might provide him from Paris. "Stocks are beginning to sink, so that if France should act as if she intends a war, they will soon fall 8 or 10 percent."

Deane's financial frustration had deepened after Congress, despite his repeated pleas for blank privateer commissions to meet high European demand, had sent only "three sets of the papers we wanted. But we shall want more, and beg you will not fail to send them by several opportunities." So in addition to Bancroft's stock schemes, in early 1777 Deane took a percentage in a privateer, *Tartar*, whose captain carried a commission specially arranged in America by Robert Morris, one of the ship's investors.

Two years later Congress would investigate an allegation that Deane had "misapplied the public money" to buy into the vessel for personal gain. Part of a barrage of charges brought by Arthur Lee against the compatriot who'd participated in Hortalez & Company without him (and, Lee suspected, profited hugely), it was based on the hazy recollections of Deane's secretary in Paris at the time. Lacking any supporting evidence, the allegation could not have been expected to stand up against accounting records properly kept. But Deane didn't keep proper records. Combined with his history of expediency and, in Lee, a relentless antagonist bent on revenge, his habitual carelessness made it hard to prove his innocence against the increasingly common presumption that government officials who flourished in wartime were thieves and possibly traitors.

But at the turn of the year between 1776 and 1777, more fervent than Deane's involvement in privateers and London stocks was the project he and Beaumarchais had initiated more than half a year earlier—loading eight ships with two thousand tons of supplies for the Continental Army. The effort had been delayed at every turn by the interference of British authorities acting on Bancroft's spy reports, but finally the largest of the vessels, *Amphitrite*, was launched, steering for New England once it cleared the port of Le Havre.

The next vessel, *Seine* left in late January and headed to Martinique, from where Bingham forwarded north its 350 tons of powder, tents, mortars, and blankets. The last transport got away that spring, concluding a tortuous process that exhausted Deane and Beaumarchais and bankrupted Hortalez & Company. The project cost $50 million, a tab that, as Deane understood the arrangement, Congress would repay as soon as possible.

Writing in his diary soon after launching *Amphitrite*, he described himself as a "humble agent" and credited those in France "whose exalted station gives them the ability and their greatness of soul the disposition of extending such relief to millions struggling under oppression's heavy hands." France's generosity, he wrote, "would be equaled only by the endless gratitude of the numberless millions rising into existence in a new and extensive world."

The supplies delivered aboard Deane's vessels would figure significantly in the Revolution's pivotal battle, the American victory at Saratoga the next October—a battle whose rout of the enemy's attempt to sever New England from the other colonies profoundly shook the prevailing worldview that Britain was invincible.

Yet the great irony of Deane's career is that, while his pursuits in war trade, stock jobbing, and privateers drew justifiable scrutiny, it was his role in dispatching those vessels—his finest contribution as a patriot—that ultimately turned his countrymen against him.

1776

John Paul Jones, commissioned as a Continental Navy officer in December 1775, was disgusted by the privateering phenomenon. "The common class of mankind are actuated by no nobler principle than that of self-interest. This and this only determines all adventurers in privateers, the owners as well as those whom they employ."

Though perfectly fond of money (in 1777 complaints were filed alleging that Jones wouldn't pay his men their wages "without their first signing a power to him to be their agent"), he viewed it mainly as pragmatic motivation to fight. Thus he denounced a navy proposal to grant "joint shares" to the entire fleet for prizes seized by individual vessels. No other commander approached his aggressiveness in raiding enemy shipping, and he saw no justice in not keeping for himself and his men "all that they can take."

He lamented that as long as navy men drew a "paltry emolument" in comparison with privateers, "in sober sadness we are involved in a woeful predicament." He wrote Congress seeking to raise a crew's prize share from one-half to two-thirds of its value (and 100 percent if it was a warship). Even after it was adopted, however, the increased distribution did little to slow the manpower drain. The navy did offer sailors a half-pint of rum per day and a $400 death benefit to families. And similarly to privateers, a man's prize share doubled if he was first to sight an enemy vessel and tripled if he was first to board it. But the navy's requirement to attend "divine service" twice a day and to discourage "cursing and blasphemy" had no place on a privateer. This moral leniency, together with privateering's elective

John Paul Jones despised privateers for draining manpower away from naval service. Yet there would come a time when privateering's profits tempted him to become an investor.

approach to battling the Royal Navy, its bigger signing bonuses, and better prospect of getting paid, made it by far the majority choice.

Continental sailors, unlike civilian mariners who signed up for one cruise at a time, lacked leverage under their long-term enlistments to demand swift payment. By contrast, the market pressures of privateering forced owners to make good on prize awards regardless of bureaucratic delays if they wanted to attract crews in the future.

There were other advantages. Privateersmen could sell their shares in advance of a voyage, accepting a lump sum from buyers who hoped to redeem them for a profit should the voyage hit big. And creditors accepted sailors' pledges of future earnings to settle debts. If earnings exceeded the amount owed, creditors kept the difference. In exchange for that privilege, debts were cleared even if the voyage came up empty. Many of these deals were unfair and probably coerced. One man, to pay off a loan of 42 shillings, sailed for eight months after granting his creditor "all my right and share of prize money that shall be taken," signing his name at the base of the agreement and indicating under it, "Indian."

Investors traded privateer shares at a premium or discount depending on whether, based on the quality of the ship and the competency of its officers, odds favored success or failure. Prize courts opened in Philadelphia and Baltimore, and the turnaround time between a prize's arrival in port and its legal settlement narrowed from months to weeks, streamlining the efficiency of an already booming industry.

The frenzy was especially fierce in Providence. While stationed there with the five-vessel Continental fleet in the fall of 1776, Jones raged at those who "wink at, encourage, and employ deserters from the navy." In frustration he took matters into his own hands, calling for the execution of deserters and employing surprise inspections to snatch away servicemen who'd jumped ship to private vessels.

Now it was the businessmen who howled. If the young captain didn't desist, "Division, confusion, and frequent bloodshedding must be the inevitable consequence."

He cursed their hypocrisy. "What punishment is equal to such baseness? And yet these men pretend to love their country!"

They in turn shot back with their British adversary's favorite slur. "Captain Jones," they said, "has been guilty of an act of piracy."

Four

Trust not your happiness in the hands of Fortune.
—*Nathanael Greene, August 1772*

One of Nathanael Greene's first business ventures was to pay "an unheard-of" price of £300 for seven acres of supposedly silver-rich land near his home in Rhode Island in 1768. He was talked into the purchase by his younger cousin Griffin. That it turned out a flop didn't discourage him from engaging in future projects with Griffin and other ambitious relatives.

Greene's scornful contention that "merchants in general are a body of people whose god is gain" concealed an inveterate attraction to deals that might in one shot free him financially to devote his energies to his wife, children, and army career. Possessing neither confidence nor acumen when speculating on his own, he preferred to be a silent partner who contributed money and later his famous name to deals conceived and arranged by others.

He narrowly had avoided another £300 loss when his company's rum was seized by *Gaspee* in 1772. His refusal to join in John Brown's retaliatory burning of the sloop reflected the rivalry between their families, a rivalry characterized by personal dislike and, from the well-to-do Greenes toward the filthy-rich Browns, envy. Six years earlier the Browns had diversified from shipping and candlemaking into iron production, mining ore and blasting it into raw pig iron at their furnace in the village of Hope. When they added a forge to refine the material, they intruded on the specialty of Nathanael's father, a Quaker minister whose foundry manufactured ship anchors and other wrought iron products.

The firms rancorously coexisted. The Greenes complained of

overpaying for Hope pig iron. The Browns complained of having been sold poor quality anchors; in a power play indicative of their superior status, they successfully dictated the terms of reimbursement. The families also clashed over the relocation of Rhode Island College. Nathanael submitted a last-minute petition to build the school near his home in Kent County, offering to top any other bid. The Browns countered that Providence had more religious diversity, meaning fewer Quakers and more Baptists, an argument the Greenes resented not least because it prevailed.

Nathanael was no fan of Quakerism. Constrained by what he called its "superstitious" piety, his education was limited to Bible study. He didn't attend college, and received instruction in Latin and mathematics only after pestering his father for a private tutor. Blaming his family's business mania for his lack of scholarship ("very early when I should have been in the pursuit of knowledge, I was digging into the bowels of the earth after wealth"), he equally criticized his habitual indecisiveness as a factor in all his shortcomings.

Words Greene wrote in 1770, when he was twenty-eight, expressed a lifelong refrain. "I am at variance with myself and am continually distracted and torn with civil feuds of my own disturbed imagination." A potentially crippling trait in a military leader, it hardly predicted his eventual emergence as George Washington's favorite and most capable general. But if "tumult and uproars from the contention of opposite interests" didn't hamper him on the battlefield, it filled much else in his life with anxiety.

Greene suffered from asthma and a congenital limp. The suddenness of his marriage in 1774 (it was announced days beforehand) to nineteen-year-old Catherine Littlefield suggests a preemptive strike against second thoughts on her part or his. "Caty" was pretty, feisty, and flirtatious—mistrusted by women, adored by men. When war later separated wife and husband, rumors arose of her infidelity, though a relative reported, "She confesses she has passions and propensities and that if she has any virtue 'tis in resisting and keeping them within due bounds."

Greene described his marriage as "Venus's War." If there was friction between them, there were sparks as well. His letters to Caty convey a fond intimacy and also the pressure he felt to keep her content. Intimidated by sophisticated society, he fretted about her behavior and incurred her wrath for correcting her spelling, her dress, and her wine drinking. "Nothing but the affection and regard I feel for you makes me wish to have you appear an accomplished lady in every point of view."

She enjoyed parties and expensive clothes, and was worldly enough to know what premium comforts lay just beyond their means. He hoped to change that through success in business, another reason why—given his desire to support Caty in style, his Quaker heritage, and his chronic self-doubt—his leap into an army career couldn't have been more unlikely.

In the years leading up to rebellion, his fiery opinions about British "chains of slavery" contrasted with an almost paralyzing ambivalence on other matters. (One self-critique described a man "perpetually falling out with himself.") Unwilling to defy his family's pacifist faith in order to join the local militia, he provoked dismissal from the Society of Friends by visiting, with his cousin Griffin, "a place in Connecticut of public resort where they had no proper business."

The year of his marriage, Greene joined a volunteer outfit called the Kentish Guards expecting to be designated a lieutenant. The members rejected him due to his limp, causing him particular "mortification" by doing so in a public announcement ("No one loves to be the subject of ridicule however true the cause"). But rather than resign he stayed on as a private.

After minutemen and redcoats fought in Lexington in April 1775, Rhode Island incorporated its scattered militias into a single army. In a mystifying move, the General Assembly named Greene, with only military book-learning and a private's experience of drills and parades, to lead the unit after two colonels turned it down. Instantly elevated to the rank of brigadier general, his career would feature several such leaps when intangible qualities of character won him unexpected favor. Accustomed to his peers' high esteem, Greene would, as a result, be painfully baffled when charges of ethical misconduct were later leveled and widely believed.

In June, Greene, not quite thirty-three, led 1,800 soldiers to join Washington's army outside Boston. Caty soon discovered she was pregnant and hired a carriage for the day's ride north to tell her husband after first stopping in Providence to buy herself a new wardrobe. During the next five years she bore four children, two in army camps. She alternately roughed it and "spent lavishly," enduring hard travel and primitive quarters in order to be with her husband in the field, pampering herself with parties and luxury goods for the extended periods they were apart. Temperamentally at odds with her Quaker in-laws, her extravagance and buoyancy clashed with what Nathanael termed their fascination with "the black pages of human life." But caught up in the war, he had little choice but to leave Caty in their care. He did the same with his finances.

He earned $125 per month as a brigadier general. How well it supported him is tricky to gauge in an era when Congress and each colony had its own currency; when foreign coins were legal tender at varying exchange rates; when debts were settled with gold or silver, with exchangeable bills of credit issued from local governments, with bartered goods, or with mutually agreed-upon services such as fixing your fence or plowing your land—and all this before war threw the economy into real havoc.

Clearly Greene's salary was ample, almost twenty times what Continental privates earned (today a brigadier general makes eight times what a private does). Certain factors marred the picture, however. American officers, like their British counterparts, were obliged to provide for themselves while on campaign—pay for quarters, provisions, and a domestic staff commensurate with their rank. Combat performance eventually gave rise to standards of merit based on results, but even in the more egalitarian American service gentlemanly trappings conferred leadership status on officers who, in the early stage of the war, had little real claim on command. Wartime inflation of Continental currency was another huge drain on their income. Intermittent pay hikes nowhere near offset the plunging dollar. And Congress's fiscal lapses increasingly meant the army didn't get paid at all, reducing budget worries down to the soldiers' grim joke that even something valueless was "not worth a Continental."

Still, in the summer of 1775, Greene, who'd been prepared to go to war as a private if need be, was in a solid situation financially. He'd won his settlement from the *Gaspee* seizure. The iron forge was running full tilt under his brothers' management, with Nathanael, per the terms of his late father's estate, receiving a share of the earnings. His partnership in Jacob Greene & Company promised good returns through speculation in shipping and trade. And finally, though he was slow to realize it, his prestige as a general in Washington's army gave him serious sway in Rhode Island business affairs.

The notion surfaced in correspondence received during his first months in command, a subtle, between-the-lines deference to a newly important person. A flattering note from his dour brother Jacob prompted Nathanael's modest mention of "the great defects I find in myself." Rhode Island Governor Nicholas Cooke, a former distiller and shipmaster (that is, smuggler), wrote in lavish praise of Greene's role in a recent skirmish near Boston. The general countered that the British in fact had won the engagement, "though at too dear a rate for them to rejoice much at their success."

Then came a letter from Providence that opened dramatically, "Having the cause of our bleeding country much at heart," before going on to offer a business deal that required a slight favor beforehand. The proposition was for Greene to buy into a privateer currently under construction. The favor was for him to use his influence to obtain a commission to license the venture—not an easy thing to do, since the Rhode Island Assembly had yet to follow Massachusetts's lead in authorizing private warships. But as a member of the Assembly, the letter's author, Nicholas Brown, knew such authorizations were imminent, and, crafty as ever, he was looking to get a jump on the competition.

Greene declined. By that time, February 1776, Jacob Greene & Company was running powder voyages to the West Indies like most every trading firm in Rhode Island. Privateering was the logical next

Nathanael Greene, despite an introspective and hesitant tempera-ment seemingly ill-suited for combat command, would emerge as one of America's greatest generals. Yet even as his battlefield prowess helped the Patriots to victory, his hefty speculation in privateers filled him with dread of personal ruin.

step. Nathanael was uneasy with the move, however. Legality wasn't the issue. Rather, he cited a soldier's priority. "It is necessary for some to be in the field to secure the property of others in their stores." Aware of privateering's reputation as a financial sure thing, he was wistful nonetheless. "Were I at liberty, I think I could make a fortune for my family."

The combat Greene experienced in coming years made him rethink his position. By 1778–after bloody fighting in New York and Rhode Island; after Trenton, Valley Forge, and Brandywine–he'd grown embittered by reports of former associates who'd stayed home amid "domestic pleasures" and now were getting richer by the day.

Squeezed by his wife's spending and the difficulty in even collecting his depreciating army pay, he wrote Jacob angrily, "Why therefore should a few zealous officers be made a certain sacrifice for the common good? What is to become of them after the war?" To persevere in the military while civilian businessmen prospered "must render the condition of the officers infinitely more wretched than other parts of society. Is it reasonable that men should be exposed to all the hardships of war, be constantly exposed to sudden death and broken bones without any compensation?"

Greene's argument was mostly with himself–to rationalize his already-made decision to get involved in privateering. Beginning in late 1776 his letters to Jacob and Griffin increasingly inquired about "navigation," "fishing," and a seaborne "golden harvest." These were coded references to privateer expeditions in which the family, including Nathanael as a discreet partner, owned shares.

The young general had found a way to participate in the wartime boom that met his standard of consistency "with the public good." Honorable patriots throughout the colonies were daily making the same calculation to the benefit of their country, their families, and their pocketbooks. Surely now it was his turn.

The British occupation of Boston had been great for the Rhode Island economy. In the absence of competition from the larger port forty miles north, Providence became New England's primary entry point for European goods imported via the West Indies and for commodities and foodstuffs brought in from elsewhere in the colonies, notably Philadelphia flour and southern tobacco. And because the British evacuation in March 1776 had left Boston in disrepair with a business community diminished by the departure of many wealthy loyalist families, Providence was able to retain its advantage through the remainder of that year–almost.

The December 6 landing of six thousand British troops at Newport sealed off Narragansett Bay and abruptly severed Providence's route to the Atlantic Ocean. That area merchants endured and in some cases flourished during Newport's subsequent three-year occupation testifies to their legendary ingenuity at overcoming trade obstacles. Boston's long commercial dormancy had forced the development of land routes linking Providence to other New England ports, and new business relationships had sprung up throughout the region to replace those no longer centered in the Massachusetts capital. Merchants therefore were ready with alternate strategies after the Royal Navy imposed from its base in Newport a smothering blockade of the bay.

Yet no amount of resiliency could fully offset the loss of sea access. Even the canniest entrepreneurs couldn't sustain the economic boom that had propelled Providence between March and December of that year, that is, in the period beginning with Congress's legalization of privateers and ending with Newport's fall. All of Providence's merchant clans—Bowen, Howell, Clark, Nightingale—had prospered in that period, but the Browns dominated. Though their candle business collapsed from the war's effect on the whaling industry (candles were rendered from the "head matter" of sperm whales), their shipping expertise, ironworks, and market savvy aligned perfectly with wartime developments that put Providence, for those nine months in 1776, at the forefront of frenetic expenditure from Congress and private speculators.

An early inquiry from the General Assembly into the possibility of their manufacturing cannon had set John, Nicholas, and Joseph Brown to a rapid conversion of the Hope furnace to military production. (Moses, dedicated to spiritual and altruistic endeavors, including the charitable support of seven thousand civilians impoverished by the war, kept apart from his brothers.) They consulted experts in the process, financed "the necessary additional works" with earnings from their West Indian powder voyages, and in January 1776 declared the facility open for business. They priced their cannon at £35 per ton with three contractual conditions: clients supplied the powder to test the guns; the Browns were not liable for faulty guns that, once purchased, exploded under use; and payment was due in full even if hostilities ended and the guns were no longer needed.

Congress immediately ordered sixty twelve- and eighteen-pounders for two frigates being built in Rhode Island as part of the effort to launch thirteen such vessels from shipyards up and down the coast. In what would prove a frustrating effort, none of the thirteen sailed before 1777; four never got to sea at all; two were sunk in battle; and the rest were captured by the enemy one by one after spotty careers in which their few prizes barely dented Congress's huge investment in the enterprise. At one point before the last vessels were completed, Washington advised Congress to scuttle them rather than waste more money on the project.

Construction of the Rhode Island frigates was especially onerous. Bloated costs and suspected graft dogged the process. The Rhode Island Frigate Committee was no help in correcting problems because, conveniently, the targets of most of the allegations, John and Nicholas Brown, were the Committee's leading members.

Their fiercest critic was one of their gun factory's first customers. John Langdon, former member of Congress now back running his Portsmouth wharf, had sought the post of New Hampshire's maritime agent specifically to keep shady officials from "doing wrong or unjust things." He became suspicious when his order for twenty-six cannon from the Browns for the Continental frigate *Raleigh* being built at Portsmouth went unfilled for months. He traveled to Providence several times to verify their excuse that Rhode Island's frigates were almost finished and therefore first in line for the guns. Finding this to be untrue, he protested to Congress. "There seemed to be a secret determination not to let me have the guns at any rate whatever." Not even, he said, at the "extortioners" price of £100 per ton.

Congress scolded the Browns for acting "against the public good" and ordered the immediate delivery of Langdon's cannon. John and Nicholas balked, claiming they were working "to the prejudice of their own interest" on behalf of the government. Facing congressional charges of "interested motives" that "bear hard on the characters of the committee men," the Frigate Committee formed a commission to investigate. John Brown headed the inquiry and duly exonerated himself and his brother, freeing them to scrap the deal with Langdon. The Frigate Committee, to bolster its case for keeping the guns for use within the state, resorted to unseasoned lumber and novice craftsmen to expedite production, ultimately turning out "the two worst of all our frigates," according to Robert Morris.

Langdon was similarly snubbed by suppliers in Massachusetts and Connecticut. He accused officials of refusing to help him for fear of losing sales commissions. A principled patriot, the thirty-five-year-old Langdon discounted or refused entirely any fees for himself on government purchases. "If these guns belong to the Continent how they can be sold on commission I know not unless the Continent is to pay for them twice." He raged at the greed of his colleagues. "My blood now boils."

Most irksome was the actual abundance of guns—a "considerable number," he wrote, but they were earmarked "for private ships." This was the root of the problem. Unlike Congress, whose dilatory accounting meant bills got paid months late in depreciated dollars, civilians paid in advance for guns and often kicked in extra upon delivery to compensate for inflation. Too, a "jealousy of one state against another" inclined suppliers to favor local buyers.

Through the fall of 1776, Langdon's *Raleigh*, which Morris rated "a very fine ship," languished in Portsmouth while the agent scrounged for arms. The delay drove five hundred potential navy crewmen to enter "on board privateers very fast, all this for want of guns for our ship. The people do not like to enter without guns, as they want to be out after prize money." In the meantime sixty-five Rhode Island privateers were commissioned with full complements of cannon, almost all of them provided by the Browns—"my worthy friends at Providence," Langdon wrote sarcastically.

With efficiency gained through long commercial experience, the brothers outfitted their own ships and marketed them as well. They hired street musicians to sing of quick fortunes ("come all you young fellows of courage so bold / come enter on board and we will clothe you with gold") and posted broadsides promising congenial captains, ample alcohol, and a thrilling opportunity to smite "the tyrant's pilferers."

They matched the best crews with the fastest boats and dispatched them with crisp instructions. Operating in packs had become the privateers' preferred tactic. That June, for instance, an armed British transport passing through Massachusetts Bay had fended off twelve marauders over seven hours until finally surrendering with "six soldiers killed outright and nine more wounded, our ammunition mostly expended." Brown-owned privateers, on the other hand, were told not sail in packs lest they have to split prizes taken in joint captures, "but if it cannot be well avoided to agree to share according to right." And since demand had driven up values enormously, their captains were always to be on the lookout for better ships to which they could upgrade.

In addition to voyages they funded themselves, John and Nicholas engaged in countless partnerships to spread out their risk exposure. (A sixteenth share of a small privateer went for £56 at the time.) They pushed the Providence prize court to speed up trials, and in contrast to Massachusetts, where privateers that captured African slaves were "forbidden to sell them or in any manner to treat them otherwise than is already ordered for the treatment of prisoners," the Browns applauded Rhode Island's policy of pricing slaves as part of a prize's usual "appurtenances and cargo."

Their maritime ventures supplemented an array of other projects, including attempts to corner the regional market for flour and, crucial for its qualities as a food preservative, salt. They'd begun stockpiling the stuff in 1775 as trade bait for gunpowder and European goods. After government price controls were imposed in 1776 to protect "humbler folk" from the "oppression of rich merchants," the Browns refused to sell until price ceilings were raised. Shortages became so acute they were legally compelled to offer the commodities "at the price affixed by law." Sales revenues were three times costs, even so.

Their privateering profits are harder to measure. But the forty-one prizes brought into Providence between April and November 1776 were appraised in excess of £300,000, a value "double the property of the whole town two years ago," and the Browns were the biggest beneficiary. Moreover, John was sufficiently enthused by the enterprise—and sufficiently flush with money even after the lengthy British occupation of Newport—to consider building a massive thousand-ton privateer in 1779. He would abandon the project only after the state's other ironworks, whose pig iron he needed to produce the cannon required for his vessel's multiple gundecks, refused to give him a bargain price.

Esek Hopkins, a former slave ship captain who'd come out of retirement in December 1775 to command the small Continental fleet at Providence, initially deemed privateers inconsequential to naval operations. He dismissed the warnings of John Paul Jones and others to expedite government prize payouts or else face dire manpower shortages. "As for the division of the plunder it gives me no concern," Hopkins sniffed, "and I take notice that those who are most clamorous about the matter least deserve it."

The commodore's laissez-faire attitude extended to combat operations. Instructed by Congress to clear Chesapeake Bay of enemy warships, he took to heart a line in his orders advising him to risk getting trapped in the bay only if the enemy were "not greatly superior" in strength. Sailing south from Providence in frigid January weather, he elected even before reaching the Chesapeake to proceed instead to the warm Caribbean and raid the British island of New Providence (Nassau). The *London Chronicle* subsequently broke the news that "a British fleet was totally defeated by Admiral Hopkins after a dreadful slaughter on both sides."

Not quite. The island was lightly defended, and the Americans seized 78 cannon and a small supply of gunpowder with no casualties except sailors felled by too much celebratory drinking. Hopkins expected this happy boost to the patriot armory to mollify Congress's irritation at his freelancing. Sighting HMS *Glasgow* off Block Island on the last leg of his voyage home, he tried to further polish his image by attacking the cruiser with a five-to-one advantage.

"Good News for America!" headlined the *Salem Gazette* in reporting the battle. The *Newport Mercury* sang the same song, mocking the beaten British vessel "yelping from the mouths of her cannon (like a broken legged dog) in token of her being sadly wounded." But as details emerged, the story took a different look.

The purported three-hour battle had lasted a fraction of that time before the ships broke contact. *Glasgow* suffered one man killed. Three Continental warships were left shattered with ten dead and fourteen wounded, while the two others, from ineptitude or cowardice, had never entered the fight at all.

Hopkins, after initially claiming that his obligation to safeguard the "precious cargoes" seized in New Providence "was the sole cause of *Glasgow* making her escape," soon had to admit that he'd quit the fight because his flagship's rudder had been shot away and "some that were on board had got too much liquor out of the prizes to be fit for duty." In a flash his reputation slid from golden hero to cantankerous bungler.

Congress held an inquiry while he awaited judgment in Providence. The wait coincided with the explosion of Rhode Island privateering and opened his eyes to its drain on recruitment. His plea to the General Assembly to freeze privateer activity until his fleet was fully manned failed, he wrote, "owing to a number of members being deeply concerned in privateering." Retained in command thanks to the influence of John Adams, who defended his support of the commodore as a necessary stand against "that anti-New England spirit which haunted Congress," Hopkins prepared his ships to sail again.

December came. British forces launched their amphibious invasion. "The inhabitants of the town of Newport favored their operation I believe too much" was Hopkins's excuse for the astonishing ease of the enemy victory, which had, in a stroke, trapped the Continental fleet ("as they term it," the British leadership sneered) up the bay in Providence. Nicholas Cooke, who as Rhode Island governor had helped stonewall outside requests for cannon, was furious that his desperate call on the eve of the attack "for the assistance and aid of our sister states" had not prompted enthusiastic compliance. But

John Langdon followed the letter of the law in seeking to outfit the Continental frigates under construction in New Hampshire. Thwarted at every turn by the popular lure of privateers and the unwillingness of weapons manufacturers to sell at government prices, he tried to recoup his losses by funding a private warship, a lapse in principle that earned John Paul Jones's contempt but made Langdon a wealthy man.

Congress focused its wrath on Hopkins for his fleet's lack of resistance and sacked him within a few weeks.

One ship of the fleet was safely at sea at the time of the Newport invasion—John Paul Jones's *Alfred*, a merchant vessel refitted for twenty-six guns. Jones had captured sixteen prizes during a six-week cruise out of Providence earlier that fall. By good fortune he'd left port again in November to keep his men from the lure of privateering. With Narragansett Bay now inaccessible, he shifted his base to Massachusetts in early 1777 before ending up in Portsmouth that spring to take command of *Ranger*, an armed sloop being built by John Langdon.

Langdon would seem to have been the sort of staunch patriot the prickly Jones could respect ("he does not improve on acquaintance," an associate once wrote of the captain). But it wasn't long before Jones was insulting him as someone "who was bred in a shop and hath been about a voyage or two at sea under a nurse," which was to say, as someone incompetent to build a warship. Jones's scorn aimed at more than the agent's inexperience. He hated privateers for the competition they posed for ships and men, and Langdon, himself long critical of the enterprise, had become an avid investor.

Still stymied in obtaining cannon for his frigate *Raleigh* ("the most humiliating circumstance of my life"), Langdon had collected an assortment of smaller guns for *Ranger*, personally laying out $40,000 at a time when two-thirds of "my little fortune" was frozen overseas in prewar deals with British merchants. Five months earlier he'd turned down an offer from Robert Morris to invest together in a New Hampshire privateer, "not that I've the least doubt but much might be made in this way." But with Congress leaving him stranded with outstanding expenses, he'd been forced to change his tune. He bankrolled several privateers and asked Bingham to receive their prizes in Martinique and "dispose of them and their cargoes to the greatest advantage."

Jones was furious that his civilian superior in Portsmouth had succumbed to privateering's lure. Fighting fire with fire, he composed a recruiting poster for *Ranger*'s crew that emphasized "the possibility to make their fortunes" alongside the chance "to distinguish themselves in the GLORIOUS CAUSE of their country."

The selective capitalization showed where his sentiments tilted, but even he wasn't immune to self-interest. At least one contemporary deemed Jones outright hypocritical in that regard. "Under the guise of despising money he is aiming and grasping all he can." This was too harsh. But still, having made $3,000 from prizes seized last fall, he used the period of delay in outfitting *Ranger* to research how best to invest it.

Jones and Robert Morris had corresponded frequently in the past about Marine Committee matters. But in a letter written that summer, Jones buried within his usual litany of suggestions and complaints a nervous request for advice. After first reminding the financier of an earlier "kind offer of interesting yourself in my favor when any private enterprise should be adopted," he proposed that "we get a small squadron together." He didn't mean a squadron of government ships. "It would give me pleasure to bear a second or a third part in any private enterprise under the conduct of gentlemen of superior abilities from whom I could receive instruction and improvement."

Since privateering was notoriously disreputable, Jones went on, "I must rely on you to guard me from future connections with illiterate men of incapacity." No sooner had he floated the idea, however, than his rectitude kicked in and he hedged, "But I have already gone too far. I leave my present and future destination to the gentlemen at whose disposal I am and whose orders shall govern my actions as servant of the public."

Jones's "future destination" was Europe. He vowed "to draw off the enemy's attention by attacking their defenseless places," a plan fulfilled the following spring in his daring hit-and-run raid on the port of Whitehaven, which panicked the British people by bringing the war to English soil. However, as to his prediction that he "would do infinite damage to their shipping," that goal was nearer approached by the swarms of privateers he despised and in whose enterprise he never wound up investing. It was glory over gold for Jones. He would have liked to get both, of course. When he died at age forty-five in France nine years after the war, he pretty much had neither.

As for Langdon, he finally got his beloved frigate *Raleigh* armed and launched in late 1777. A year later the vessel surrendered under enemy fire, was rechristened HMS *Raleigh* by its captors, and subsequently participated in the British capture of Charleston, South Carolina, in the summer of 1780.

1776

BROOKLYN, NEW YORK

Whitby, a decrepit transport that once carried livestock for the British Army, dropped anchor in Wallabout Bay on the Brooklyn side of the East River in October 1776. Its hull was dismasted and stripped of its fittings, portholes were barred, and a ten-foot barrier, notched for the muskets of British guardsmen, was erected between the main deck and the elevated quarter-deck at the stern.

Six weeks later the governor of Connecticut received a letter from Timothy Parker, a navy lieutenant imprisoned aboard *Whitby* along with 250 other Americans. It detailed their "miserable circumstances" with a desperate decorum that, to read it today, gives an impression that things weren't really so bad. Two-thirds rations, being "crowded promiscuously together without distinction or respect to person, office, or color," and the necessity of "tubs and buckets" to do "what nature requires" seem unequal to the "lingering inevitable death" the lieutenant foretold for himself and his companions.

The matter alarmed George Washington, however. Having long believed that the enemy's treatment of American prisoners "ought to be exactly observed upon our part to those we take prisoners from them," he now warned his British counterpart, General Howe, that unless conditions on *Whitby* improved, the Continentals "will, if forced to it, most assuredly retaliate." But conditions didn't improve. Overcrowding led to illness and malnutrition. British bitterness over the prolonged war led to willful cruelty toward prisoners and indifference to their suffering; that most were civilian "pirates" contributed to the vindictiveness of their treatment. Even Lieutenant Parker distanced himself from those pariahs, stressing that he'd been taken "in the service of our country and cannot be deemed a common privateer."

British captives taken at sea generally complained of the Americans' rude behavior rather than of any systematic abuse. Vastly outnumbering Continental and state warships, privateers did most of the capturing. Applications for commission required them to pledge a bond as high as $10,000 to guarantee "the greatest humanity and tenderness" toward captives. This didn't prevent occasional "cruel usage" (a phrase connoting anything from being cursed to being flogged), but there are few recorded claims of mortal mistreatment at the hands of privateers, and prosecutions of violations that might have resulted in bond forfeitures were rare.

Theft of captives' personal property was common. Some skippers offered reimbursement in Continental dollars, itself a potential scam since captives usually spent it; whereupon, faced with no job prospects in an alien port, "they must starve unless they enter on board privateers which are always ready to receive them."

Constantly short of experienced crew, privateers no less than the Royal Navy cajoled prisoners to switch sides and join the ship's company. Americans by and large resisted this pressure ("a man had better curse mother and father and be killed at once than live such a life," said one). British seamen, especially those off the merchant ships, flipped more easily, though there were many instances when they banded together to take control of a privateer once the dispatch of prize crews thinned the number of colonials on board down to a vulnerable few.

Detaining a prize's officers served a legal purpose; at settlement trials their testimony helped establish the legality of certain captures. Yet in most cases privateers considered captives mere baggage and freed them at the first opportunity. This blasé disregard, critics argued, reduced America's leverage to force exchanges for prisoners held in British jails.

William Bingham shared that opinion. As his Martinique privateers grew increasingly successful, the island's prison filled with enemy seamen. A British emissary alleged they "were starving and dying each meal there," but Bingham ("styling himself the agent of the American Congress," clucked the emissary) declared that none would be released "until the Americans should be discharged by the English from their prisons." The same objective later motivated Franklin's involvement with privateers in Europe. Though other officials were in it for the money, "The prisoners to exchange for Americans are all the advantage I have for my trouble," he wrote

In Britain, Forton and Mill prisons received more than four hundred seamen in the first months after opening in April 1777. Eventually that number reached three thousand, with inmates, almost all New England privateersmen, ranging in age from nine to sixty. Getting there in the holds of warships was often the worst part of the ordeal. British humanitarians called conditions below deck "barbarous" and described disembarking colonials as resembling "persons in a hot bath, panting, sweating, and fainting for want of air." Once the prisoners arrived at Forton or Mill, the Commission for Sick and Hurt Seamen, which administered the facilities, strove to provide decent food, clothing, and medical care. In five years only a hundred men died.

To be consigned to the hulks of Wallabout Bay, however, posed a different fate entirely. In one "obstinate engagement" between a Salem privateer, *Jack*, and an enemy brigantine late in the war, the privateer's first officer (his captain and many mates had died in a point-blank volley after the two ships tangled in one another's rigging) took a boarder's bayonet through his thigh, which then "entered the carriage of a bow gun, where I was fastened." Even so, by exhorting his men to remember "the sufferings of the prison ship," he got them to fight for two more hours before capitulating.

Whitby was gone by then, set afire in 1777 by prisoners who preferred immolation to imprisonment. But seven other vessels took its place, including *Jersey*, a converted three-deck battleship that housed one thousand prisoners. If *Jack*'s survivors wound up there, odds were three in four that they never left. Fewer than a thousand were exchanged off the prison ships during the war. Some twelve thousand died, bearing out Timothy Parker's dark prediction to his governor.

Most of the dead were privateersmen. Their bodies were thrown overboard or buried by fellow inmates in the sand banks edging the bay. In the decades since, bones unearthed during construction of the Brooklyn Navy Yard were interred in a large crypt at nearby Fort Greene. A 148-foot Martyrs Monument was erected above it in 1908. Designed by famed architect Stanford White, its tower featured a lighted beacon and an elevator to carry visitors up for a sweeping view of New York. After the 1930s it fell into disrepair due to lack of funds and community interest.

Five

I flatter myself I am not dependant upon the state of Rhode Island for either my character or consequence in life.
—*Nathanael Greene to John Brown, September 1778*

The esteem that developed between George Washington and Nathanael Greene derived mostly from shared defeat. Resiliency and perseverance were their only solace after repeated setbacks in the summer and fall of 1776. In advising the commander in chief that September, "'Tis our business to study to avoid any considerable misfortune," Greene was telling Washington nothing he didn't know. Washington always had sought to injure the enemy without being drawn into conventional battle against a vastly superior force. The only question was whether to launch selective tactical strikes, dig in and make a stand, or pull back lest his army be overrun and the rebellion lost at a stroke.

Anticipating that the enemy, having quit Boston in March for temporary refuge in Halifax, would strike New York next, Washington had moved his army to Long Island in expectation of an attack from the east. Instead, a British task force landed on Staten Island in July, then crossed New York Bay and flanked the American positions in Brooklyn.

Washington was slow to recognize the threat of his army's entrapment on the far side of the East River away from retreat routes into the mainland. His last-minute evacuation on August 29, brilliantly executed in small boats at night, followed a stinging defeat in the Battle of Long Island in which his conduct had been "inept and indecisive," according to the historian David McCullough.

Washington then vacillated on the matter of abandoning New

York altogether. Greene, incapacitated by illness during the recent fighting, argued for withdrawal in order to spare the army for future battle, a course Washington chose only after needlessly losing more men and equipment in inconclusive skirmishes that fall.

But their roles reversed in November when Greene persuaded Washington to leave behind a heavily armed garrison at Fort Washington overlooking the Hudson River across from New Jersey. Despite Greene's assurance of its impregnability, the fort fell to an overwhelming assault at a loss of 146 cannon and 54 men killed, 100 wounded, and more than 2,800 captured, two-thirds of whom died in the next eighteen months aboard prison ships anchored in Brooklyn's Wallabout Bay.

Both commanders were roundly criticized. Members of Congress and some fellow officers hinted that they should be fired. But Washington retained Greene despite the Fort Washington debacle, and Greene reciprocated with an admiring loyalty whose fundamental view ultimately mirrored history's. "His Excellency George Washington never appeared to so much advantage as in the hour of distress."

Soon they would taste success against the Hessians at Trenton and Cornwallis's redcoats at Princeton. Countering the British advance into Pennsylvania later in 1777, Greene, under Washington's direction, would lead troops in battles at Brandywine and Germantown in which the Continentals were driven from the field only after inflicting casualties in such numbers the British leadership was rattled, French confidence in the American rebellion encouraged, and the patriots' spirit renewed.

But when the army settled at Valley Forge in the winter of 1777–78, logistical problems exacerbated by what Greene called "neglect of some and the designs of others" turned a relatively mild winter into a crucible of cold and hunger. "Our troops are naked. We have been upon the eve of starving and the army of mutinying. Our horses are dying by dozens every day for the want of forage, and men getting sickly in the huts."

Greene had excelled at managing logistics during the siege of Boston, and his placement of storage depots in advance of the army's retreat through New Jersey had indicated a talent for contingency planning. So while still at Valley Forge, where almost a quarter of his men would die, Washington tapped him to revamp the army's supply system as quartermaster general.

Though Greene's brothers and his cousin Griffin were "very anxious I should accept," he consented only because "His Excellency presses it upon me exceedingly." He was unhappy to be removed from battle's "line of splendor" and wrote a colleague, "All of you will be immortalizing yourselves in the golden pages of history while I am confined to a series of drudgery to pave the way for it." As a concession, Congress allowed him periodically to couple his quartermaster duties with field command.

The preceding quartermaster general and his staff had shared a 5 percent commission on all transactions. Greene, fearing to appear greedy, asked in letters to Washington and Congress to serve only at his current salary as a major general. But to entice into public service the two businessmen he wanted as aides—John Cox, a Philadelphia merchant with extensive area connections, and Charles Pettit, who would keep accounts and manage the cash—Congress allotted the three men a 1 percent commission to be divided among them.

Greene's two year tenure in the department saw a dramatic improvement in the army's supply situation. Though subsequent winters were harsher, the agonies of Valley Forge weren't repeated on anywhere near the same scale, and his system of field depots contributed to the tenacity of Washington's pursuit of British forces evacuating Philadelphia for New York in the summer of 1778. Yet he detested the job and asked several times to resign. Like every procurement official, he was constantly harassed for payment of government bills. At one point, more than three months passed before his pleas to Congress for money were answered—and these were in letters sent from Pennsylvania and New Jersey rather than, as from William Bingham and Silas Deane, across the Atlantic Ocean.

His dislike of his duties ("humiliating to my military pride") made him defensive of his accomplishments. "It is confessed by everybody that the army could not have got from Valley Forge at the time they did had it not been for the extraordinary exertions we made." One aspect of his work worried him, however. It was making him rich.

In a replay of the solicitations that came to him as he'd risen in rank earlier in the war, Greene's appointment as quartermaster general brought a rain of business offers. His relatives were first in line. To dodge "impositions" for trading across state lines, Griffin Greene asked to move his merchandise on military wagons, whose loads weren't subject to such fees. He asked also for a right of first refusal on military contracts provided it was "consistent with your honor."

Merchants from throughout the colonies sought similar deals, each of which promised commissions for the general. "Nothing shall ever induce me to depart from the line of honor and truth in any business committed to my care," he wrote his brother Jacob–but lest others not interpret matters in the same light, "You must not let people see my letters as they contain sentiments that I would not wish made public."

Questioned by Washington about the wisdom of doing business with family, Greene explained that the army's desperate need for supplies forced him to cast a wide net. "I have given extensive orders almost without limitation for the purchase of these articles." Persuaded that pragmatism and expediency "save the public millions of dollars," Washington's concern was assuaged–another instance, Greene wrote, of the "partiality that His Excellency General Washington has always shown to my advice."

The young general was less sanguine in private. He nervously asked Jacob to "write me the public sentiments respecting transactions in the quartermaster's department and how the public views me." And Griffin's pushiness in exploiting their connection forced Nathanael to temper, "for fear you should mistake my intentions," a letter of hearty recommendation to the deputy quartermaster in Baltimore. Do not engage Griffin in any way "which will interfere in the least degree with the duties of your office or effect its reputation," he wrote. More specifically, "Neither must you lend Mr. Greene any public monies."

He had cause for worry. In purchasing the army's food, clothing, ammunition, arms, and medical supplies, building its camps, and securing horses and wagons to transport its gear, quartermaster officials could profit through commissions or through embezzlement for which "a thousand opportunities would daily present themselves without the possibility of detection." All Congress could do to limit "peculation" from "piddling, pilfering plunderers in the characters of deputies and deputies' assistants" was to hold the quartermaster general "responsible for their conduct." Responsible, that is, personally.

There's no evidence that Greene inflated purchases in order to increase his commissions. He didn't have to. Just prior to his appointment he'd implored his brothers to dissolve their father's estate and to buy out his stake in Jacob Greene & Company. "Let it be valued, and I will either give or take." He'd needed immediate cash to support his family and maintain his staff, and saw no way to raise it short of liquidation. But the quartermaster job was "flattering to my fortune" from the start, a fact corroborated by the almost instant disappearance of money worries from his personal letters.

Those worries had centered on Jacob Greene & Company's heavy involvement in privateering. Caught up in fighting the war, he'd taken little notice of their vessels' poor performance. Besides, as important as turning a profit was the damage they did to British morale. "Remember, while it rains upon us, the sun does not shine upon them. We must balance accounts in national suffering." But as the realization sank in "that fortune is no friend of ours in the privateering business," his offhand inquiries into the family's "navigation matters" took an urgent tone.

By mid-1777, after learning of the capture of two family-owned vessels, *Florida* and *General Greene*, he was ready to support his brothers' call to quit the enterprise. "They have met with so many losses, they had better stop before all is gone." But the family was still involved a year later due to his insistence, "I am not for quitting yet." If the reason he gave his brothers to stay the privateering course seems fatalistic—"It is a long lane that has no turn"—his prediction to Griffin was much bolder. "Great things may yet be done by speculation."

He was in position to know. Expenditures out of the quartermaster department approached an annual rate of $32 million soon after Greene's appointment. This brought him commissions worth more than half a million dollars in today's terms, far above his general's salary and one of the highest assured incomes of any man in America at the time.

Though he downplayed his improved situation to his wife ("My fortune will be small but I trust by good economy we may live respectably"), they were doing better than ever before. When visiting Greene in the field, the twenty-five-year-old Caty socialized with the loftiest couples in the army, including Martha and George Washington, who joked of stealing Caty from her "Quaker preacher" while they danced for hours at a time. When in Rhode Island, she and their children lived in a large farmhouse in Westerly. There, she wrote, "I have been visited by the finest circle of ladies I have seen for a long time."

Because he was paid in Continental dollars, which could lose half their value in a month, Greene was compelled to spend his money as soon as he got it. Without banks or stocks available as investment vehicles, and with government loan certificates paying a negligible return in those same plummeting dollars, his best options were real estate, ships, and commercial ventures. With no time to manage his affairs, he depended on his brothers and cousin to arrange deals. In addition, he formed partnerships with his aides, Pettit and Cox; with Samuel A. Otis, an emerging leader in Massachusetts privateering; and with the army's commissary general, Jeremiah Wadsworth, a merchant and former seaman one year younger than Greene.

In 1779 Wadsworth and Greene put up the capital behind Barnabas Deane & Company. Barnabas Deane was Silas's brother, and like his sibling had more ambition than cash. He and Wadsworth were longtime associates whose careers, typically of the era, combined self-interest with significant contributions to the Revolutionary cause, including shipbuilding, powder voyages, and iron production.

Placing the company in Deane's name was an acknowledgment that even honest officials often found their public service rewarded with criminal investigation. "However just and upright our conduct may be," Greene wrote Wadsworth in 1779, "the world will have suspicions to our disadvantage. By keeping the affair a secret I am confident we shall have it more in our power to serve the commercial connection than by publishing it."

Privateers figured big in Barnabas Deane & Company's operations. Records of August 1779 show an interest in nine of them worth £25,000, and at times its roster of ships at sea numbered in the dozens. Similarly invested through his other partnerships, Greene's involvement deepened just as privateering reached new levels of risk. The Royal Navy began putting copper sheathing on the hulls of its ships in 1778. The copper repelled wood-boring worms and reduced the accumulation of seaweed and barnacles that hindered performance. As a result, enemy vessels patrolled the seas for longer periods and were faster and more nimble in battle.

And there were more of them, thanks to Britain's 1777 authorization of anti-American privateers. Parliament had been reluctant to take this step since it seemed implicitly to recognize America as a legitimate state. But once legalized, one hundred loyalist warships launched from New York and more than a thousand from Britain and the West Indies, another species in a crowded sea of predators.

American privateering remained a growth industry. Applications quadrupled between 1778 and 1781, by which time there were almost five-hundred private warships at sea and less than ten Continental ones. General Washington praised the Boston community for "the valuable prizes that have been lately brought into your port. We stand in need of all your activity to increase our supplies by these means."

To promote sea raiding, he'd directed that "ammunition from the Continental magazine" be made more available to the public. "They should not be suffered to want so essential an article." But businessmen who were paying close attention realized that privateering's easy pickings were a thing of the past. "The case is very different now," was the word around Boston in 1778. "More than half the vessels that have been fitted out this winter have been taken."

Greene remained largely oblivious. Distracted by military "cares and applications of every kind" and insulated from the shock of failed voyages by his quartermaster cash flow, he was almost flippant in his commitments. "I should have no objection to sporting with five or six thousand dollars in that business, providing there was a good vessel with a lucky captain."

His main motive for dabbling in privateers continued to be their connection to "the business of my present profession," meaning warfare. "I don't wish to become an adventurer. Indeed, I should have little or no inclination to be concerned in privateering but for its being calculated to annoy the enemy and consequently to favor our cause."

In other words, privateering was serious to Greene in strategic terms. But as a financial endeavor it was "sport," a cavalier view he could well afford in this time of plenty of money.

Back in Providence, the economic fallout of the British occupation of Newport was felt by everyone. John Brown complained that it "ruined the place, that shipping was rotting, that wealth was being invested elsewhere." He was exaggerating. While trade indeed was hurt, industries such as paper mills and saddleries flourished, as did ironworks owned by the Browns and others.

But his point that "privateering successes were few" was accurate. A series of letters from John R. Livingston, a young fortune-seeker from New York, chronicle the downturn. Livingston shared Greene's poor business timing. He arrived at Providence at the peak of its boom in October 1776, two months before Newport fell. He wrote his family excitedly, "The many captures that are daily made convince me that it is best to lay out our money in privateers." True, local merchants were a crafty lot, "But I shall endeavor to play them like a trick." His confidence swelled when his first bet struck gold—"I have made £800 by the *Beaver*"—though in hindsight it seems a classic instance of the early blind luck that keeps a gambler too long at the table.

Three months later he was in Boston, whose rebound from enemy occupation got a boost from Rhode Island's maritime shutdown. "This harbor really looks brilliant and grand, as full of ships as in the most flourishing state of commerce." Unapologetic in his quest to profit by war, he worried that peace, "if it takes place without a proper warning, may ruin us."

Before long, however, a closer look at his privateer investments persuaded him to cut back. "I am rather too deep. I wish I could take all my property from the vessels I am concerned in." With a stake in four ships totalling £4,882, he unloaded one at "25 percent on what I gave, and the other at 30 percent." This was the business advantage of "persons on the spot" that Morris had described, an advantage General Greene, preoccupied with military concerns, didn't enjoy.

Meanwhile the Browns flourished. Having long resisted doing business outside Rhode Island, they now funded privateers in Boston, Philadelphia, and Baltimore. They also expanded their arms clientele up and down the coast, ultimately selling three thousand cannon at roughly £2,000 apiece, bringing in revenues approaching $1 billion in today's terms.

And how did Rhode Island fare overall? Soon after the British pulled out of Newport in late 1779, a French visitor was amazed by the "large tracts of country cleared and many houses recently built" outside Providence. Even the most conservative citizens were "money crazy," he reported.

The colony's nervy temerity likewise never lagged. In 1782, a French military force passed through Providence on the way to joining the Continental Army. Town leaders subsequently billed the French government 4,600 silver dollars for property damage caused by its soldiers. The foreign ministry denounced it as an "exorbitant sum" and paid it under protest.

1778

BARBADOS, WEST INDIES

A sad maxim of war suggests that it's often the best officers who get killed in combat, that bravado under fire and fierce commitment to duty aren't conducive to long life. No one exemplified this better than Nicholas Biddle of the Continental Navy. "I fear nothing but what I ought to fear," he wrote his family in 1775. "I am much more afraid of doing a foolish action than of losing my life."

In 1777 Biddle was given command, at twenty-eight, of the thirty-two-gun *Randolph*. The Marine Committee, fearing the loss of yet another new frigate, cautioned him "to avoid two-deckers or engaging when there is more than one in sight." Aspiring to "character of conduct as well as courage," he vowed "never to throw away the vessel and crew merely to convince the world I have courage."

Biddle's conscientiousness wasn't matched by his luck. On its first cruise, *Randolph*'s main mast snapped in two and its crew was ravaged by fever from which many died. While under repair in Charleston, the vessel twice was struck by lightning, splintering two replacement masts. Biddle dealt with more illness among his men and had to put down a mutiny before finally relaunching in August. Over the next eight months he captured several prizes and small warships in West Indian and European waters.

Praise from the Marine Committee contained a revision of its original order. He was now "to strike a stroke" against Britain's "Jamaica Fleet." Though still obligated to dodge enemy frigates sailing in pairs, "if you meet either single we hope you can and will take them." Near Barbados in March

1778, Biddle tried to do that. The vessel he took on, perhaps mistaking it for something smaller in the 8 p.m. dusk, turned out to be HMS *Yarmouth*, a sixty-four-gun ship-of-the-line.

He fought brilliantly, outsailing his opponent and getting off three volleys to each one of *Yarmouth*'s, leaving it "greatly shattered." Misfortune superseded bravery and seamanship, however. A South Carolina privateer, *General Moultrie*, swept in to support the Continentals, a blessing that turned negative when its first volley struck *Randolph*, severely wounding Biddle and forcing him to direct his vessel while slumped in a chair on the quarterdeck.

Then *Randolph* exploded—probably from a spark in the powder magazine. *Yarmouth*'s captain wrote later that "our ship was in a manner covered with parts of her." The debris included burning spars and, eerily to witnesses, "an American ensign, rolled up, blown in upon the forecastle, not so much as singed."

In an event the British captain called "very remarkable," he picked up four survivors clinging to some wreckage five days later. The rest of *Randolph*'s crew—301 men—were gone. It was America's costliest naval battle of the war, with almost twice as many sailors killed as in John Paul Jones's victory over *Serapis*.

In total, 832 Continental seamen died in Revolutionary combat. Harder to measure is the number killed among what the U.S. Navy's official compilation of war documents terms that "peculiar comrade-in-arms, the privateers." But statistics out of the coastal towns of Essex County, thirty miles north of Boston, offer a clue. Newburyport listed twenty-two vessels destroyed and a thousand men dead. Salem lost almost one-third of its fifty-four registered privateers; Gloucester lost all twenty-four. Their postwar populations of adult males were roughly half what they'd been before the war. Two-thirds of Beverly men between eighteen and sixty were captured at sea at one time or another, some of them more than once. One-third of the women in Marblehead were widowed, and more than one-fourth of the children were fatherless. Hundreds of tax abatements were granted to families whose breadwinners were listed as "missing at sea," "taken and sick," "died abroad," "in the hands of the enemy," "long absent, supposed to be lost."

Roughly 10 percent of all privateers seized by the British hailed from Essex County; warships under American flags eventually poured out of Boston and other New England ports, Maryland, Virginia, the Carolinas, the West Indies, and, in time, Europe. But if wider consequences can be inferred from one county's experience, it's clear that untold thousands died in the enterprise.

The government editors of *Naval Documents of the American Revolution* acknowledge, "Hundreds of sea fights occurred between our privateers and British merchantmen, between United States and British privateers, and between our privateers and British naval vessels, but all such actions we have omitted. Privateers were not part of our navy."

Six

Thousands of schemes for privateering are afloat in American imaginations. Out of these speculations many fruitless and some profitable projects will grow.

—John Adams, August 1776

After seizing Newport and blockading Providence in December 1776, Admiral Richard Howe advised his captains that the rebels would now "assemble their chief maritime strength at Boston."

John Adams would have liked nothing better. An avid supporter of privateering, he'd predicted that Massachusetts would lead the way in launching a citizen armada once Boston was free of enemy occupation. So fervent was his cheerleading for his home colony, he disliked hearing, weeks after the British pullout, that "Continental cruisers have taken so many and the provincial cruisers and privateers so few prizes. Our people may as well fight for themselves as the Continent."

Adams considered Massachusetts mariners tops in courage and skill. He blamed Congress's "languor, censure, and complaint" for administrative delays in translating those qualities into hordes of marauding warships. A year later, reflecting on Rhode Island's early success in mounting voyages, he revised his view. "At Providence, I fear, there has been a system of selfishness, and at Boston of incapacity."

He was right to narrow his disappointment down from Massachusetts as a whole to Boston in particular. Though the town was beginning to reclaim its eminence as the center of New England commerce, recovery from occupation was slow. Despite the reopening of its harbor and the return of many merchants, business remained at "low ebb" into 1778. The colony's true strength lay in its Essex County ports of Beverly, Salem, Marblehead, and Newburyport, which got a head start in expanding their maritime industries thanks to the capital's sluggish revival.

Until recently, Boston-based enemy frigates had suppressed the county's fishing and sea trade to such an extent that almshouses swelled with record numbers of needy and coastal communities had to seek relief from the annual province tax and to accept grain from Quaker charities in Pennsylvania. Prizes taken by Washington's Continental schooners over the winter of 1776–77 had nudged the stalled economy forward. The momentum built to a torrent after the Royal Navy abandoned its Boston station in March.

Before the year was out more than forty privateer commissions were granted and more than eighty prizes captured. The first of the 350 armed vessels that ultimately sailed from Essex County were former fishing sloops and schooners, small and lightly armed. Through new construction or refitting old vessels, larger brigs and brigantines with upward of twenty cannon and one hundred crewmen became the preference.

Finding armaments remained a challenge, "but with what they dig up on wharfs and at the corners of streets," one visitor marveled, "they have made out heretofore very well." One source of metal was the many local statues of British royalty, which could be melted down and recast as musketballs "to assimilate with the brains of our infatuated adversaries."

The county was "privateering mad." Ports swarmed with seamen attired in "Dutch cap, check shirt, canvas trousers, with coarse shoes and brass shoe-buckles . . . rolling and rollicking along with their pockets full of hard money, singing songs, chewing tobacco, smoking cigars, drinking at all the public houses." Recruiters worked the waterfronts like carnival barkers. Taverns were pasted with broadsides advertising voyages to "anyone meaning to make his fortune in a short time" and offering signing bonuses of up to $100 (Congress was giving $40) to go along with a $20-monthly wage, prize shares, and ample allotments of grog, a sailor's "liquor of life."

The many prize captures were manifested in a glut of goods and commodities still scarce in Boston. And while ocean trade remained an important component of the region's resurgence, men who'd pushed for the legalization of privateers and whose speculation in commerce raiding equaled or exceeded their involvement in traditional trade were making the greatest leaps in wealth and influence.

There was, however, something different about what was happening. In Providence, established business leaders, the Browns foremost, used their experience and family wealth to grab the greatest rewards of the wartime boom. The same was largely true in Philadelphia. (Robert Morris was an exception: he'd been successful before the war but no titan, and lacked the lofty social ties of most of his associates.) Boston likewise featured an ensconced upper class of interconnected merchant families, but since many had been loyalists forced to flee with their British protectors, a vacuum was left that the entrepreneurs of Essex County quickly filled—first as provincial elites; later, after many moved their homes and businesses to the capital, as new-minted Boston Brahmin.

Of middling prewar status for the most part, these men included Joseph Lee, Josiah Batchelder, Jr., and John and Andrew Cabot of Beverly; Richard and Elias Hasket Derby of Salem; and Nathaniel Tracy of Newburyport. Captains in their hire, notably Hugh Hill and Simon Forrester, used prize earnings to buy vessels of their own. Israel Thorndike, a cooper's apprentice in Beverly, skippered a privateer at age nineteen before going on to amass one of New England's largest fortunes in banking and textiles.

At least one common sailor, Joseph Peabody, made the transition from teenage deckhand to privateer investor over the course of nine voyages between 1777 and 1783, initiating his rise toward becoming Salem's largest magnate with eighty-three ships and eight thousand employees. And the lawyer John Lowell, originally of Newburyport, outearned his privateer clients through fees collected by brokering partnerships and helping to settle more than a thousand prizes.

They were the Revolution's nouveau riche, daring, grasping, brazen. Their future heirs would exemplify American old money at its most genteel.

John Adams pushed to legalize American privateering at a time when many of his congressional colleagues still recoiled from its shady reputation. But while thrilled with privateering's success against enemy shipping, he was shocked to see his beloved Boston consumed with speculation and materialism thanks to the industry's soaring profits.

John Hancock, Congress's president through October 1777, was even more impatient than John Adams to see Boston thrive again. Adams, a lawyer, rooted for the town out of civic pride rather than financial interest. But Hancock had been Boston's wealthiest merchant ever since inheriting his uncle's estate in 1764. Nothing he did as an anti-British agitator before the war or as a politician during it was completely divorced from his business interests.

In 1768 one of Hancock's vessels, *Liberty*, had been seized for failure to file proper papers on a cargo of wine. A subsequent mob riot had forced British authorities to quarter two regiments in town as a police force whose rankling presence ignited the Boston Massacre eighteen months later. Hancock similarly was tied to the Boston Tea

Party in 1773. Confronted with a $90,000 influx of duty-free East India tea, Samuel Adams had proposed dumping it into the harbor out of fear that if landed and brought to market it would prove an "invincible temptation" to the people. Hancock concurred. Though an ardent patriot, he was also, by virtue of his commercial stature, one of those "certain men who had a large financial stake in smuggled tea."

Hancock owned one of Boston's largest wharfs, shut down by British decree during the occupation. In naming a protégé, John Bradford, to be Congress's prize agent in Boston less than a month after the British evacuation, he anticipated profitable returns once the town's maritime industry got up to speed. The Marine Committee hastened that result when, in a favor typical among political colleagues, it had Bradford direct "all the Continental prizes that arrive in your port to our worthy president's wharf and transact the whole of their business there." The agent's subsequent report that two British transports "now are an ornament to the finest wharf in America" shows the zeal with which he carried out the order on behalf of his benefactor.

The captains of Washington's original Continental schooners weren't pleased to make Boston their exclusive "port of rendezvous" to service their vessels and send prizes for settlement, transactions that would generate commissions for Bradford and business for Hancock. Agents elsewhere in Massachusetts were also peeved. Bradford was a latecomer to a process that after months of confusion was starting to run smoothly. At privateering's Beverly–Salem epicenter, the partnered agents William Bartlett and Jonathan Glover had laid out personal funds to outfit Continental warships in expectation of reimbursement with interest. Now they'd been summarily fired in notices signed by the new "Navy Agent of Massachusetts Colony."

Glover rode to Boston in June to confront Bradford. He left their meeting with an understanding that Bradford would "superintend over the whole" but not displace local agents. Then Bradford did the math. Hancock had appointed him on April 23, 1776. That was three weeks before the young Marblehead skipper, James Mugford, captured the British transport *Hope* with its rich cargo of one thousand muskets and five hundred barrels of gunpowder. *Hope* was scheduled for trial in Boston on June 21. Such trials were termed "libels" and provided a chance for "any persons concerned therein" to claim rights to the vessel and cargo before they were sold at auction. With thousands of dollars in commission at stake, Bradford reasserted his status as the colony's ranking agent, dismissing his predecessors in Essex County as "the late agents."

Glover and Bartlett protested that his appointment was unofficial. It was true. Hancock had installed Bradford through an informal communication. The technicality delayed Bradford's taking office until after *Hope*'s libel trial. But still hoping for a piece of the vessel's proceeds, he begged Congress for a written order while at the same time undertaking a letter campaign to Hancock and Robert Morris in which he trashed his rivals' abilities and reputations.

With Hancock, he pulled no punches in accusing Glover and Bartlett of running a shabby operation. Their captains, he said, were "all at variance, each taxing the other with being a thief, a robber, a coward." He passed along rumors that the agents were cheats, buying up sailors' prize shares "for a fourth part of their real value." And he noted that despite the many prizes settled in Essex County, he had "not the least probability of coming at any money from Glover and Bartlett," the implication being that they were embezzling government funds.

He was more circumspect with Morris, burying his wish to be "vested with greater powers than the present" under large dollops of praise for the chairman of the Marine Committee, "so important a station in the Grand Council." But four days before *Hope*'s scheduled auction on July 18, he penned a frantic follow-up. Glover and Bartlett "pay no regard," he whined. "The powder ship was taken weeks after my appointment, yet they've advertised to sell the powder without consulting me."

Hope and its cargo sold for more than $1.5 million. Details of the auction are unknown, but by rule, bidders would immediately have put up 5 percent of the purchase price in cash. The buyers they represented—Congress being but one of them, and with no greater right to the munitions than any private entrepreneur—increased that amount to 10 percent, with the balance due within three days or else the downpayment was forfeited.

Still not empowered at the time of the sale, Bradford went after his 2.5 percent commission retroactively. In addition to lobbying Hancock again, he laid a groundwork of innuendo against Glover and Bartlett in a pair of letters to George Washington, who'd appointed the two agents the previous year. After pouring on the flattery, Bradford wrote with aggrieved righteousness of local seaports full of "men too little impressed with the honorable service they are employed in." He reported that "great complaints are made" about the prize process but dared not specify Glover and Bartlett by name. They were Washington's guys, after all.

Both agents had already written their former boss to argue the case for keeping their jobs. They cast Bradford as an interloper whose abrupt promotion was an insult to the commander in chief's expressed satisfaction with their performance. But Washington had no time for this fraught correspondence. He was preparing his army to defend New York.

With not "the smallest inclination to interfere in any degree in the matter," he forwarded the letters to Hancock and thereby cut ties to the agents, the Continental schooners, and their privateer offshoots. After the war he would reflect that sea power was "the pivot upon which everything turned." His forbearance in unleashing that power through the unruly and ungovernable privateers is perhaps reason enough to claim, as did one naval historian in 1932, "George Washington as our first great admiral."

Bradford received his official designation as the sole Continental agent in Massachusetts on August 8, 1776. He promptly published it in the *New England Chronicle*. When he showed it to Glover in triumph, however, the Salem agent pointed out that Congress had dated it July 30, not April 23 per Bradford's informal notice from

Hancock. The technicality caused Bradford to miss out on all of *Hope*'s sales commission.

He embarked with a vengeance on his new duties. He demanded detailed ledgers from former agents, informed the captains of the schooners ("our little navy," he called them to Hancock) that he was their representative now, angled to manage prize shares for the schooners' crewmen, and set about purchasing cannon for two Continental frigates, *Boston* and *Hancock*, recently constructed in Newburyport. Finally, he contacted French merchants to let them know that, "as Continental Agent, it probably will be in my way to do business with you." At the close of the letter he put in his first order: tea and brandy, "for my account."

Having already alienated agents in Massachusetts, he quickly got on the wrong side of John Langdon by knocking New Hampshire ("the cruisers from this state don't shine in taking prizes") and by urging the Marine Committee to settle Portsmouth prizes in Boston because "it's a notorious fact that vessels nor cargoes will sell for more than half they would sell for here." Langdon retaliated by warning friends in Congress that Boston, like Providence, had become a place where "there are schemes on foot to keep everything in their own hands."

More damaging to Bradford was the distrust of his sailor clients, whose grumblings turned ugly when he was caught manipulating prices at the January 1777 auction of *Lively*, a valuable British transport. The episode highlighted an agent's difficulty in serving the interests of captors, who wanted a maximum return on prizes, and the interests of the government, which sought to pay no more than a reasonable price for munitions and supplies culled from captured cargoes.

Lively's cargo included thousands of suits, shoes, and blankets desperately needed by Washington. As Bradford later told Congress, "the exigency of the army being such, I was obliged to send forward large quantities of goods uninvoiced." Men from the Continental schooners that had captured the vessel were furious that the goods, rumored to be worth as much as £25,000, had been dispersed without payment.

They got even angrier during *Lively*'s auction when a Baltimore merchant, William Turnbull, presented himself as a military procurement agent there to bid on the remaining cargo. Out of patriotic generosity, the public sometimes withdrew from bidding on items needed for the health and welfare of Continental soldiers; that way, government agents didn't have to pay top dollar. This benefited the cause but not the prize's captors, who were never pleased when bidding was artificially dampened.

When they saw other buyers refraining, men from the schooners began bidding against Turnbull in an attempt to boost prices. He prevailed easily, but then came the scandal, which Bradford described to his superiors with careful understatement. "It seems at the close of the sale a gentleman offered Mr. Turnbull 100 percent on his purchase. This got about the sailors and created great bickering and uneasiness."

Bradford had reason to be nervous. Because it had been stored in crates unseen by the general public, only he and Turnbull had known that *Lively*'s leftover cargo consisted purely of civilian goods—wine, women's clothing, and housewares. Turnbull's military procurement ruse had been proposed by Bradford as a way to hold down competition and clean out the ship at a bargain. What Bradford gained in the deal is unknown, but word soon spread that he "could not be trusted." Shunned by clients, he retained his position thanks only to Hancock's clout.

Three months after the *Lively* travesty, the Marine Committee formed a three-man oversight commission to monitor Bradford's books. "We find complaints are made by the officers and seamen concerned in the capture of prizes that have fallen in your hands." Though he remained in office until the end of the war, his authority was vastly diminished. In a last laugh, the sailors' grievances had been compiled and sent to the committee "by Mr. Glover, their agent."

Bradford blamed his job woes on "this growing evil" of avarice, but he was ill-suited to the waterfront scene from the start. The seamen, said to "pant for the expiration of their enlistments in order to partake of the spoils of the West Indies," shocked him with their rudeness. Even officers were "vulgar enough to quarrel on the Sabbath morning." They behaved "like pirates," he said.

He blackballed captains who balked at sending him their prizes, withholding government funds needed to mount new voyages; they in turn continued to divert much of their business to Essex County. After taking fifty-five prizes since its inception in 1775, the Continental squadron fell into disarray. By the end of the year its schooners had been sold and its captains commissioned in the navy, though all but one would eventually switch to privateering.

Bradford's efforts to launch the frigates *Hancock* and *Boston*—part of Congress's original call for the construction of thirteen Continental warships—were only marginally more successful than his stint with the schooners, but he caught so much grief in the process that it merits some sympathy. Like Langdon, he constantly contended with privateers for armaments and crew. And it didn't help that the two men assigned to command the frigates, John Manley and Hector McNeill, despised one another.

Manley, famous for capturing the ordnance ship *Nancy* in November 1775, had taken several more prizes since then. A popular hero, he wasn't without detractors. John Paul Jones passed rumors that he was illiterate and ridiculed him as "a boatswain's mate" who fatuously flew a commodore's pennant. Jones resented that his commission predated Manley's but that Manley ranked higher on Congress's officer seniority list. "That such despicable characters should have obtained commissions as commanders in a navy is truly astonishing and might pass for romance with me unless I had been convinced by my senses of the sad reality."

Among his men, however, Manley was considered "blunt, honest, and extremely popular." This despite a temper that, when annoyed by a junior officer's insubordination, for instance, caused him to strike the man "with a cutlass on the cheek with such force that his teeth were to be seen from the upper part of his jaw to the lower part of his chin."

He was also generous—and often with diminished means. The Salem court had awarded him and his crew £2,500 in April 1776, of which £30 went to the lowest-rung sailors and £250 to the captain. (A Boston family at the time could live comfortably on about £50 a year.) But of his richest prizes, the supply-starved army "had stripped ordnance from *Nancy*, coal from *Jenny*, and clothing from *Concord* without placing a value on the goods." *Nancy* didn't receive its official valuation of £20,500 until ten months after capture, too late to garner money for its captors.

Even so, after pestering Washington for a ship "of equal footing with the enemy" and receiving a promise to command *Hancock*, Manley put up his own money to outfit the frigate after months of delay. "Persons who scarcely know the difference between a ship and a wheelbarrow" had gotten the lucrative construction contracts through inside connections. "Captain Manley," the Massachusetts General Court noted of *Hancock*'s progress in November 1776, "has therefore exerted himself to get her round and has been obliged at very considerable expense to execute this business."

He'd felt secure enough to contribute toward his ship's preparation on the basis of a judgment of £1,000 due him for *Elizabeth*, a transport seized during the British evacuation of Boston that had been loaded with valuables stolen from local homes. Unfortunately the cargo subsequently was ruled private property and the judgment overturned before Manley or his crew got paid—only to be restored again in October 1777, far too late for it to be itemized and sold.

His counterpart aboard the frigate *Boston*, Captain Hector McNeill, though admittedly inexperienced "in the way of taking prizes," shared his friend Jones's disgust at being ranked below Manley. McNeill considered Manley an illiterate primitive whose leadership was suited only to "such creatures as himself." Ordered to serve as his subordinate, he agreed to "follow as the jackal does the lion, without grumbling except in my gizzard." In fact he grumbled plenty, to John Bradford.

"Impudent" was the agent's opinion about the many snippy missives he received from McNeill, in one of which McNeill bluntly grouped Bradford with "the set of men who can only be called drones." The letters often griped about money, but their most common refrain was personal derision of Manley. The general opinion that McNeill's vanity was primarily to blame for the spat did little to resolve the problem of two navy commanders sailing in tandem, who, "like the Jews and Samaritans," a friend advised John Adams, "will have no connections or intercourse." Yet sail together they would—and, to further complicate matters, they would do so in company with nine privateers.

The plan to deploy Continental and private vessels in a joint operation had been adopted grudgingly. It arose out of mutual acknowledgment that antagonistic competition for ships, cannon, and crewmen was hurting both sides. Privateering's huge popularity (a "moderate computation" at the time put the number of New Englanders participating at "not less than 10,000") had led the government to place embargoes on privateers in hopes of quelling the demand that was depleting Continental ranks.

The embargo was predicated on military manpower quotas. Until a town had fulfilled its assessment, it could dispatch neither privateers nor merchant ships without official permission. Businessmen protested the policy change. "The government has been forward in encouraging private adventurers," complained one consortium of investors with £12,000 tied up in a grounded privateer, "and in consequence of that our ship was fitted at great expense."

Cooperation soured between the public and private sectors. When asked to lease vessels to the state, Elias Hasket Derby drove such a hard bargain ("I shall be willing if the terms suit me, together with five percent commission"), it was a slap at lawmakers. One of them, James Warren of the Massachusetts General Court, came to "execrate the policy of stopping our privateers" for the rancor it caused, the corruption it promoted, and the relief it gave the British from "the amazing damage we should have done them."

John Adams concurred. "I am sorry the embargo was ever laid. I am against all shackles upon trade. Let the spirit of the people have its own way."

One compelling argument to remove the embargo was tactical. Royal Navy frigates, based now in Halifax, were still patrolling Massachusetts Bay to devastating effect. Aboard HMS *Milford*, "foremast

John Manley captured the Revolution's first and last significant prizes. After a maritime career that won him the devotion of his men and the respect of his British adversaries, Manley, like his relentless detractor John Paul Jones, fell into postwar obscurity. Unlike Jones, he remained there.

men" who earned bonuses for sighting colonial vessels had made £140 each in recent months on their prize shares. Because the frigates usually "cruised single," a flotilla of American warships seemed the best way to defeat them.

But privateers were averse to the yoke of Continental command and in any event avoided taking on the Royal Navy except as a last resort. Such confrontations usually went badly. Daring as they were, most privateersmen were seafaring novices who "could not find a rope in the night" much less match the gunnery skills of British professionals. A 1777 engagement in the West Indies was typical. Though the warships—one private, the other Royal Navy—were of equal firepower, the battle left two British casualties versus, on the American side, "16 killed and near 40 wounded. Two have since died of their wounds and many others likely to meet the same fate."

An awareness of such grim statistics had accounted for an inglorious episode earlier that spring. *Cabot*, a sixteen-gun Continental brig on its very first day at sea, had been left in the lurch by a pair of state-leased privateers when *Milford* bore down to do battle. The sight of his fleeing compatriots had led *Cabot*'s commander to abandon ship under a rain of cannonballs. Boston newspapers tried to minimize the loss after the vessel turned up in Halifax as HMS *Cabot*. "The good, loyal, run-away Tories (from this town) who remain there were congratulating each other on the glorious (as they said) acquisition. Deluded creatures! They think the fate of America depends on a single brig."

A court investigation into whether the privateers had "failed in a point of duty" cleared their captains on grounds that bad weather had disrupted communication; and indeed, bravery wasn't an issue. The state skippers, John Fisk of *Massachusetts* and Jonathan Haraden of *Tyrannicide*, distinguished themselves in combat both before and after the incident. But privateering's ingrained calculation of reward versus risk was a hard habit to break.

On April 23, Warren informed Adams that *Milford* and several other frigates were again in local waters. "We are endeavoring to get out Manley and McNeill to take her." Several days passed as privateers debated joining the effort. Their hesitation gave way when a British warship, under a flag of truce, sent a boatload of American prisoners ashore "with a message and a challenge to Manley and McNeill and all the armed vessels in this harbor." Continued Warren to Adams, "This has roused the indignation of the officers and tars [seamen], and given us an opportunity which many of us thought should not be neglected. We shall get the Continental ships and the privateers to sea and meet the challengers."

Even with pride at stake, negotiations to integrate privateers into a manageable fleet under Manley's leadership were testy. Chain of command, prize shares, ship-to-ship signals, and compensation to civilian crewmen "in case they lose life or limbs" had to be worked out. Beyond providing ammunition and other supplies, the government had to cover any losses to privateer owners that exceeded prize earnings. There was one more owner stipulation. "The Court will take off the restrictions with respect to manning." After four months of spotty enforcement, the embargo was lifted.

Privateer sailors were as stubborn as their employers. They wanted something better than government-issue "stinking New England rum" to drink. And they demanded that the joint deployment be given a fixed time limit. Without it, "The owners are willing, the men are not." Their participation was capped at twenty days.

Warren's labors in hammering out the agreement led Adams to push Congress to create the Eastern Navy Department with Warren as its lead member. "The profit to you will be nothing," he wrote his friend, "but the honor and virtue the greater."

On May 21, the little fleet left Boston and headed north toward Cape Ann. One of Manley's first communications was to remind the largest privateer, *General Mifflin,* "not to part with us upon consideration whatever. If we should fall in with two British frigates you are to engage one with the ship *Hancock.*"

General Mifflin responded that some of its crew had suddenly taken ill with smallpox and the ship must depart the fleet at once. Two months later, the privateer was cited in a Liverpool newspaper for having chained the skipper of a transport seized off the coast of Ireland below deck for several weeks, leaving him crippled and causing "his flesh to swell to a shocking degree. All his prayers and entreaties were in vain. The inhuman tyrants had no compassion."

And *General Mifflin* wasn't the first privateer to bail. *Sturdy Beggar* and *Satisfaction* had stuck around less than two days, and within a week the Continental frigates were sailing on their own.

Flying false flags several miles ahead of McNeill, Manley lured into range HMS *Fox,* twenty-eight guns, subduing it after a ninety-minute battle in which four Americans and four British were killed. Witnesses aboard *Fox* reported that Manley, hollering through a voice trumpet, declared his vessel "an American rover" before unleashing his first broadside. During the fight he "ran continually from one end of the ship to the other, flourishing and swinging a great cutlass around his head and with the most horrid imprecations swearing he would cut down the first man who should attempt to leave his quarters."

Boston, arriving late to the scene, pumped a volley into *Fox* after the British warship already had struck its colors. This—and McNeill's immediate claim on half of *Fox*'s prize value—infuriated Manley, and the captains icily continued their expedition with *Fox* in tow. Continued quarrels over signals and course directions came to a bitter head when the vessels encountered a pair of large enemy frigates, *Rainbow* and *Flora*, forty-four and thirty-four guns, off Nova Scotia in July.

The engagement was a forty-hour zigzag affair during which the Americans appeared to *Rainbow*'s commander, Sir George Collier, "irresolute and undecided as to their course and conduct." This was an understatement. Manley mistook *Rainbow* for a giant ship-of-the-line and wavered before attacking, giving *Flora* time to enter the fray. The prize master aboard *Fox* sailed ineptly and was unable to lend fire support to *Hancock*. And McNeill, concluding that the enemy was unbeatable, tacked for the horizon, an act Manley understandably "execrated with many oaths."

The last hours of the battle were severe, with multiple dead on both sides. Given an ultimatum to strike or die, Manley ran up extra sails in a last effort to escape. Collier wrote in his after-action report, "I therefore poured a number of shot into him, which brought him to the desired determination." *Hancock* and *Fox* surrendered. "His capture will be extremely dispiriting to the rebels," the British captain exalted, "as they placed the entire direction of their navy in him."

When news of the debacle reached Boston in August, James Warren lamented the "sad reverse" and confided wearily to Adams, "I sigh for private life and incline to resign."

Bradford offered a captive British officer to "redeem poor Manley" from imprisonment. When the exchange was completed eight months later, Manley returned to Boston to face court-martial for surrendering *Hancock*. During his absence, McNeill had supplied much lurid testimony about his colleague's "blunders and misconduct" in the engagement against HMS *Rainbow*. The tactic backfired. McNeill, with his "overbearing haughtiness and unlimited conceit," was found guilty and dismissed from the service while Manley was acquitted.

Unable to secure another Continental command, Manley signed

on to the 16-gun privateer, *Cumberland*. Its owners' design of a flag for the vessel signified their high confidence in their famed captain. Said to be "unusually large," it featured the image of a pine tree, a snake with thirteen coils chopped into thirteen pieces, and the motto, "Join or Die." Unfortunately, just weeks after sailing for the West Indies in January 1779, *Cumberland* fell to HMS *Pomona* and Manley was jailed with his crew in Barbados.

Past performance was the primary gauge of a privateer captain's potential for success. Given the business's dicey nature, fortune rather than experience became the quality most valued by investors. Manley, after bribing his way out of the Barbados jail, went on to skipper other vessels; his Revolutionary career was barely at its midpoint. After losing their entire investment, however, *Cumberland*'s owners likely would have concurred with whispers about him that circulated when he returned to Boston in quest of a new assignment. In contrast to 1776, when word around Washington's headquarters had been that "good fortune seems to stick to him," Manley was a two-time loser now. As a result, Revolutionary privateering's first star was considered "an unlucky commander."

In those days even a tainted skipper didn't stay unemployed for long. In June 1779 Manley set sail in *Jason*, a twenty-gun vessel with a crew of one hundred. A few miles out of port, he was hailed by a state sloop and told, on order of the General Court, to quit his voyage and join a combined fleet of government and private warships. The debacle of the *Hancock* experience two years earlier had been forgotten. Officials had organized another joint operation on an even larger scale in an effort to expel a garrison of redcoats from Maine's Penobscot Bay.

Fifteen privateers and twenty-four civilian transports, two-thirds of them from Essex County, would join three Continental brigs for the mission—the largest American naval expedition of the Revolution, and Manley wanted nothing to do with it. After agreeing to submit to the court order, he set his course in the opposite direction and headed off to raid loyalist transports off New York. It would prove a smart move.

His fortunes remained mixed, however. He captured several prizes, including, after an especially "warm engagement," a pair of British privateers, one of which carried two sacks of gold dollars it had captured from a Spanish trade ship. But in September, *Jason* was overhauled by HMS *Surprize*. After suffering eighteen killed and a dozen wounded, most of *Jason*'s crew "broke open the forehatches and ran below, refusing to fight against a frigate." Manley struck his colors.

When the British captain brought him aboard, he observed that the rim of Manley's hat had been shot off during the battle. "You've had a narrow escape," to which came the reply, "I wish to God it had been my head."

In 1777 Manley's captors had treated him with dignity, believing him the commander "in whom the Congress place all their confidence, and who is the only man of real courage they have by sea." But this third capture provoked no respect. Unlike in 1777 when his vessel had been a Continental frigate, this time he was skippering a privateer. As such, he had no rights under the British legal system and no honor in the eyes of his adversaries. The rules of Parliament's "Pirate Act" now applied.

Next stop for Manley was Mill Prison, thirty miles from his birthplace in England. He would be there for two years.

1779

PENOBSCOT, MAINE

Massachusetts tried again to assemble a joint fleet of privateers and Continental frigates in 1779, two years after its failure with *Hancock* and *Boston*. The goal this time was to drive seven hundred redcoats from their foothold at the mouth of Maine's Penobscot River. The outpost threatened the region's fishing and lumber industries, gave haven to loyalists, and posed a standing insult to New England's maritime resurgence.

Puffed with confidence over the success of its privateers, the state assembled an amphibious task force for the mission. Newburyport, Essex County's northernmost port, immediately pledged four armed vessels. Other towns initially showed "no general sense of urgency." Their hesitancy was a negotiating position from which, after four weeks of dickering, they got the state to indemnify them from any financial losses resulting from the expedition and to allot ship owners 100 percent of any captured booty.

Ground forces were led by Massachusetts natives, including one of Boston's favorite sons, Paul Revere. Dudley Saltonstall commanded the fleet of three Continental brigs, fifteen privateers, and twenty-four transports. With a personality hard to like (John Paul Jones, no sweetheart himself, called him "rude, unhappy"), Saltonstall possessed two distinctions that would prove significant. He was from Connecticut (Silas Deane's brother-in-law, in fact), and he was a Congress-appointed officer.

The expedition, a sure snap against a vastly overmatched foe, was a fiasco. In multiple councils of war aboard Saltonstall's flagship, the ground and sea commanders argued over who should initiate the assault on the Penobscot garrison. The former demanded a preliminary naval cannonade; the latter feared to sail too far up river lest "the enemy send a reinforcement of heavy ships. In that case they may block us all in and may take the whole of us." As they dithered, a battle fleet under Sir George Collier arrived from New York and did exactly that.

One American vessel, offshore at the time, escaped. The others all fell to the Royal Navy ("transports on fire, men of war blowing up") or grounded themselves in the river shallows, crewmen and soldiers fleeing on foot back to Massachusetts, an arduous slog in the summer heat that claimed the lives of hundreds.

Boston newspapers were ruthless in their derision. "Our irregular troops made an irregular retreat; it is in imitation of an irregular brigadier and a new-fangled commodore, without any loss excepting the whole fleet."

An inquiry by the state's General Court ruled that the disaster was entirely Saltonstall's fault. Meanwhile "each and every" state and private skipper was found to have "behaved like brave experienced good officers." But recent studies, notably George E. Buker's *The Penobscot Expedition*, reveal a concerted "Massachusetts Conspiracy" to make the Connecticut captain the scapegoat.

The motive was simple. Costs to the state, which was on the hook for private losses as well as its own, exceeded $7 million. Nailing Saltonstall as the sole culprit shifted liability to Congress, his sponsor. Buker's review of the expedition's records reveals that, of all its officers, Saltonstall was the most aggressive and impatient for action. But opposite testimony provided by the Massachusetts men on his staff gave the Court grounds to force his expulsion from government service.

One typical example read, "I have been told by one who fell into the enemy's hands that Britons spoke highly in praise of the commanders of the land forces as being judicious in their movements; but that the commander of the fleet they would hang for a coward." Unfortunately, any further examination of this hearsay was impossible because the witness was "since deceased." Congress subsequently paid Massachusetts $2 million in compensation for Saltonstall's "uniform backwardness" and his "want of proper spirit and energy" in the Penobscot debacle.

Only one state officer was cited for misconduct—the artillery colonel Paul Revere, whose alleged "disobedience of orders and unsoldierlike behavior tending to cowardice" led to his brief arrest. Humiliated, Revere spent the next three years trying to clear his name, finally securing a statement from the Court in 1782 that granted him "equal honor as the others in the same expedition."

A year earlier, Saltonstall had written the owner of a transport named *Minerva* requesting a job as its captain. The owner, who'd lost a privateer at Penobscot, replied that he wanted Saltonstall to skipper the vessel "as a cruiser rather than as merchantman, and chiefly that you may regain the character with the world which you have been most cruelly and unjustly robbed of."

They converted *Minerva* to a warship. Among its prizes was *Hannah*, a transport carrying cargo worth £80,000. One of the top investors in the venture was Paul Revere.

Seven

They have taken up eleven bodies. The water was covered
with heads, legs, arms, entrails, etc.

—Connecticut Courant, *July 1776*

During the action, no slaughterhouse could present so bad a
sight with blood and entrails lying about as our ship did.

—London Chronicle, *August 1776*

One shot took off three midshipmen's heads who happened
to stand in range.

—Pennsylviania Gazette, *August 1776*

Dire was the slaughter of the Rebel crews, and many a man-
gled corpse the decks bestrewed; while all down meandering
on their sides issued in purple streams the sanguined gore.

—New York Gazette, *August 1777*

Manley's commodore's pennant from *Hancock* was delivered as
a trophy to George III. Britons exalted over the "utmost bad
consequence to the rebels" of losing the man understood to be "the
chief executive officer of their navy." It gave another push to the
pendulum of war sentiment whose swings were becoming extreme.

British newspapers regularly printed letters from distant
correspondents—travelers, merchants, military men. Their random
news and often clashing viewpoints constituted the freshest perspec-
tives available about the state of the war. A typical sequence in May
1777 featured one letter assuring London readers that naval patrols
"have been very successful against the Americans and almost
knocked up their trade by the many captures they have taken," and

then a few days later another letter passing a frantic rumor that forty out of a fleet of sixty transports had fallen to privateers on a recent voyage from Ireland to Grenada.

Similarly, a letter exhibiting utter confidence ("Whatever people may say or think in England, everybody here is satisfied that the rebellion is dying apace") was followed by one full of worry. "These islands swarm with those vermin of American privateers. A day does not pass but they take some vessel."

The editorial whiplash was constant. A gentleman on shipboard in America published an editorial in Liverpool that began, "Put no confidence in any news favoring the rebels." Another groaned in the same paper, "Nothing is safe here. We cannot help thinking ourselves much neglected." And a letter pronouncing that "the rebel force is everywhere rapidly declining" was countered with another's hysteria. "God knows, if this war continues much longer, we shall all die with hunger."

Unlike its strategic progress, the war's impact on the British economy wasn't in question. Maritime losses in the West Indies alone stood at £2 million by mid-1777. During the Seven Years' War, insurance premiums had peaked at 6 percent of a cargo's replacement cost. In the first eighteen months of the Revolution, that number increased fivefold. Newspapers had chronicled the "great pain" of merchants and underwriters from the beginning, and now editorials from the business community were frequent and howling. Trade was "ruined," the Royal Navy "pitiful," French complicity "iniquitous," and Parliament content "to stand neuter."

Many British armchair tacticians had ideas to help turn the tide. Most aimed at squashing French meddlers in the West Indies, who, it was said, "enjoy all the advantages of war without any of the inconveniences." Two frigates assigned to blockade Martinique would make a good start, one merchant opined in the *London Chronicle*. "No step the Ministry could take would distress them more."

Another said threats of "British thunder" against "French and other neutral ports" that were trading with the rebels would smoke out duplicitous allies. "An open enemy is much better than a secret enemy, and we trust Britain will yet take severe vengeance on every pitiful associate of the American rebels." The view reflected people's growing awareness that Britain had other secret enemies besides France.

The crews of privateers bearing congressional commissions, especially those signed by William Bingham, were increasingly of mixed nationality. Indeed, the only English spoken by many West Indian privateers was the "Strike to Congress!" they yelled as they closed on their prey. Spanish and Danish islands known to deal with American blockade-runners were now said to receive, with only perfunctory stealth, British prizes for settlement. As for the Netherlands, a diplomat's observation that "these Dutch browse in all pastures" struck a sour note in London after reports that the fort at St. Eustatius had returned the cannon salute of a visiting Continental brig, *Andrew Doria*, in November 1776.

The gesture, which signified respect for sovereign flags, fueled British paranoia that the Netherlands was now "so far debased" as to recognize the American nation. After France officially entered the war on America's side in 1778 and St. Eustatius replaced Martinique as the foremost "nest of spies and rogues who carried on clandestine trade with the enemies of Great Britain," that paranoia proved justified.

Even in the face of such two-faced behavior, merchants generally stopped short of demanding an all-out military escalation against their European neighbors and against the rebels as well. Their early hope for a quick victory had banked, in the French foreign ministry's analysis, on "the idea that all the ports in America would be blockaded and their ships burned. They had not taken into consideration the impossibility of guarding a coast 1500 miles long."

Reports filtering back to America indicated that many British businessmen were "petitioning for an accommodation with the colonists upon commercial principles only." Benjamin Franklin, writing for the Committee of Secret Correspondence, had counted on just such frustration. "We expect to make their merchants sick of a contest in which so much is risked and nothing gained."

Britain's hawks remained steadfast. Their usual rebuttal to any defeatism was to call it subversive. Victory was assured, argued London's *Public Advertiser*. "All reports to the contrary are manufactured here by interested stockjobbers or by disappointed statesmen." Negative war news was disinformation put out by Congress to deceive its own constituents. "They have no idea of their real situation; losses are concealed, defeats made victories, and French assistance represented as at the door. By such subterfuges, three-fourths of the rebels are engaged in nominal support of a desperate cause."

There was concern that hostilities with America had been "carried too far to retract" and that initiating peace talks with Congress would, in the eyes of European rivals, "be manifesting their real weakness if they now consented to grant what they have so constantly refused." Too, there was a visceral element to British belligerence. People resented America's hit-and-run combat style on land and sea, deeming it an "unmanly way of fighting." A perception of the privateers in particular as "bragging, cowardly banditti" was reason enough to persevere.

One report of the capture of a supply ship alleged that "rebels stripped the killed and wounded, robbed every article of clothes, bedding, and provisions belonging to the sick, burned the cutter and added every insult to the distress." And any foe that would, "against the laws of God and Man," fire on a vessel under a flag of truce deserved, it was declared after one such incident, "all the horrors of rebellion," by which was meant no mercy.

Disgust with the "unequal terms" on which Britain was engaging the rebels—that is, the conduct of honorable warriors versus lawless rabble—was expressed by one of the Royal Navy's ablest captains, Andrew Snape Hamond of the forty-four-gun HMS *Roebuck*. Stationed in American waters since early 1776, Hamond complained of "treating them with openness and generosity while they are daily practicing every kind of art, treachery and cruelty to destroy us."

He particularly deplored the privateer trick of rigging abandoned vessels with "combustibles" that caused powder magazines to explode after British seamen took possession, a scene "horrible to behold," one witness wrote. "It went off like the sound of a gun, blew the boat into pieces and set her into flame." Before long, however, Hamond and other commanders resorted to "piratical" tactics that once would have shamed them, including such *ruses de guerre* as flying phony colors or distress signals and painting over their gunports to imitate defenseless merchant ships.

The captain found it worrisome that so few American captives opted to switch sides. But Ambrose Serle, who as Admiral Howe's secretary wrote out "pardons for rebels," filed a contrary report that applicants were "coming in for them by hundreds." Serle took this as evidence "that the hostile business will be settled in the next campaign." Writing on the very same day, a Royal Navy officer in Newport warned that American mariners "have employed themselves with such success to the southward that they have collected the means to prosecute this diabolical war for three years."

Britons were unready for such a long struggle. Charles Garnier, a diplomat in the French embassy in London, believed that his host's maritime pride, which, he said, "exceeds national pride by several degrees," would crumble over time. He assured the foreign minister in Paris that "the great superiority of the English navy consists in the confidence which reigns in it—a spirit founded on the success and experience of its officers who are accustomed to master their element." Undermine that confidence through "a slow war devoid of glorious adventures" and the Royal Navy and ultimately the British people "would be without strength and credit."

That was Captain Hamond's fear when he lamented the "defensive kind of war" Britain was waging. Dutiful optimism sustained him for a while ("Englishmen always rally when things are at the worst"), but after his crew suffered dozens of fatalities during the winter of 1776–77, some in battle, most from illness, he acknowledged "the great success the rebel small privateers have met with." Meanwhile the land war, with its "sad blot" of British defeats at Trenton and Princeton, continued to sputter due to one "favorable moment" after another failing to be exploited by army commanders.

Most dispiriting was the apparent futility of the navy's operational

Twenty-four-year-old William Bingham excelled at what he called "the art of uniting war and commerce." The vast network of privateers he managed in the West Indies unsettled Congress with its unruliness but decimated enemy trade in the region and won him the bitter respect of the British press, which marveled that Bingham's international status rivaled that of Britain's ambassador to Paris.

success. More than 120 American vessels were captured in the West Indies between November 1776 and April 1777. Losses ran into millions of dollars. Hundreds of casualties had been inflicted, thousands of prisoners taken. Yet the devastation, Hamond noted with puzzlement, "has been of very little consequence in distressing the enemy."

This paradox was integral to the American game plan. Though fewer British transports were lost in the same period, the greater wealth and breadth of British trade corresponded to a higher value of its individual cargoes—the difference between, say, an American sloop carrying barrel staves and a fat British "Indiaman" packed with sugar, textiles, or slaves. "They have much more property to lose than we have," Robert Morris wrote with typical pragmatism. William Bingham, who knew better than anyone the state of the maritime scorecard, concurred. "Upon casting up accounts, the balance will be immensely in our favor."

By mid-1777, the French foreign ministry, observing from the sidelines, had received confirmation of its early prediction that Britain possessed "insufficient resources in men and money to sustain a prolonged war at sea." Most telling was the public outcry—"disturbances in several places," was how a French newspaper reported it—against the government's impressment of seamen for the Royal Navy.

Impressment, or "the press," was the age-old way that warships were manned whenever there were shortfalls in volunteers. Its techniques ranged from mere marketing to brute force. Sometimes it was enough to set up recruiting desks in waterfront pubs and let officers and sailors spin tales of world travel and *esprit de corps*; signups were taken on the spot. And sometimes, especially during war, press gangs were used. These were comprised of moonlighting navy men or hired local toughs. Paid up to 40 shillings per head, they filled quotas by snatching citizens from the private workplace and herding them to His Majesty's ships.

The legal warrants under which the coercive "hot press" was authorized were much disputed. In his study of the Royal Navy in the eighteenth century, *The Wooden World*, N.A.M. Rodger notes the fundamental conflict between the navy's manpower needs and the people's instinctive resistance to "any extension of government's power to control and regulate. Thus, in the midst of war, public opinion and the law still worked strongly to hamper the Navy."

In the midst of this war particularly, with its pressures of unconventional combat on land and sea, traditional dissension against impressment turned virulent. Elaborated upon by the French ambassador to Britain, Marquis de Noailles, those earlier "disturbances" in fact were bloody riots against the press gangs. "The sailors of the India Company fought back, as well as sailors from some privately owned ships. A naval lieutenant was killed, and there were about thirty men drowned or wounded."

To avoid such eruptions, the Royal Navy preferred to replenish its crews at sea. It was standard procedure to seek converts among enemy captives; the persuasion could be comradely or severe. In addition to pressing foreigners, the navy was allowed to grab sailors off British transports as long as it was done offshore. The remove from public scrutiny combined with the merchantmen's sailing experience and penchant for seafaring made offshore presses the Royal Navy's most consistently productive. Shipping firms condemned the practice, of course, even though their demand for warships to defend transatlantic convoys was a major cause of the manpower squeeze. Their hypocrisy was cited by some members of Parliament as evidence "of the unpopularity of the present barbarous war."

Parliament's hawks, on the other hand, defended the press as unpleasant but necessary. "Two very striking features" of the current rebellion forced the issue in their view. First, in the past the Royal Navy had included some thirteen thousand Americans in its ranks. "It is unnecessary to say where they are now. They are making reprisals upon our defenseless trade." Second was the "mysterious conduct" of France and Spain, both of whom were expanding their navies. If they moved against Britain, "fifty, sixty, seventy frigates and sloops" would be required to repel them. And where were those ships? "Almost all in America." More were needed, along with sailors to man them. Otherwise, lamented a former admiral to his fellow lawmakers, "things have an extreme disagreeable appearance."

Soon it wasn't just the maritime community that felt the sting of impressment. "It is beginning to snatch away servants from behind their master's carriage," the French ambassador gloated. When news of an upcoming sweep hit the dockyards of London's Thames River, "most of the men withdrew into the city for protection." Their flight, and the collusion of those who hid them, engendered a scofflaw culture hardly helpful to the government's selling of the war to an increasingly dubious public.

Local officials obliged to enforce impressment procedures began to work against them. This was especially true in places unaccustomed to the coarse presence of roaming gangs. Three naval officers were arrested for running a hot press outside the London stock exchange. They had legal authority but briefly were thrown in jail anyway. Ambassador de Noailles gave Vergennes the good news. "There you have the first example of resistance by civil authority since impressment began."

Forced to maintain the press despite rising opinion against it, British leaders enacted other controversial measures in order to keep a posture of stern resolve. George III issued a proclamation assuring punishment "to the utmost severities of the law" to any Briton found serving on a foreign vessel—a situation prevalent on American privateers, whose skippers often marveled at how readily British merchant seamen threw in with them. In addition to a money reward, the king offered a one-year amnesty from naval impressment to anyone turning in such an offender.

Prime Minister North's infamous Pirate Act of 1777 likewise sought to harden British resolve. John Paul Jones spoke for all American mariners in protesting their designation under British law as "Traitors and Pirates and Felons! Whose necks they wish to destine to the cord!" But the act was widely criticized in Britain as well. It was called "cruel, persecuting"; "ill-advised and intemperate"; "unconstitutional"; "shocking to humanity"; and sure to bring "oppression and tyranny through every part of the realm." For the five years it remained law, it was a rallying point for antiwar and humanitarian activists, for whom it exposed "the precarious tenure on which the liberty of England is held." The controversy gave American leaders a useful gauge of anti-government feeling in Britain. Indeed, the first reports of the act to reach Philadelphia contained both its technical details and the encouraging news "that the city of London had ineffectually petitioned against it."

On the heels of its passage came the admiralty's announcement that the prisons at Forton and Mill were ready to receive captives taken at sea. "A shocking place," wrote Jonathan Haskins, the first American to enter Mill. He was the surgeon on *Charming Sally*, a privateer out of Martha's Vineyard seized in January after a brief cruise in which it took one prize. Others who'd suffered long confinements on prison ships and in their captors' holds had a different view. One man "rejoiced greatly" at the change of scene. Another likened it to "coming out of hell and going into paradise."

As the prisons filled, problems of sanitation, food, and the "negligence or connivance" of the guards rendered them less congenial. Illness, lice, and "the itch" (mange) were rampant. Inmates called their treatment "more cruel than Turkish enemies" with punishments that included flogging and up to six weeks' lockup in tiny windowless cells known as "black holes." The open-ended detention permitted by North's Act added to the duress. By August 1777, most prisoners believed their welfare depended totally on American victory. Should Britain "conquer the country or even get the upper hand, we are positive the gallows will be our destiny."

The admiralty tried to exploit this anxiety in order to entice them into Royal Navy service. After the war, Franklin, who despite North's Act successfully negotiated exchanges for small groups of Forton and Mill inmates, praised their resistance to "the allurements that were made use of to draw them from their allegiance to their country." He called it "a glorious testimony in favor of plebian virtue," and pointedly noted that "This was not the case with the English seamen."

The facilities drew considerable public curiosity. In coming to ogle the exotic rebel pirates ("Can they talk? Are they white?"), Britons were amazed to discover, wrote Charles Herbert of the captured privateer, *Dalton*, "They look like our people, and they talk English." When prisoners were later indentured into the population as laborers and apprentices, their savage reputations were further humanized, planting seeds of sympathy that eventually led to underground networks dedicated to helping escapees elude capture and slip out of the country.

Initiatives on behalf of the prisoners sprung up at all levels of British society. Churches and charities donated food and clothing. One hundred Londoners met at a pub in December and raised £1,300, an amount quickly tripled by contributions from three members of the House of Lords. The money was distributed to inmates according to rank and went for the purchase of tobacco, tea, books, and writing supplies; a lot went for gambling and drinking as well.

The cause of prisoner relief inevitably became linked with Britain's peace movement. In Parliament, opponents of the war supported fund drives and dispatched representatives, with pointed skepticism, on fact-finding missions to Forton and Mill. Newspaper editorials against the war added humanitarian pathos to their economic argument for reconciling with America. Reading them in prison, Charles Herbert sensed that Britain was "little short of civil war." Though an exaggeration, the impression no doubt heartened him and his fellow prisoners, not to mention observers in America and Europe equally impatient for British resolve to crack.

To go along with North's Act and the opening of two prisons for American seamen, Parliament took another aggressive measure by legalizing British privateers in March 1777. The resolution followed deliberations along the lines of Congress's debates the previous year, with privateering's potential for social chaos weighed against the damage it would inflict on the enemy.

It was out of such chaos that support for the policy had first arisen. Merchants on Antigua, center of Britain's West Indian commerce, had been ravaged by rebel privateers. In reprisal, they began launching unauthorized warships against American trade in late 1776. Soon frantic reports of enemy privateers "cruising for northward vessels" filled American newspapers. France took note as well, fearing its trade would be ensnared in the melee.

Ambassador de Noailles, blind to the irony of decrying the same scourge he'd formerly applauded, demanded an explanation from the admiralty. The assurance he received of British merchants arming their transports strictly in self-defense echoed the indifferent replies he'd given the admiralty when the tables had been reversed. "The government being unable to attend to all the needs of merchant shipping, there is no other remedy but to encourage private shippers to protect their own interests."

But the Antiguans took things to extremes. As their warships logged growing numbers of captures, the lucrative flow of prize cases through the island's maritime court tempted British merchantmen to jump to privateers. When Royal Navy sailors began deserting for the same reason, civilian shipowners were warned by Admiral James Young, commander of the Antigua-based Leeward Islands squadron, to cease their illegal enterprise.

They ignored him. "This adventure is not in opposition to the Navy but to the rebellious Americans, and to make recaptures for our very heavy losses."

It was another dispute Young didn't need. For more than a year, he'd been trading letters with the governor of Martinique about that island's dealings with American rebels. To call their correspondence confounding doesn't do justice to his utter aggravation at the governor's blithe dismissal of countless testimonies of American ships and British prizes popping in and out of the port of Saint-Pierre under the management of "one Bingham."

Similar activity was occurring at St. Eustatius. In the period since its fort had saluted *Andrew Doria*, Young had learned that island merchants were "giving all manner of assistance to the American rebels, and daily suffer privateers to be manned, armed, and fitted in their port." Governor Johannes de Graaff refuted the charges with the same flowery circumlocution ("I flatter myself that your Excellency will see great cause to suspect many current assertions") used by his counterpart on Martinique. Rendering it still more infuriating was Young's certainty that de Graaff, the richest merchant on St. Eustatius, was "an avowed abettor of a scene of piracy and depredation" who not only tolerated privateers, but invested in them.

No less frustrating than the stonewalling from foreigners was the continued minimization by Young's superiors in London of the maritime challenge he confronted. He'd long complained that his area of operations (which now included the Danish Virgin Islands, lately reported to support "illicit traffic notwithstanding the orders and directions of their governor") far exceeded the capacity of his squadron. "I take leave to assure your Lordships," one of his many imploring letters began, "that these seas now swarm with American privateers, several of them vessels of considerable force." But rather than grant his request for "not less than fifteen ships," the admiralty authorized six.

To compensate, he refitted a number of captured sloops into eight- and ten-gun warships skippered by lieutenants and sailing masters. The *London Chronicle* reported admiringly, "It is said these armed cruisers have within a few months taken upward of fifty sail of American vessels, some of them privateers."

Young's appreciation for tactical improvisation didn't extend to Antigua's privateers. This was surprising given the fright instilled at Martinique and St. Eustatius by the prospect of being targeted by British raiders, something the admiral might have welcomed after the smug duplicity he'd endured. When seizures of neutral shipping inevitably occurred, how could he not have relished the Dutch outcry against British "brigands" or the Martinique governor's panicky condemnation of "the acts of violence committed against our commerce by British pirates in a manner contrary to the terms of treaties"? But Young was nothing if not a proper professional and so agreed to correct any British misdeeds, though he did offer a jab about those islands' "clandestine disposal of the cargoes of English vessels."

True to his word, he demanded that Antiguan merchants immediately stop their privateering activity on grounds that it was "not only illegal but highly derogatory to the King's authority." Refusing to risk an international incident with one of Britain's ostensible allies "for the sake of gratifying a few individuals," he threatened these "robbers on the high seas" with arrest and warned that his cruisers would fire on private British vessels that refused to submit to inspection.

When the island's attorney general ruled that Young's decree undermined the merchants' right to seek redress for stolen property, the admiral asked his superiors for "an issuance of orders" to clarify official policy on the matter. Before any orders arrived, the merchants took matters into their own hands. In what an observer called "a bold and unprecedented affair," they deployed "a whole herd of lawyers" to sue Admiral Young "for seizing and sending into port the armed vessels employed by them." Then they had him thrown in jail.

He took it pretty well, considering. His letter to the admiralty begun on the morning of March 8, 1777, alluded in passing to the merchants' talk of initiating "actions of trespass against me." In a "P.S." added that evening, he was compelled to "further acquaint your Lordships" with news that he indeed had been briefly jailed and forced to put up bail of £1,100. Any outrage he felt was conveyed in his closing request for the admiralty's "support and protection, which may hereafter prevent any commanding officer from being publicly insulted." Another letter followed soon after—a request for transfer home from Antigua. "Three years in this climate is full long enough," he wrote.

Word of Young's arrest reached America within weeks. The *Pennsylvania Journal* mocked the merchants for humiliating the admiral for "spoiling the sport" of their greedy ambitions. But the broader ramifications were sobering. "The people at the Grenades, Dominica, Montserrat, Nevis, St. Christopher's, Anguilla, and Tortolla have followed the detestable example of the Antiguans. They have many pirates out, and have been very successful."

The real eruption of British "piracy" began three weeks after the admiral's arrest, when George III approved Parliament's decision to commission private warships "for the seizing and taking of all vessels, goods, wares, and merchandize belonging to the inhabitants of the colonies now in rebellion." The proclamation constituted a resounding answer to Young's request for clarification of the government's position on privateering. That policy was now crystal clear. America was due for payback.

Admiralty courts in Britain, Antigua, Halifax, and British-held New York were flooded with applications for privateer commissions and letters of marque. Estimates of the war's total number range as high as 2,600, with New York's Tories leading the way in vengeful expeditions against the patriots who'd so disrupted their lives.

Though "in no way authorized to run down ships of other powers," the abundance of armed vessels on the prowl for plunder vastly increased the likelihood, as Ambassador de Noailles fretfully put it, of "hostility toward neutral flags."

The degree to which the Atlantic now teemed with international vessels at cross-purposes of trade and predation is evident in an amazed report from a loyalist skipper sailing in convoy from Bermuda to Barbados later that spring. Sighting more than 150 ships along the way, he found the sea "alive with privateers" trying to pick off straggling transports like wolves circling an animal herd. "One son of a bitch ran amongst us but was too small to attack our convoy."

A British slave ship, *Derby*, was similarly beset as it entered West Indian waters, no sooner driving one off one marauder than finding itself targeted by another. The vessel's hard voyage (its first mate reported leaving Nigeria "with 349 slaves, and buried ninety and ten white men on the passage") ended with capture near Barbados by two American privateers, *Fly* and *St. Peter*.

The ship and its human cargo were sold "at Martinico" under Bingham's direction. Island officials skimmed a few slaves for themselves in what had become a customary payoff—though the agent was said to be "dissatisfied at their taking so many," because, he told a colleague, "he should not be paid for any of them." After *Derby*'s settlement, some of *St. Peter*'s men used their prize money to purchase the vessel and convert it to their own privateer commissioned, of course, by Bingham.

Marquis de Lafayette, writing from shipboard en route to America in May 1777, acknowledged the heightened perils of sea travel in a letter to his wife. "At present we are in some danger because we risk being attacked by English vessels." But once ashore, he assured her, "I shall be in perfect safety. The post of general officer has always been regarded as a warrant for long life. Ask any of the French generals of which there are so many."

Meanwhile in Europe the shoe was on the other foot when it came to privateers. In 1776 the French foreign ministry had shrugged off British complaints about American "pirates" with barely concealed amusement. "Shall we say they are pirates? They do not commit any acts of piracy against us." But by the fall of 1777, Ambassador de Noailles was regularly sending the admiralty furious accounts of British privateers harassing French transports.

The admiralty, to say the least, was not quick with sympathy. "We may venture to assure you that none of the vessels complained of are ships belonging to His Majesty. There is great reason to believe they were some of the piratical vessels fitted out by His Majesty's rebellious subjects in America. Unless you can furnish us with names or a more minute and circumstantial description of those vessels, it will be impossible for us to cause those enquiries to be made which you have desired."

De Noailles relayed this unhelpful response to Vergennes in Paris. The foreign minister was neither surprised nor alarmed. France's naval buildup was almost complete. Its fleet in the West Indies had been expanded and modernized. With just a little good news from the American mainland, France would throw off the veil and enter the war. He told his ambassador not to worry. "We are going to put things aright."

1779

Christopher Vail was seventeen when, in his eagerness to join the Continental Army, he secretly assumed the place and name (Paul Pain) of an acquaintance eager to desert it. He subsequently found himself on Long Island in 1776, cut off from retreat by William Howe's redcoats. Ferrying Vail's unit under fire across the Sound to Connecticut were the Essex County watermen commanded by John Glover, who a year earlier had leased Washington the ill-fated armed schooner, *Hannah*, and installed his friends and relatives as its officers and agents.

When Vail's enlistment ended nine months later, he joined the crew of *Mifflin*, a Continental warship based in New London; and then *Warren*, one of Congress's original thirteen frigates that later would be Dudley Saltonstall's flagship in the disastrous assault on Penobscot.

In January 1779 he headed for the West Indies on the privateer *Revenge*. Capturing a transport bound for Halifax, he went aboard as one of its prize crew. Two days later a British privateer engaged them with the particular viciousness of combat between civilian warships. Outgunned, Vail's vessel struck its sails in surrender. Even so, the enemy pumped several more volleys into its hull before boarding "with drawn swords in hand." The Americans were herded to the side of their vessel and forced to leap the span of water to their captors' ship. "I think the distance I jumped was 12 or 14 feet to avoid a cutlass." Vail and his mates were then delivered to the Royal Navy prison at Admiral Young's base on Antigua.

After five failed escape attempts (ignorant of Britain's "Pirate Act," he'd been shocked to learn "there was no exchange of prisoners"), Vail was shipped from Antigua to Britain. En route, warships under the command of Sir George Rodney pressed them into service. Vail manned a cannon on HMS *Suffolk*, seventy-four guns, against the French fleet off Martinique in April 1780. The initial bout was a "ship to ship slogging match" involving almost forty battleships and lasting three and a half hours. The British suffered eight hundred casualties, the French at least twice that number.

In the midst of the fighting, Vail's ship had "an accident. A number of cartridges took fire and blew up 36 men." The British flagship was no less hammered. "Our ship was next to Admiral Rodney in the action. I counted 24 shot holes that went through his ship between the two tiers of guns, and so many above that I could not count them." Its decks later were washed with seawater that ran out the scuppers. "I saw plenty of blood on the Admiral's ship's side after the action."

For several days the fleets maneuvered for advantage. The French were arrayed in a battle line, and Rodney decided to strike its rear section in order to cut off those vessels from the main force and destroy them piecemeal. His captains misunderstood his signals, however, and instead attacked the heart of the enemy's strength. Vail's ship led the way. "At 6 p.m. our ship struck the center of the French line but found it impregnable and bore away with the loss of nearly 100 men as she took the fire of four ships at once. The second came up in the same manner and was repulsed as the other." In all, fifteen British ships in succession tried vainly to break through.

The enemy counterattacked the next day. "The French brought their whole force of 23 sail of the line to fight 16 of the English." After another slugfest in which opposing warships mingled "all much together" as they blasted one another, each fleet withdrew, rendering the battle "inconsequential" in history's view. "We lost a great many men and our ships very much damaged," Vail wrote. He noted, too, that the battle considerably changed the attitude of his Royal Navy shipmates:

"The first time that we were going into action with the French, the whole crew seemed elated, being sure of success. They told me two English ships could take three Frenchmen any time. I really must acknowledge that the English fought well in the action, but came off second best. After this I heard no more said about the French not fighting."

The next time the crew was called to quarters, Vail and the other American conscripts refused to report. The captain threatened to flog them but didn't carry it out. Vail overheard one of the ship's officers grudgingly commend their resistance. "Damn them, I like them better for their conduct."

Transferred to HMS *Action*, the Americans again refused to fight. It drew only scorn from the British this time. As an example to his comrades, one was selected for flogging. He was stripped and given ten lashes. The resistor, Ebenezer Williams, still wouldn't serve. "Damn him," *Action*'s captain snarled, "whip him until he will do duty." More lashes followed. At last Williams relented "after being cut into jelly."

First chance he got, however, the captain unloaded the stubborn captives onto a passing transport. "Our living on board this ship was horrible beyond description," Vail wrote. Its provisions, "condemned six months before," consisted of "black beef, yellow pork, sour oat meal, and blue butter."

His next stop was Falmouth, England, where he snuck away and joined *Amazon*, a British privateer hunting French and Spanish prizes. One incident during the cruise was particularly evocative of privateering's mortal uncertainties. Off Portugal's Cape St. Vincent, "We chased a large ship one day, and at 8 p.m. came alongside and hailed her but received no answer." The vessel's sails lay slack against the mast. He and some others rowed over in a longboat. "She mounted 20 guns which was all loaded and the matches lighted and a barrel of brandy opened on the larboard side of the deck. There was not a man on board."

At Lisbon, Vail jumped ship and made his way to Cádiz,

on Spain's southern coast. There, Richard Harrison found him a place on a French warship. Harrison had been Congress's agent at St. Eustatius early in the war. One of William Bingham's business partners, he'd gone there undercover as a sufferer of venereal disease seeking a tropical cure. He'd left the island after political change in Europe killed its commercial advantages.

Vail's vessel hailed a privateer flying American colors—false colors, it turned out. He fired his gun twenty-four times at the British impostor before both ships sheared away "completely cut to pieces." During the fight some of his shipmates had "run from their quarters. I hollered to them to stick to it like good fellows. Every time I fired I was very careful and took good aim, and when I fired the captain says, 'Huzza for the American 12 pounder!'" Afterward the relieved French captain "gave every man a bottle of wine."

While in Cadiz to make repairs, Vail found a Massachusetts privateer, *Thomas*, preparing to head home to Salem. The four-week journey was disagreeable in one serious respect. The captain was a teetotaler, denying his men "one drop of spirits of any kind to drink nor even did he thank us for our services."

From Salem, Vail returned to New London in May 1781, "which makes two years, four months, and five days absence." Two days later he hopped another privateer and took off again to sea.

Eight

It is our business to force on a war, for which purpose I see nothing so likely as fitting our privateers from the ports and islands of France. Here we are too near the sun, and the business is dangerous; with you it may be done more easily.

—*William Carmichael to William Bingham, June 1777*

I have by no means neglected what Mr. Carmichael so strongly recommends in regard to precipitating a war betwixt France and England. I have always been fully convinced of the policy of irritating the two nations, of affording them matter for present resentments, and of renewing in their minds the objects of their ancient animosity. The attempt has not been altogether unavailing.

—*William Bingham to the Foreign Affairs Committee,
October 1777*

One of the excuses France offered Britain for its treaty violations was that its people were "turbulent spirits eager to run after adventures." Since "adventure" meant both financial speculation and personal thrill-seeking, the characterization was dead on. Money above all drove Frenchmen and other Europeans to join, as crewmen or investors, still-illegal privateer expeditions. But the excitement of tweaking the British "lords of the ocean" was clearly part of the draw.

Most Americans in Europe at the time likewise operated with mixed motives, combining their patriotic endeavors with capitalist ventures in privateering and the export home of munitions and trade goods. Though Benjamin Franklin (and later John Adams, who replaced Silas Deane as a commissioner in the American mission in 1778) was an exception in his business indifference, men like Deane were typical in working for fame and fortune along with American liberty. Deane told his partner Caron de Beaumarchais that he preferred "not to live" if the Revolution failed. If that was to be his fate, however, his incessant wartime speculation shows he meant to go out rich.

William Carmichael was rich already. The young Marylander's family wealth enabled him to join the staff of the commissioners in Paris as an unpaid volunteer. A self-described dilettante "covetous only of reputation, and now and then a pretty woman," he took a position as Deane's secretary to be "near the sun" of great events unfolding in Europe. Carmichael was a minor figure historically. Yet along with many others of similar background he occasionally wielded no little influence thanks to the presumption of authority that often attached to socially connected, wellborn gentlemen despite their lack of demonstrated merit.

France in 1777 was full of such Americans. Chronicles of the period blur with the names of businessmen, maritime agents, Continental representatives authorized or self-designated, and assorted relatives, wanderers, and hangers-on, most of whom were split into bitter factions over money, access to French officials, and the comparative purity of one another's allegiance to the patriot cause.

Some fifty or sixty gravitated to the port of Nantes on the Loire River where many mercantile houses with ties to the colonies were based. The preeminent American there was Tom Morris, younger brother to Robert, the member of Congress said to chair "all the committees that can properly be employed in receiving and importing supplies." Tom had represented Robert's firm, Willing & Morris, since the start of the war. His nepotistic promotion to the post of Congress's top commercial agent in France, which should have cemented his high stature, coincided with the terminal phase of his alcoholic tailspin.

When Tom left Nantes on a binge in the summer of 1777, his brother sent John Ross, a Scotsman, to rescue the company books from chaos. Described as "puritan" in his ethics, Ross clashed with another upstanding accountant, Franklin's nephew Jonathan Williams. Williams's assignment from his uncle to cull any Continental receipts from among the cargoes and prizes Tom Morris had overseen inevitably put him at odds with Ross, who was there in the interest of Willing & Morris. They were driven into an uneasy détente, however, by charges of graft leveled at them and at many others by Arthur and William Lee of the powerful Virginia clan of soldiers, statesmen, and planters.

William Lee had relocated from London to Paris after his brother became Congress's third diplomatic commissioner. That each today is labeled "troublemaker" in the scrupulously benign *Encyclopedia of the American Revolution* constitutes some consolation to anyone who hopes villains will be called to account in the historical record if not in their lifetimes. The fact that they aimed to murder reputations rather than lives hardly mitigates nastiness committed in an era, and among a social set, in which the two were more or less equivalent.

The Lees' relentless slander of their fellow expatriates furthered a lust for prestige more than profit. Arthur, angling to be Congress's sole delegate to France, wanted his brother posted to the court of Frederick the Great in Berlin, Franklin sent to "respectable and quiet" Vienna, and Deane removed to Holland. He was jealous of the stature accorded Franklin by France's government and the affection he enjoyed from its people, a feeling aggravated by the distaste and rebuff Arthur engendered on various congressional errands around Europe. But his loathing for Deane was personal.

Having conceived with Beaumarchais the original idea of a dummy firm to funnel arms to America, he believed Deane had usurped what should have been his role in Hortalez & Company. Deflected by Franklin from participating in diplomatic talks, he was similarly kept in the dark about Deane's efforts to obtain arms and outfit privateers on behalf of Congress. Certain that Deane was making a secret fortune, Lee decried his "faithless principles, dirty intrigue, selfish views, and wicked arts" in countless letters to influential contacts in America, including his congressman brother, Richard Henry Lee, and Richard's friends, John and Samuel Adams— "the L's and the A's," Arthur termed them.

Ultimately he hoped to implicate every American in France "through whose hands the public money has passed," he wrote Richard. "If this scheme can be executed, it will disconcert all the plans at one stroke, without an appearance of intention, and save both the public and me."

William Lee chimed in, promising "proofs to come" to verify the brothers' sketchy but ominous charges. To their voices was added that of Ralph Izard, another scion of southern wealth hanging around Paris in hope of advancement. "The three men gave themselves great airs," writes Helen Augur in *The Secret War of Independence*, "and misdirected attention from the fact that they were doing nothing but adding to the witch brew."

The trio did little damage to those able to defend themselves. Williams and Ross kept impeccable records of their work in Nantes and so were never seriously jeopardized. Franklin, repeatedly accused by the Lees of embezzling funds, was untouchable by virtue of his years, experience, and established record. "I have been a servant to many publics through a long life," he wrote in answer to one "malignant" attack. "There is not a single instance of my ever being accused before of acting contrary to their interest or my duty."

Izard, less than half Franklin's age and with no accomplishments to speak of, didn't hesitate to call the old doctor "haughty, and not guided by principles of virtue or honor." When no evidence could be found of Franklin's supposed perfidy, Izard took that as proof in itself. "His tricks are in general carried on with so much cunning that it is extremely difficult to fix them on him."

Contemptuous barely captures Franklin's opinion of Izard: "little, hissing, crooked, serpentine, venomous." Still, the mudslinging hindered but didn't derail his discussions with the French foreign ministry about formalizing a Franco-American alliance. The atmosphere at Franklin's residence in the Hotel de Valentinois in the exclusive Passy section of Paris continued to reflect his manner of relaxed improvisation, which, as a negotiating style, was all the more effective for being true to his nature, earnest and elusive at once.

For example, William Bingham recently had accepted Martinique's demand of a 1 percent fee on all services to American privateers; he persuaded a dubious Congress that receipts verifying French payoffs, if made public, would "quicken the resentments of the English." Thinking along similarly devious lines, Franklin dismissed the conventional wisdom that French ships leased to British merchants seeking immunity from privateer attack undermined the American cause. He predicted that shipowners would, "with a little encouragement, facilitate the necessary discovery" of British cargoes despite the supposed protection of sailing under a French flag. That encouragement, namely bribery, could then be leaked to the British with predictable outcries of French treachery.

When Franklin (with what his adversaries called "insidious subtlety") encouraged American privateers, increasingly prevalent in European waters, to bring their prizes to French ports rather than sail them back to America for settlement, he pushed the boundary of diplomatic decorum to the point of impertinence. France could turn a blind eye only to a degree; in the face of blatant indiscretion, a sharp scolding was due its American guests if only to mollify British outrage. Franklin crafted slick apologies for the infractions that were mindful of French dignity while still pushing sly proposals to transfer captured cargoes onto French ships at sea or to conduct prize sales just outside the harbor in technically international waters. He rarely gave ground completely, in other words, leaving each issue slightly nudged toward maintaining friction between France and Britain.

He could play the game harder if need be. His effusive expressions of remorse to the foreign ministry "when any vessels of war appertaining to America, either through ignorance or inattention, do anything that might offend," often carried reminders, lest France forget the commercial windfall which an alliance might bring and which Anglo-American reconciliation would certainly snuff, that its "protection to us and our nation will always be remembered with gratitude and affection."

Yet even as he outwardly backtracked from encouraging privateers, he supported Deane's continuing call for Congress to send more blank commissions to Europe. "This mode of exerting our force should be pushed with vigor."

Franklin and Deane conferred almost daily. "The latter appears to be the more active and efficient man," a British intelligence report said, "but less circumspect and secret, his discretion not being always proof against the natural warmth of his temper, and being weakened also by his own ideas of the importance of his present employment."

In running the mission's maritime operations under Franklin's far-thinking but often chaotic leadership, Deane puffed up his role because he thought its significance underappreciated. "I repeatedly gave my sentiments in favor of sending cruisers into these seas," he told anyone who'd listen. "They have been of infinite prejudice to our enemies, both in their commerce and reputation."

Franklin praised his colleague's contributions. "He daily proves himself an able, faithful, active, and extremely useful servant of the public." When the Lees questioned why most of the mission's commercial documents bore Deane's signature alone, Franklin explained that Deane "consulted with me and had my approbation in the orders he gave, and I know they were for the best and aimed at the public good." But he knew this about Deane as well: "I perceive he has enemies."

Having enemies was no rarity in those times. But Deane was vulnerable because his store of well-wishers was thinner than he realized. When the Lees' charges against him first circulated in Congress, they'd been countered by the strong advocacy of Robert Morris. But when Robert learned that fall of Deane's efforts to remove his brother Tom as the top American agent at Nantes, he renounced their friendship—and Deane didn't find out for months.

Communication lapses between Paris and Philadelphia also kept Deane from realizing the extent to which his commissioning of French fortune hunters as Continental officers had angered people like George Washington and Nathanael Greene. Greene almost resigned over the elevation of a French artilleryman, Philippe du Coudray, over General Henry Knox. Du Coudray's drowning near Philadelphia in September 1777 resolved the matter, though not before it opened a permanent rift between Greene and John Adams, who condemned the general's refusal to bend to Congress's civilian will.

Franklin too was besieged with applications from French aristocrats and thus came to sympathize with Deane's difficult position during his early months abroad. But there was little chance that colleagues in America could appreciate the isolation and stress that had led Deane, without funds or commodities to pay for supplies obtained on credit, to accept French officers in order to placate their wealthy families.

It didn't help Deane's reputation that his two steadiest companions in Paris were Beaumarchais and Franklin's American-born secretary, Edward Bancroft. Beaumarchais was essentially viewed as a French Silas Deane, a clever insider who couched his avarice in idealism; while Bancroft's frequent travel between France and Britain, the nation of his citizenship now, hinted at the apolitical opportunism underlying his shady business deals and his employment as a British spy.

But most exploitable by Deane's enemies was his work with privateers, whose notorious success in New England and the West Indies brought instant connotations of lawlessness. Franklin, through his tireless efforts to free American mariners from British custody, would be revered by sailors as "the patron saint of prisoners." Deane earned a less beatific title as the one "who watched over the sea captains." He enjoyed the work for its saltwater, daredevil milieu. His critics among the L's and the A's suspected that he enjoyed its plunder as well.

For years, France and Spain had shared the view that "England is the monster against which we should always be prepared." Vergennes, the French foreign minister, wasn't yet ready to get "actively offensive," however. He had twenty warships in the West Indies and another thirty-two in France prepared to support America "whenever it can be done with advantage." But he wanted further proof from the battlefield that the Continental Army stood a chance against British ground forces.

Comte de Vergennes, the wily French foreign minister, leaped at the opportunity to undermine Britain by offering secret military aide to Congress and granting safe harbor to American privateers. Confident that the American rebellion could be exploited to France's advantage, he didn't imagine that his gamesmanship might someday contribute to the fall of his government.

Spain's longstanding dispute with Portugal, a British ally, over territories in South America had led its king, Charles III, initially to back Vergennes's clandestine maneuvers against Britain with a hefty loan to Hortalez & Company. But those disputes had been resolved in Spain's favor by mid-1777, cooling the king's enthusiasm. He'd also begun wondering, with good reason it turned out, if a free and empowered United States might someday be a threat to Spanish possessions in the New World.

This wavering gave Vergennes pause, for he knew his monarch, the ever cautious Louis XVI, was loath to go to war without Spain at his side. As one historian later wrote, such considerations were "in strict accord with classic diplomacy, which indulged in no philanthropy and was much addicted to lying."

The need for American fighters to make a good show was therefore more important than ever. British spy reports gauged the situation bluntly. "The great object of Messrs. Franklin and Deane is to obtain some open declaration in favor of America. This must soon happen; instantly indeed if Mr. Washington should gain any decisive battle against Sir William Howe."

But good news was scarce. British troops still held Newport and in April 1777 had rampaged through western Connecticut. Having prevailed in numerous small skirmishes from Vermont to Georgia, they retook Fort Ticonderoga and its precious store of military supplies in early July. The action called attention to General John Burgoyne's advance from Canada into New York with 8,000 men, alarming Congress with the prospect of Burgoyne linking up with Howe's army in the lower Hudson valley and effectively cutting the colonies in two.

Deane painted a desperate picture to French officials. "The United States will be distressed to the last degree, if not absolutely ruined, in the next campaign unless relieved from some quarter or other." But Franklin stayed optimistic, assuring Congress that war among the European powers was, if not imminent, inevitable. "When all are ready, a small matter may suddenly bring it on."

Almost a year earlier, Deane had successfully lobbied, with French help and over British protests, for the release of Captain John Lee from a Spanish jail. Freeing the Newburyport privateer had established that, despite their outward amity, Spain and France didn't share Britain's belief that American commerce raiders were criminals. Neutrality agreements still forbade the material support of one another's foes, but the public affirmation of Spanish and French disregard of British grievances marked a big step toward open hostility.

Rebel activity in European waters had increased after the Lee decision. Occurring just across the English Channel, the provocations were even more maddening to Britons than those in the West Indies. The main sore point was that under terms of their treaties, nations could receive any vessel in "distress caused by weather or want of provisions." This loophole enabled visitors to feign hardship or disrepair in order legally to enter neutral ports to refit and meanwhile do business. When France and Spain invoked the clause to justify the American presence in their ports, Britain scoffed at the claims yet was helpless to disprove them.

The majority of American vessels in Europe were private transports engaged in the same commodities-for-arms trade that Congress was pursuing. The privateers among them were independent operators that had ventured across the Atlantic in search of prey. *Tyrannicide* and *Massachusetts*, after the shabby episode in which they'd abandoned the Continental brig *Cabot* to HMS. *Milford* off New England earlier in 1777, proceeded to take twenty-five prizes off the British coast that spring. *General Mifflin*, which on the excuse of illness afflicting its crew had deserted John Manley's navy-privateer fleet six days after leaving Boston, subsequently prowled the Irish Sea and sold prizes at the French port of Morlaix.

Rising States and *Freedom* from Massachusetts and *Montgomery* from Maryland also carried prizes to France. Reminding their skippers of the restrictive "treaties and ordinances," Franklin recommended "some convenient place on the coast where the business may be transacted without much observation and conducted with discretion. I suppose this may be done because I understand it has been practiced in many cases." More commonly, privateers provisioned in French and Spanish ports but didn't linger and rarely sold prizes there, dispatching them instead to America.

The first warship that sought entirely to base its operations in Europe was the sixteen-gun Continental brig *Reprisal.* Under its captain, Lambert Wickes, *Reprisal* had delivered Bingham to Martinique in mid-1776 and Franklin to France in December. Wickes had seized prizes on each trip, giving his eminent passengers a persuasive look at commerce raiding in action.

He'd sold his prizes openly in Martinique, but at Nantes had hastily unloaded them at half value to avoid attracting the notice of British observers. They got wind of it anyway, and within weeks London newspapers were calling it more evidence of French duplicity. "Is this not acknowledging the American privateer's commission? And is not *that* an acknowledgment of the independency of America?"

Winter weather froze *Reprisal* in port through January 1777. During the hiatus Wickes joined Deane's circle in Paris. Centered at Deane's hotel, the high-living group included Carmichael, Bancroft, Beaumarchais, Franklin's teenage grandson William Temple Franklin, and any number of "privateer masters who needed rest and relaxation" courtesy of their gregarious host. One visiting skipper wrote of the scene, "Carmichael and myself are constantly driving about in Deane's coach, and have missed but one night of opera, comedy, or masquerade since I came to town."

After the February thaw, Wickes took *Reprisal* on a three-week expedition in the Bay of Biscay that netted four British merchantmen and, at the cost of eight American casualties, the armed "Lisbon packet" carrying mail from Portugal to London. Returning to France, he let the prizes go cheap at 100,000 livres (about £4,000) to merchants who, in exchange for a bargain, "are willing to take upon themselves all consequences as to the illegality."

Hushed up though they were, the transactions were immediately known to Lord Stormont, the British ambassador. His source was Bancroft, Deane's friend and fellow partygoer. Paid by the British to uncover "intelligence that may arrive from America, the captures made by their privateers, and how the captures are disposed of," Bancroft regularly hid notes in a tree near the Tuileries for pickup by his handlers. Through working as Franklin's secretary and carousing with the affable, loose-tongued Deane, his access to American secrets was limitless. Thanks to Bancroft, Stormont's complaint to Vergennes about Wickes's activity was supported by an itemized list of prize sales.

Embarrassed to be caught red-handed in its tolerance of illicit behavior (he'd expressly demanded of his maritime officials that "the registers must not contain any item or any indication of this connivance"), the foreign minister gave Wickes twenty-four hours to leave port and face enemy warships waiting offshore. At once the captain claimed *Reprisal* had sprung a leak and provided a carpenter's report as evidence. To British dismay, for it was all but certain that Wickes had poured seawater into his hold, a stay was granted on humanitarian grounds so that *Reprisal* could make repairs. The stay lasted three months, outlasting the Royal Navy blockade.

The prizes listed by Stormont meanwhile were snapped up by local merchants after registrations bearing false names and manifests were filed with the government. On May 22 the French naval secretary, Antoine de Sartine, informed the British ambassador with regret that "if there had been fraud, it would be very difficult to trace it now."

By that time, Deane had added two vessels to Wickes's command: Captain Henry Johnson's Continental brig, *Lexington*, which had arrived in April with two prizes in tow; and *Dolphin*, a refurbished cutter recently purchased by the commissioners and skippered by Samuel Nicholson, a drinking buddy of Carmichael's.

The "three American privateers," as the British press called them, sailed on May 28. Circling Ireland twice during a month-long cruise, they seized eighteen vessels, sending eight to French ports, releasing three, and sinking seven. The squadron "most effectually alarmed England," prompting forty British transports awaiting departure in the Thames River to shift their loads to French vessels, closing down a fair in Chester near the Irish Sea out of invasion panic, and generating, no doubt to the crown's particular annoyance, glowing newspaper testaments from British passengers "of the humane treatment they met with from the commanders of *Reprisal* and *Lexington*, both of whom endeavored to make the situation of their prisoners as easy as their unhappy circumstances would admit."

Reprisal barely made it back to France. Chased into Saint-Malo by HMS *Burford*, Wickes had to heave his guns overboard to lighten weight. His report to Deane included a straight-faced gripe at his pursuers for ignoring the legal boundary of France's territorial waters as the distance from shore of a cannon shot. "They pay very little regard to the laws of neutrality," he complained.

In a replay of the aftermath of *Reprisal*'s February cruise, Stormont filed a protest with the foreign ministry. The main offense was the sale of prizes, and as before the speed with which they were purchased undercut any response that might have satisfied the British. It also—unfortunately for the cash-strapped commissioners—meant that no profit was generated. Deane explained, "The prizes are sold without condemnation and consequently to a great loss, as the whole is conducted secretly." On the positive side, "Though these cruises have not been profitable to us, they have been of infinite prejudice to our enemies."

At minimum, Stormont wanted the American warships banished. Vergennes rebuked Franklin and Deane ("this conduct offends the dignity of the King my master at the same time it abuses the neutrality which His Majesty professes"), but stopped short of expelling Wickes's squadron from port. Rather, he had it "sequestered and detained there until sufficient security can be obtained that they will return directly to their native country."

Since the Royal Navy again was poised to ambush Wickes upon departure, Vergennes's order was really a disguised pledge of sanctuary. Stormont argued the point to no avail. "Vergennes insisted," he reported with dismay after their meeting, "that no ship is ever sent forcibly out of a neutral port as long as cruisers that are in wait for her are within sight of the coast." There was no such rule. It was just another instance, the ambassador fumed, of the foreign minister's "usual frivolous answer."

Meanwhile Vergennes told his staff that he was prepared to squabble along these lines indefinitely. "This sort of war will not be dangerous so long as governments do not meddle with it."

After a two-month layover that featured parties and parades in the Americans' honor, *Reprisal* and *Lexington* (*Dolphin* was unfit to sail) made a dash for home. Prior to sailing, Wickes instructed Captain Johnson to destroy, "if you are taken," their codebook of ship-to-ship signals. "I will do the same." He looked forward to their rendezvousing in New Hampshire. "The wind is now fair. I shall depart immediately."

Neither man reached his destination. *Lexington* was overtaken off Brittany by HMS *Alert*. The journal of the British warship gives the cold facts: "5 a.m. saw a sail to eastward . . . fired a swivel to bring her to . . . he hauled down English colors and hoisted American colors . . . gave us a broadside which we returned . . . half past 2 she struck . . . the enemy had seven men killed and 11 wounded . . . the loss on our side was three men wounded and two killed."

Many of the injured were "in need of amputation of arms or legs" London's *Daily Advertiser* reported. Captain Johnson was sent to Mill prison along with 60 crewmen, including a large number of Frenchmen whom he blamed for his defeat because they "would not stand to their guns."

Meanwhile *Reprisal* eluded the enemy but foundered off Newfoundland in heavy winter seas. According to the lone survivor, three massive waves swamped the ship and "carried her down" along with 128 men. Franklin notified Congress of Wickes's death. "This loss is extremely to be lamented, as he was a gallant officer and a very worthy man."

Beyond his personal fondness for the captain, which dated from their voyage to France in 1776, Franklin appreciated Wickes's concern for "the distressed situation" of American mariners held in British prisons. Speaking for himself and his officers in a letter to Franklin, Wickes earlier had pledged, "We ourselves will readily and willingly assist them as far as our money or credit will go."

With the "three American privateers" having taken a hundred captives in their European sorties, Franklin offered a prisoner exchange to Stormont, whose snippy reply conveyed his frustration on many fronts. "The King's ambassador receives no applications from rebels, unless they come to implore His Majesty's mercy."

Franklin's response was no less astringent. "We received the enclosed indecent paper as coming from your Lordship, which we return for your Lordship's more mature consideration."

Unsurprisingly, it would be almost two years before the two sides got together to exchange Americans held in Britain for Britons held in France. The deals would be grudging and the numbers skimpy even then.

1780

NEWFOUNDLAND, CANADA

The 18-gun sloop *Ranger*, outfitted at Portsmouth, New Hampshire, by John Langdon in 1777, had wreaked havoc off Scotland and Ireland under John Paul Jones. After Jones was detached to command *Bonhomme Richard* two years later, *Ranger* returned to refit for a cruise to the Caribbean.

Visiting the town waterfront with his father one day, young Andrew Sherburne found it a stirring pageant of color and industry. "Ships were building, prizes taken from the enemy unloading, privateers fitting out, standards waved on the forts and batteries, the exercising of soldiers, the roar of cannon, the sound of martial music and the call for volunteers so infatuated me that I was filled with anxiety to become an actor in the scene of war."

His father let him join *Ranger*'s crew only because it was "in service of Congress" and not a seedy privateer. Despite the precaution, life on shipboard introduced the boy to boxing, drinking, and the "abominable practice" of cursing. "There was a necessity for it," Andrew wrote in his memoir many years later. "To counterbalance my guilt I became more constant in praying. I prayed every night to atone for the sins of the day."

Seasick most of the time, he waited on *Ranger*'s officers and "in time of action" carried ammunition to "the third gun from the bow." One prize, the three-deck *Holderness* loaded with cotton, sugar, rum, and spices, made the voyage a hit. And because it was armed with twenty-two cannon ("her crew was not sufficiently large to manage them"), the transport was designated a warship and thus awarded 100 percent to its captors.

Sherburne's naval salary was $6.66 a month. His share of

Holderness's loot was "one ton of sugar, from thirty to forty gallons of fourth-proof Jamaica rum, about twenty pounds of cotton, approximately twenty pounds of ginger, logwood, and allspice, and about $700 in paper money equal to one hundred dollars in specie." At age fourteen, he'd become his family's star breadwinner.

In the spring of 1780 *Ranger* took part in the failed defense of Charleston against an assault of British land and naval forces. It was Sherburne's first heavy combat. The explosion of an artillery shell "within a few feet of me" left him "much alarmed" and "in continual apprehension" for the much of the battle. Captured, he was shocked by the spectacle of redcoats "hurried into eternity" by accidentally sparking a storehouse of gunpowder. "I saw the print of a man who had been dashed against the end of a brick church thirty feet above the ground."

Since orderlies were paroled along with their officers, Sherburne got back to Portsmouth within a few months. He found his family in shambles. His father and older brother had been lost at sea aboard trade ships. His mother, now that "the avails of my former cruise were pretty much exhausted," was working as a seamstress to support her two daughters and youngest son.

"Almost sixteen and pretty well grown," Sherburne gave in to a recruiter's persuasion to "take a short cruise in a fine schooner and make your fortune." He joined the "jovial company" of the privateer *Greyhound*. "She had a full complement of officers, two or three ordinary seamen before the mast, and between twenty and thirty boys, some of them not a dozen years old."

Dispatched with a small crew to sail *Greyhound*'s first prize back to port, Sherburne soon detected that his prizemaster was "completely deranged," tending to bark out orders to imaginary subordinates and then replying "as though they answered him." The man had deserted from the Royal Navy and was consumed with dread of recapture. His anxiety drove him to fold his clothes neatly on deck one night and jump naked over the side, never to be seen again.

Run down and boarded by British privateers whose threats to execute them were defused at the last moment by their captain, "who appeared more rational," Sherburne and the rest of the prize crew were incarcerated in a Canadian village previously "visited" by American raiders who'd plundered its stores and terrorized its citizens, an affront that disposed Sherburne's jailors to starve him to death in retribution. Fortunately a Royal Navy ship, *Duchess of Cumberland*, came to take the prisoners to Newfoundland for exchange.

On the way, a gale whipped up and drove the vessel onto the rocks. "Her decks began to open." A column of seawater "eight or ten inches in diameter" gushed into the hold. The ship pitched so violently its officers started "raving and swearing, crying and praying." The helmsman was thrown overboard and crushed between the hull and the rocks "as quick as you could crush an egg shell in your hand."

Two sailors swam to shore clinging to a wooden spar to which a rope was tied. After the rope was looped around a boulder, Sherburne was the fifteenth man to pull himself along it through the raging surf; ten had made it alive so far. The survivors from among the ship's company then trudged to the nearest port, where the Americans were remanded to a British transport bound for Plymouth, England.

There, a court of "elderly judges, and all wore large white wigs," sentenced Sherburne to Mill Prison "for rebellion, piracy, and high treason on His Majesty's high seas." When released in the spring of 1781 malnutrition had taken its toll. "I walked poorly even with two canes."

Disembarking in Salem, he learned that *Greyhound* had taken a valuable prize and its original crewmembers were entitled to "sixty-three pounds sterling each." But having left his mother power of attorney in his absence, he found that she'd drawn his money and spent it.

Still lame and gaunt from his captivity, he signed on to *Scorpion*, a transport carrying eight small guns and a letter of marque permitting it to take prizes during its trade run to the West Indies. He would have preferred to remain on land and convalesce, "but this business would not do to live by."

Eighteen months later he would return to Portsmouth after trekking overland from Rhode Island. Meeting him at the outskirts of town, his younger brother almost fainted at the sight of "my bones projecting" beneath the skin. Sherburne staggered the rest of the way home on his brother's arm and collapsed into bed, where he remained for twenty days. "I was very unwell," he wrote.

Nine

The equipping of armed vessels in the ports of France to act under commissions from the Congress against the English, being contrary to treaties and therefore disagreeable to government here, cannot possibly be complied with.

—*Benjamin Franklin to a French merchant, August 1777*

England is extremely exasperated at the favor our armed vessels have met with here. To us, the French court wishes success to our cause, winks at the supplies we obtain here, privately affords us very essential aids, and goes on preparing for war.

—*Benjamin Franklin to Congress, September 1777*

Irish-born Gustavus Conyngham was twenty-eight when he'd skippered a powder voyage to Holland for his cousin's Philadelphia trading firm in late 1775. The experience gave a glimpse of commerce raiding as seen from the other side when his vessel was captured and placed under the command of a Royal Navy prize crew. En route to Plymouth, England, Conyngham and his men retook the ship by force and sailed on to Amsterdam. But thwarted by British officials from exchanging his cargo for munitions, he'd sold his vessel and journeyed to Dunkirk in search of a job.

Located on France's northwest coast near the narrowest point of the English Channel, Dunkirk was unique among French ports in that a British commissioner resided there with international authority to make sure it wasn't fortified against amphibious attack. The stipulation was part of agreements signed after France's defeat in the Seven Years' War and aimed to prevent Dunkirk from arming and harboring privateers so near the British coast. Britons had a proprietary view of the place as a result, which gave treaty violations occurring there an especially irksome sting.

William Hodge, another young go-getter attached to the American mission, went to Dunkirk in early 1777 on assignment from Deane and Franklin to procure two packet boats to improve communications with Congress. Hodge recently had arrived in France via Martinique bearing blank congressional privateer commissions. Having observed Bingham's daring deployment of privateers, he was eager to convert one of the new vessels to a warship.

John Ross, the Scotsman in Robert Morris's employ, recommended Conyngham as a captain, and in March Franklin commissioned him as a Continental commander. The appointment proved problematic. Though it placed Conyngham in government service, his ship and crew were 50 percent financed, due to the mission's chronic lack of funds, with private money. The pitfalls of this hybrid arrangement loomed large when disputes later arose over his expeditions' prize payouts. "I always acted under the orders of the commissioners and none other," the captain later testified in a bid to claim his share. "I understood (merely by hearsay) that money was advanced by private persons but did not know the terms of such advance."

After buying the mail boat *Peacock*, Hodge snuck aboard four cannon and ten swivel guns at night outside Dunkirk harbor, then renamed it *Surprise*. He was one of its investors—as possibly was Deane, though the only evidence is testimony given by Carmichael to Congress eighteen months later. Carmichael had brought Conyngham his sailing orders from Deane. His later suggestion that his boss held a stake in *Surprise* was officially discounted due to its basis in hearsay. Deane's critics, however, never doubted that he'd taken "an active part in this piratical enterprise."

Conyngham and his twenty-five-man crew sailed on May 2. One day later he snagged his target, *Prince of Orange*, the "royal packet" plying between Holland and the British port of Harwich. Its hoped-for cache of £10,000 in government gold wasn't on board; still the capture brought headlines if not treasure. London's *Public Advertiser*

Benjamin Franklin was seemingly available to every portraitist that asked him to take time out for a sitting—he's depicted here in Paris during the war. Franklin's casual manner belied his crafty manipulation of privateers to stir up mistrust between France and Britain, and he was tireless in working behind the scenes to aide American privateersmen in British prisons facing the hangman's noose as "pyrates."

railed, "The capture of the *Orange* is a complete refutation of what we have been so often told of the reduced state of the Americans. They have hitherto kept us in sufficient play on their own coasts, and now, in their turn, they even venture to assail ours."

Rumors flew in Britain of "no less than thirty" privateers fitting out in France with international crews said to include "a number of our best seamen, allured by the prospect of getting a great deal of prize money." Insurance rates on shipments across the Channel jumped another 10 percent as unverified sightings of privateers "infesting" waters from Ireland to Spain poured in.

Rancor mounted in Britain's maritime community as merchants

criticized local privateers for avoiding battle with their American counterparts and preferring instead to "cruise the latitudes of the enemy, where they joyfully succeed in taking prizes." And British newspapers mocked "the secretary and clerks of the Admiralty" for their rosy war reports and began highlighting demeaning incidents such as transports surrendering to privateers armed with wooden guns "for deception" and a Royal Navy frigate accidentally discharging a celebratory holiday volley into an adjacent troop ship.

When Conyngham returned to Dunkirk with *Prince of Orange* and one other prize in tow, a storm of diplomatic fury greeted him. Dunkirk's delicate political status made the move "imprudent" in Franklin's view and "stupid" in Vergennes's. On Louis XVI's decree, *Surprise* was confiscated, its prizes restored to Britain, and Conyngham thrown in jail. This pleased Stormont ("a temporary triumph," Deane shrugged) and drew praise from George III, who called it "strong proof that the Court of Versailles means to keep appearances."

Many Britons were less sanguine, deeming Conyngham's "mock confinement" a phony gesture. Vergennes didn't care. "It matters little to His Majesty whether His determination has or has not excited the gratitude of the English."

Confident of his nation's dominant position in its negotiations with Congress, Vergennes saw no rush to enter the war. "Whatever may be the strength of the English army, it appears that the Americans are in a position to face them." Time seemed on France's side. A year earlier, he'd downplayed the need to help America win at any cost. "If they fail, we will have entertained with them, at least momentarily, a trade exchange which is obviously to our advantage." He still held that view, noting that Britain's woes presented a rare opportunity for France's maritime interests. "It is to be hoped that our sailors will have the good sense to profit from the circumstance."

This languid pragmatism worried the Paris commissioners. Knowing the precariousness of America's finances and fighting ability, the commissioners resolved to push British pride beyond its limit by perpetrating more treaty violations under French auspices. After all, it made no difference whether France or Britain initiated hostilities against the other as long as one of them pulled the trigger soon.

Franklin continued to play a double game with his hosts. He privately cheered reports of British privateers snatching French transports; it was another pinprick that might "occasion the two powers to stumble on a war whether either really intends it or not." But his official response was to express deep regret for any inadvertent part played by American mariners in provoking such illegal reprisals. Likewise, after directing Deane to entreat French authorities to release Conyngham on grounds that his return with prizes to Dunkirk had been merely an error in judgment, Franklin excitedly wrote Congress that it was "an act so notorious and so contrary to treaties, that if suffered must cause an immediate war."

When it didn't, Deane and Hodge began outfitting another, larger warship in Dunkirk in anticipation of Conyngham's release in June. The financing was murky. Half the proceeds from the vessel's eventual voyages went to the government, even though, for appearances' sake, Hodge was listed as the vessel's sole owner. His actual share was one half. Deane may personally have taken a percentage of that. John Ross, for one, referred to him as "part owner." Arthur Lee carried the presumption further, asserting beyond question that Deane bought his stake with public funds.

The vessel, *Greyhound*, was registered as a transport, albeit a singular one, "painted blue and yellow, built for the smuggling trade, and reported to be a fast sailer." Fourteen cannon and twenty-two swivels were hidden in its hold. Before approving its departure, local authorities certified that no Frenchmen were among its crew. When on the eve of its launch British officials lodged a last-minute protest of Hodge's earlier connection to *Surprise*, Hodge countered by immediately selling *Greyhound* to one Richard Allen, a little-known English sea captain of apparently spotless reputation.

The vessel sailed. Once offshore, its guns were mounted, the forty-man crew was augmented with sixty-six French "desperadoes," and *Revenge* became its new name. Under carefully worded orders conveyed by Carmichael from Franklin and Deane, the vessel was to return straight to America, "notwithstanding which if necessity obliges you to obtain provisions either in making prizes for your own preservation or in making reprisal for damages sustained."

Lest the commissioners' meaning still be unclear, Carmichael offered "verbal explanations that could not be committed to paper." As intended, this got the crew clamoring for an all-out hunt for British plunder. Having "no interest in diplomacy," their new commander readily agreed. It wasn't Richard Allen—there was no such person. *Revenge*'s captain was Conyngham.

"By his bold expeditions," Deane wrote Robert Morris six weeks later, "he is become the terror of all the eastern coast of England and Scotland. But though this distresses our enemies," he cautioned, "it embarrasses us."

The embarrassment was diplomatic. Stormont, whose fulminations had inspired French officials to turn his name into a verb, *stormonter*, was again demanding penalties against the commissioners. "There are some things too glaring to be winked at."

Vergennes at first tried to pin Conyngham's voyage on "the interposition of an English subject named Richard Allen," but the secret of that alias was out. Compelled to throw the ambassador a bone, he had William Hodge locked up in the Bastille for "changing the ownership" of his vessel in order to get it to sea.

Franklin sought his release. Vergennes refused. "I know not whether such tricks are allowed in America, but in France and Europe it is a very serious fault to tell the king a falsehood."

Commissioner Arthur Lee had been left out of the doings at Dunkirk. Now that the "illegal transaction" had soured relations with the French government, he was quick to lay blame. Speaking for himself and Franklin (who in truth had supported Conyngham's cruise), he assured Robert Morris, "It was done by Mr. Deane without our knowledge." For good measure he wrote his brother Richard as well. "Mr. Deane seems desirous of persuading us and others to be in ill-humor with the Court for taking violent measures to which they have been compelled by his unwarrantable conduct."

Lee was distancing himself from Vergennes's public displeasure—

but in private the foreign minister was less adamant. He cautioned Louis XVI that "declaring them and their countrymen to be pirates and sea robbers" risked "implanting in the breasts of the Americans a hatred and a desire for revenge which the lapse of centuries will perhaps not eradicate." His point was that Americans wouldn't soon forgive, if it came to pass, France's failure to stand by them in their bid for independence. And the beneficiary of their resentment would be Britain.

This acknowledgment heralded a shift in the ongoing negotiations. While still awaiting the right moment to exploit it fully, Franklin had understood from the beginning that France needed an American alliance. Now Vergennes understood it, too.

On September 25, the foreign minister issued revised instructions which Stormont tersely conveyed to London:

"Hodge is set at liberty."

Revenge took twenty prizes in fourteen months of operation in European waters. Its captain became "the Dunkirk pirate" in the British press, a "nightmare figure" who burned or sank an additional two dozen vessels and ransomed several others.

Ransoming, legal at the time, enabled a captor to set free a prize in exchange for a negotiated fee to be paid on the prize's safe return to its owner. (Conyngham asked that his fee be sent to the Paris commissioners.) Often the prize's captain, who signed the pledge in his employer's name, was held prisoner till payment arrived.

Britain was ransoming's leading proponent. The law helped the Royal Navy to collect on the value of a captured ship without having to spare a prize crew to sail it home for settlement. But in 1782 Parliament would declare it "unlawful for any British subject to agree to ransom any British vessel" on penalty of £500. The privateers' success forced the change in policy. "Now it was Britain's enemies whose cruising range was extended by ransom practice."

After circling the British Isles that first summer, Conyngham deposited prisoners, sold prizes, and refitted at Spanish ports. Two

Spies working for Britain's ambassador in Paris, Lord Stormont, informed him of every detail of France's clandestine aid to America. His threats of violent reprisal had little effect on French officials increasingly confident of the damage the Revolution and, in particular, the privateers were doing to the British economy—and they played into Franklin's plan to incite war between Britain and France "sooner than is desired by either party."

merchant houses, Lagoanere & Company of Coruña and Gardoqui & Sons of Bilbao, handled his affairs in a cooperative arrangement in which costs and revenues were shared "with perfect consideration," Lagoanere told a business partner in November 1777. But confusion set in when Arthur Lee got involved. After learning that Ross and Hodge were in Spain monitoring Conyngham's activities at Deane's behest, he fired off imperious letters to Conyngham and the Spanish merchants hinting at misdeeds and cover-ups.

"Mr. Hodge and Mr. Ross have no right to direct or control you," he wrote the captain, "neither had Mr. Deane any right to dispose of the prizes you made, as Monsieur Lagoanere informs us he has done." Lee demanded to review beforehand any dispersal of prize money from now on. "Individuals who may be concerned will have their share when they prove their right."

Conyngham, though puzzled by Lee's orders "contradicting those of Mr. Deane," was accommodating. He asked only that his men be paid (they wouldn't sail otherwise) and that his prize earnings, once available, be sent to his wife and children in Philadelphia in the event of his death or capture.

Ross and Hodge were intimidated, however. Through insinuations "artful and wicked," Hodge wrote his colleague, "Arthur Lee, Esquire, has been of considerable detriment to me, and has puzzled me to know how to act in regard to the accounts."

Lee's true target was Deane. In hopes of catching him in a lie, he regularly checked Deane's assertions with Ross and Hodge to confirm "whether you understand it so." The queries led Ross to warn Deane about appearing too independent. "Circumstances and my own observations lead me to see it necessary for you to act as much as possible with consent and approbation of your colleagues, lest your distinct services for the public in your present station (however well intended) may be misrepresented or misconstrued."

Undeterred, Deane continued to direct Conyngham's activities from Paris in a loose style that gratified the Spanish merchants if not Lee. They welcomed the business of other privateers and solicited colleagues to front Conyngham "all the money he will ask of you, upon drafts on us."

So well did the merchants make out, when John Adams visited Spain two years later, Lagoanere handed him $3,000 in cash. A Bayonne merchant gave Adams "a letter of credit for as much more as I should have occasion for," while another in Bordeaux offered a bill of exchange "for the like sum." Adams's travel expenses were "paid upon sight" and even his government salary, he advised Congress, could be drawn from Lagoanere's funds if necessary. The source of this largesse seemed to surprise him, "being part of the proceeds of some prizes heretofore made by Captain Conyngham."

Interestingly, Deane's later testimony to Congress described Conyngham's expeditions out of Spain in 1777 as a tactical winner but a financial drain. The first prize settled there "turned to little account," he said, "as did also some others he afterwards captured."

This was the truth as far as he knew. Though his critics contended that he discounted the vessel's profits in order to pocket them, throughout its period of operation he consistently lamented *Revenge*'s red ink to friends and colleagues. The settlement snafus that plagued New England privateering occurred in Europe as well, delaying the accumulation of revenue; what were surpluses by the time Adams arrived were deficits to Deane. Thus by the fall of 1777 he was looking to unload *Revenge* "on account of the unsuccessful, expensive cruises of that vessel."

Admitting that he didn't expect a price "equal to the first cost" of its original purchase in Dunkirk, Deane proposed that Ross buy the government's half-interest in the vessel and become co-owner with Hodge. He didn't doubt that Conyngham and *Revenge* would continue to attack British trade; he predicted that they'd operate more effectively "under private instructions." Being on scene in Spain rather than in Paris, Ross realized *Revenge*'s earning potential and agreed to buy it.

He nervously notified Arthur Lee of the pending deal, saying it was "agreeable to all parties." Lee scotched it at once "owing to some difficulties" he didn't articulate. They were clear enough to Deane and his subordinates. "The jealous disposition of Mr. Lee, which led him to apprehend designs injurious to him in everyone he dealt with, gave a general disgust and often proved prejudicial to our affairs."

There were other setbacks. In December Conyngham seized a Spanish transport bearing British cargo. His excuse that the Royal Navy often ignored neutral flags didn't assuage Spanish annoyance, and the crew Conyngham had placed aboard the prize was briefly imprisoned. Deane upbraided his captain ("in future let French, Spanish and other neutral vessels pass without detaining them") and assured Lagoanere and Gardoqui that their support would bring no further embarrassment. That Conyngham still cursed the "damned policy" didn't bode well, however.

The influx of privateers from America made such violations more common. A pair of Charleston vessels captured a Rotterdam sloop. A Massachusetts privateer, *Civil Usage*, managed to insult "two Bourbon courts" in one swoop by taking a French ship carrying Spanish goods, while a warship from New Hampshire did American diplomacy no favor by seizing a load of British beef bound for the French navy.

But the most egregious violation, occurring in May 1778, again involved Conyngham. Upon overhauling a Swedish brig, *Honoria Sophia*, he found a valuable cargo of wine, fruit, and oil. His crew, understatedly described as "not always amenable to discipline or willing to abide by the laws of civilized warfare," composed and signed a crude release. "Whereas Captain Conyngham says that he has directions not to insult any neutral flag, yet the cargo appearing so plain to be British property we have engaged him to take her and try her chance to America."

The dispatch westward of *Honoria Sophia* was the great affront in this case; it showed that *Revenge*'s men knew the capture was illegal and that their only chance for a payoff was in a prize court far from Europe. Now Sweden joined in the condemnation of "an American corsair named Conyngham," whose claim that he'd been pressured into the deed by his crew found few believers in light of his fierce reputation.

Franklin undertook the usual damage control ("it is a crime in our eyes to have displeased a power for which Congress is penetrated with respect"), while Arthur Lee spread word that the incident's fallout was dire but not his fault. In fact it subsided in a few months. Europe, in Deane's phrase, was "embarrassed with connections and alliances" that often generated more diplomatic smoke than fire.

Still, the uproar over *Honoria Sophia* convinced Conyngham it was time quit Europe. His new destination was the same place the Swedish ship had ended up for settlement—Saint-Pierre, Martinique, the most avid privateering port outside New England.

His arrival in October 1778 was welcomed by Bingham. Knowing from experience that successful privateering required a satisfied crew, the agent advanced *Revenge*'s men a "bounty" against their future prize earnings before dispatching them after "the grand object" of enemy trade. Near St. Eustatius in November, Conyngham took three small transports and a British privateer in a single day. More captures followed ("this intrepid commander," raved the *Boston Gazette*), until at last he headed home to Philadelphia in February 1779.

He arrived not to acclaim but to lawsuits. Three members of a prize crew he'd sent from Europe had filed a complaint that he'd concealed prize money through a private arrangement with Hodge, the man they said was *Revenge*'s true owner. The captain, who remembered his accusers well ("a very troublesome and mutinous disposition"), was called before Congress's Marine Committee, headed by Richard Henry Lee, to explain:

"I admit that the command I was engaged in was intricate in its nature, but I must observe that I did all in my power to prevent any obscurity in the business so far as related to myself and the commissioners under whose authority I acted. I know of no evidence existing to prove or justify the idea of the vessel being private property, nor ever did I consider myself under the direction of any private person or persons."

To support his defense, Conyngham was asked to provide "financial accounts and letters of instruction" pertaining to his voyages. It was impossible. For almost two years he'd been at sea, in prison, or darting in and out of foreign ports. Unable to make a ruling either way, Congress dismissed the matter and put *Revenge* up for auction.

Conyngham used the occasion of the inquiry to press a claim for back pay. "I also think myself entitled to two-twentieths of all prizes sent into port. This was sacredly promised to me by the American commissioners in Paris." He apologized that his estimate of monies owed wasn't exact, "but as nearly so as I was able from the information I was then possessed of."

He cited April 1778 as when the commissioners had begun giving him newly detailed instructions "for the application of proceeds of the prize money," instructions whose proper fulfillment he was certain the commissioners would verify. By that date, however, Deane had been gone from France for almost a month; and Franklin, as ever, was focused on diplomacy and prisoner relief. Conyngham's petition depended on the corroboration of one commissioner only.

Eighteen years later, the claim would remain in limbo. "Every difficulty was thrown in my way," Conyngham wrote in 1797, "by Arthur Lee, Esquire."

The year 1777 saw Deane become intensely disillusioned. His slide had begun in February when, with high hopes, he'd joined an independent privateer project under a captain named Thomas Bell. By August it had fallen apart; French go-betweens hired to procure the warship, *Tartar*, apparently fleeced the investors. The project's mastermind, the pickled Nantes agent, Tom Morris, pressured Deane to fudge his books so that *Tartar*'s funding, £1,000 of which had been put up by Tom's brother Robert, would appear "as having been paid on public account." Deane refused.

Tom went with an alternate plan, appropriating a recently arrived government cargo to fulfill, he said, an outstanding debt to Willing & Morris. When *Tartar*'s bills came in (though it never sailed, people still demanded to be paid), Deane was left holding the bag. He lost doubly as a result—his stake in the privateer and the value to the commissioners of the purloined cargo.

Beaumarchais, who also owned a piece of the ill-fated deal, bailed Deane out. William Carmichael, Deane's secretary, assumed that the Frenchman's source for the money was Hortalez & Company, a public firm disguised as a private one. He didn't keep that assumption to himself.

Then there was Deane's entanglement with James Aitken, alias "John the Painter," a twenty-five-year-old Scot who'd first sought him out at Deane's Paris hotel in November 1776, seeking help for his one-man plan to burn down the Royal Navy shipyard at Portsmouth.

Compelled by personal grievances against the British government rather than zeal for American liberty, Aitken ("his eyes sparkling and wild") had struck Deane as clearly nuts. Yet always open to schemes against Britain, he'd given the young man his blessings, an endorsed passport, and the equivalent of "about three pound" in French currency. He also gave him the name of Edward Bancroft as a contact in London.

Aitken was hanged as a saboteur in Portsmouth in March 1777, his remains displayed in a gibbet beside the harbor for almost half a century. A fire he'd set in the facility's rope house caused only £20,000 in damage, but that incident combined with his attempts to ignite incendiaries in neighboring Bristol had sent the London stock market plummeting on fears of mass arson. It also goaded Parliament to pass Lord North's controversial Pirate Act suspending the legal rights of captured American seamen.

Before his execution, Aitken named Deane ("the honestest man I know") as a supporter. He also implicated Bancroft, a potentially ruinous link for a gentleman with extensive business and family ties in London, not to mention one secretly working for the king's intelligence service. To clear his friend, Deane sent a seemingly oblivious letter asserting Deane's right as an American "to destroy, at one blow, the fleet and armaments preparing to spread devastation and bloodshed in my country" and clearing Bancroft of any advance knowledge of the attempt.

British spies intercepted the letter, as Deane had expected they would. They suspected it was a ploy, but weren't certain enough of the evidence to prosecute their valuable double agent for treason. And once the decision was made to keep Bancroft on the payroll, they ran a ploy of their own, briefly jailing him in order to convince the Americans that he truly was one of them. Deane bought it completely. "I feel more for Doctor Bancroft than I can express. He deserves much from us."

Of Aitken's hapless terror attempt, French officials were amused by "the gravity given to the matter by the British court." It was no joke to Bancroft, however. He later proved that he'd go to any lengths to erase any trace of his involvement.

In September Deane opened a June edition of the *Connecticut*

Gazette to discover a notice of his wife's death "after a long indisposition." The shocking news, he wrote, came amid "public distresses and calamities" that didn't displace the sorrow but at least distracted his mind "into a soft insensibility of its sufferings."

He'd been trying for a year to get Elizabeth and their twelve-year-old son, Jesse, to Europe. He now asked his brother Barnabas to obtain Jesse passage aboard a British man-of-war, the safest mode of transatlantic travel. "Though I am as obnoxious to England as any person living, yet they would not detain a lad who had taken no part." When Jesse finally sailed three years later, Deane embraced him as "my only hope, and almost the sole object I wish to live for."

Deane's discouragements of 1777 didn't diminish one undoubted triumph—the safe arrival that spring of the eight military transports he and Beaumarchais had launched at the start of the year. In presenting the good news to the foreign ministry, his diplomatic formality ("very seasonably arrived," he reported of the vessels) couldn't conceal his gratification over his countrymen's reaction: "unanimous and in high spirits."

Lord Stormont had a different reaction. "The two ships, *Amphitrite* and *Mercury*, had on board not less than thirty thousand stand of arms, four hundred tons of gunpowder, five thousand tents, and sixty-four pieces of field artillery. The arrival of these great succors has raised the spirits of the rebels and of their numerous well-wishers here."

Amphitrite and *Mercury* had been the first vessels sent out, followed by *Seine* and the others. "Shipped by Mr. Jonathan Williams per order of Mr. Deane," their arrival was heralded by John Langdon as "this important event." In Boston, John Bradford reviewed the list of supplies for his patron John Hancock and called it "a smile of heaven on us, for we really were distressed for want of them."

George Washington personally directed the equipment distribution. The cannon were of particular importance. Most went to a large depot in Springfield, Massachusetts, that supplied the northern Continental Army under the command of Horatio Gates.

To pay for the materials, Congress repacked the ships with lumber and tobacco and returned them to France. The commodities, valued at more than 4 million livres, were eagerly received by Beaumarchais as remuneration to Hortalez & Company and to provide, at last, commissions for him and Deane.

Arthur Lee intervened. He assured Congress that the supplies funneled through Hortalez had been given without obligation by France and Spain. Since "no return was expected," the return cargoes were public property and Beaumarchais's attempt to claim them was thievery. Lest Congress forget who else was involved, Lee noted that although Hortalez had originally been his idea, "Upon Mr. Deane's arrival the business went into his hands and the things were at length embarked."

Lee was wrong about the Hortalez operation. Louis XVI had never said the supplies were gifts. Secretly providing weapons and gunpowder to a fellow monarch's rebellious subjects had been risky, but at least if discovered it could be passed off as a commercial venture; making charitable donations in support of treason had been out of the question.

Vergennes was clear on the point. "The king furnished nothing to them, and merely permitted Monsieur de Beaumarchais to take the supplies from the royal arsenal on the condition that he replace them." Congress embraced Lee's version anyway. Its money woes were worse than ever. Once heard, the happy prospect of free stuff from France was too good to let go.

Congress's perception of Beaumarchais as a royal mouthpiece had been unwittingly fostered by Deane in his early letters to the Secret Committee. After his first meeting with his new partner in Paris in 1776, he'd giddily bragged that "everything he says, writes, or does is in reality the action of the ministry." So it's understandable that his superiors got the idea that the Frenchman's ardent support for America mirrored the sentiments, and more pertinently the generosity, of his king.

Lee strove to reinforce that impression. "This gentleman is not a merchant but is known as a political agent," he wrote of Beaumarchais." A corrupt political agent, he added, who was now trying to steal American property that "being once in his hands would never be recovered."

Unaware of Lee's letter campaign, Deane wrote Congress impatiently. "You are sensible of the necessity of sending remittances by every opportunity. I pray they may come care of Hortalez & Company as they have advanced for the arms and many other articles over and above their other large advances." Arriving just days after one of Lee's preemptive strikes about the company's thieving designs, this looked suspicious beyond belief. The dossier of Deane's purported scams grew thicker as a result.

If the timing of Deane's letter about the returning transports was poor, their arrival in America couldn't have come at a better moment. From the Springfield depot, the French-made cannon were requisitioned by General Gates. When his army battled Burgoyne at Saratoga the following October, it enjoyed the rare circumstance of fielding artillery equal to the enemy's. This enabled Gates's almost two-to-one advantage in numbers, and the aggressive brilliance of his cavalry commander, Benedict Arnold, to carry the day. Six thousand redcoats were captured along with forty-two cannon—by far the greatest American victory to date. Burgoyne's bid to split the colonies was thwarted. More importantly, British prestige was shattered.

Word of the Saratoga victory reached the commissioners on December 4, 1777. They marveled that it "occasioned as much general joy in France as if it had been a victory of their own troops over their own enemies." Beaumarchais was so excited, he crashed his coach between Passy and Paris trying to be the first to notify the foreign ministry. He may also, it was said, have been in a hurry to place a bet that the London stock market would crash on the news.

On the same day, December 4, Richard Henry Lee personally dispatched to Europe a congressional order: "Resolved, that Silas Deane, Esquire, be recalled from the Court of France."

After Saratoga, the French–American negotiation took a new dynamic. The British position clearly had weakened, improving the likelihood that peace offers might follow. That was Vergennes's worst fear. His time to dither in talks with Franklin was running out, he knew.

Still waiting for Spain to get on board, the foreign minister bought time with a loan to the commissioners of 3 million livres. Meanwhile British officials in London decided to float the possibility, through secret contacts with the commissioners, of reconciling with America. The concessions in mind were short of total independence but offered much of the political and economic autonomy the colonists had sought at the start of the war.

The job of extending those overtures fell to Paul Wentworth, a colleague of Bancroft's with an American background, an established life in Britain (he hoped to become a British peer), and proven ability as a master spy. Unfortunately for the British initiative, Wentworth arrived in Paris one day after verbal assurances had finally been given to Franklin and Deane (Vergennes detested Lee and refused to deal with him) that France, with or without Spain as a partner, would shortly proclaim a military and commercial alliance with America.

In a last attempt to derail the deal, Wentworth, in separate meetings with the two commissioners (again, no Lee) promised them "emoluments" ranging from cash to British knighthood to induce them to back out. He was rebuffed–but Franklin, keeping silent, purposely let the French ministry wonder about the outcome.

Vergennes could wait no longer. "The power which first recognizes the independence of the Americans will be the one to gather all the fruits of this war." On February 6, 1778, he and the king's other ministers signed the treaty of alliance in the name of Louis XVI and the three commissioners signed for America.

It was Franklin's triumph above all, though Lee scrambled to take credit. "With the greatest difficulty," he told his friends, Lee alone had persuaded the other commissioners "to insist on the recognition of our sovereignty and the acknowledgment of our independence. These were proposed by me, evaded by my colleagues." If Deane and Franklin dared dispute this, "They will force me to bring proofs before Congress and the public, when I am sure they will shed some of their borrowed plumes."

Deane of course was pleased by the new treaty, but his letters in the days before and after its signing were full of disenchantment. To Robert Morris, "I have no ambition of being at courts. I have seen enough of them to ease me of any such passion." To his brother Simeon, "I am most heartily tired and only wish to retire without loss or disgrace." To Jonathan Williams, "It is too much for men to spend the prime of their lives in vexation and anxiety for nothing but to be found fault with and blamed."

His melancholy presaged the March 9 arrival in France of Congress's official notice of his recall. Its wording was vague. Couched in terms "complimentary to your abilities of serving these United States," the stated reason was that "it is of the greatest importance that Congress should, at this critical juncture, be well informed of the state of affairs in Europe." But knowing there'd been a whisper campaign against him, Deane suspected trouble in store.

In order to better prepare his defense, he decided to stay put until Congress communicated the specific complaints against him. Beaumarchais changed his mind, persuading him to gather what documents he had and go make his case at once. Guessing that the charges concerned the many French officers taken into Continental service and the disputed Hortalez shipments, and knowing who was the main accuser, Beaumarchais assured his friend that "I have in my possession letters from this time-serving Lee" that verified the Virginian's support of the recruitments and his approval of the Hortalez operation "in the language of active mutual trade, and not otherwise."

Thinking a dramatic entrance would bolster Deane's reception, Beaumarchais urged French officials to deck him with tributes suitable to a returning hero. Deane was given a portrait of the king and letters of praise from Vergennes. His pessimism eased. "I am under no apprehensions but that this will turn out greatly to my advantage, and that I shall be able to retire with honor."

He sailed in company with France's new emissary to America, Conrad Gerard, aboard the flagship of a seventeen-vessel battle fleet under Admiral Charles d'Estaing. Congress welcomed Gerard's arrival on July 14. On July 15 it opened Deane's case.

The testimonials from Vergennes were read aloud—one addressed

Relentless in attacking his fellow commissioners in Paris, the envious and meddlesome Arthur Lee smeared Silas Deane with charges of corruption in the arms trade and in privateering. But Lee couldn't touch Benjamin Franklin, whose "frauds and wickedness," he alleged with typical hysteria, were kept from the public by "hush money" paid out to suppress the evidence.

to Congress praising Deane's "zeal, activity, and intelligence," the other a personal expression of the "true interest which I shall forever take in your happiness." A letter from William Lee was read next.

Like his brother Arthur, William had been on record for years with charges that Deane, Franklin, Hodge, Ross, and Carmichael "were productive of much mischief to the general interest of America." He was especially critical of their links to Conyngham's expeditions, whose combination of private and public funding afforded, he believed, a convenient ambiguity. "It is hinted now that the expense of this outfit is to be placed to the public account, for the scheme has not proved a profitable one. This intelligence has made me apprehensive."

Deane's view of William Lee ("a greater scoundrel than I imagined") was widely shared in Europe. The observation that "his character begins everywhere to stink" was literal in that he inspired dislike in courts across the continent when he was sent out on minor assignments. To have his letter received by Congress as a creditable rebuttal to France's venerable foreign minister was not a good sign for Deane.

The inquiry into his conduct consumed Congress through the summer and fall of 1778, splitting it into hostile camps with the "Adams-Lee junto" on one side and, on the other, friends of Franklin and Robert Morris, who by that time had reconciled with Deane after their falling out over Tom. Observing the proceedings, Lafayette was dismayed at their rancor. "There are open dissensions in Congress, parties who hate one another as much as the common enemy."

Deane had brought along few records of his finances. Once he understood that he'd been recalled in effect to stand trial, he had to depend primarily on his reputation and his countrymen's appreciation for his public service, both hardly a lock, to exonerate him. His fortunes rose and fell with each submitted letter that defended or attacked him. The result was that stabs such as Arthur Lee's "Mr. Deane is universally understood to have made £60,000 sterling while he was commissioner" simply canceled out Franklin's contrary commendation of him as "a man of integrity."

The hearings were in stalemate in September 1778 when Richard Henry Lee announced a new allegation. It was based on remarks overheard "some time in the last spring or winter" from Deane's former secretary William Carmichael. Richard's brother Arthur almost certainly was the eavesdropper, and the charge concerned privateering.

Almost a year earlier, when the British spy service was wondering who among the French-based Americans could potentially be bribed into becoming agents for the crown, Carmichael and Deane had topped the list. Neither was turned, but each man's indicators were the same: fond of bragging, good times, and money.

Meanwhile on the French side, the astonishing speed with which secrets of the American negotiation were getting to Stormont had led Vergennes to conclude that Carmichael was the culprit. (The actual mole, Edward Bancroft, completely escaped suspicion.) In addition to his social proclivities, Carmichael's callow air of presumption made him ripe for the flattery and promises with which spies were wooed by rival governments.

Not long after becoming Deane's secretary, for instance, he'd loftily instructed William Bingham on how to spark a war through privateering; he directed the Martinique agent, probably the world's foremost expert on the subject, to forward those instructions to Congress. More annoyingly to Vergennes, Carmichael had been known to express "a most inveterate dislike of the French" and had loudly predicted "that if America should be successful, she will never grant exclusive rights of trade to France." None of this was helpful, and as a result Vergennes and the commissioners decided "suddenly, and with but a few hours' notice," to send the young man home.

He and Deane met amiably in Philadelphia during the latter's congressional hearing. Thus Deane must have been dismayed when Carmichael suddenly appeared to testify against him. At issue were the financing of Conyngham's first expedition aboard *Surprise* and Beaumarchais's bailout of Deane after the *Tartar* privateer project with Captain Bell fell apart. But what Richard Henry Lee had characterized as Carmichael's utter conviction ("he knew that Mr. Deane had misapplied the public money") proved under questioning to be full of doubt: "I apprehended at the time . . . I think . . . I have heard . . . I do not certainly know."

Of the Beaumarchais connection, Carmichael had seen the Frenchman draw funds "to a large amount" from Hortalez & Company to pay for the government-sponsored shipments of supplies to America. "I thought it was likewise on the public credit he advanced this sum" to pay off Deane's losses on *Tartar*. He may have been correct—the Hortalez accounts would never be fully unraveled—but his shaky testimony was useless as evidence. Congress dismissed him after a week.

Arthur Lee kept the heat on. Six months after Conyngham's illegal capture of the Swedish-owned *Honoria Sophia*, he was still going on about the "great offense" it had caused. His alarm wasn't meant to explicate the international scene. It was meant to harm Deane, whose departure to America two months before the incident didn't diminish his culpability in Lee's mind. "From the beginning to the end of this business with Conyngham," he wrote the Foreign Affairs Committee after the Carmichael fizzle, "it has been so bad that Congress only can correct it by punishing those who are concerned." Since Deane was known to have directed Conyngham, there was no mistaking Lee's target.

As with Hortalez, it was impossible to prove whether the financial maneuvers behind Conyngham's voyages had been driven by greed or by the pressure of wartime necessity. That didn't stop Congress and most of Philadelphia from fiercely debating the issue for more than a year. It became a referendum on the right of officials to combine public service and private speculation.

One result was that America's fundamental argument about the role of capitalism in a democracy was sharply delineated. This in turn planted the seeds for early political parties favoring "the localist and power-weakening emphasis in the Revolution" on one side and stability, nationalism, and centralized authority on the other. The Deane inquiry was a nasty start to that grand discussion. Though in the near term it settled nothing, "The rancor it left," writes E. James Ferguson, "was for years the underlying basis of Congressional division on questions which might better have been considered on their own merits."

Deane returned to Europe as a private citizen in 1780. There had never been a possibility of retaining his diplomatic post; John Adams, chief among the L's and A's, had been named his replacement four days after Congress moved to recall him. As it was, Deane's release from the inquiry had been a close call. A congressional motion that he be indefinitely detained pending further investigation failed to pass only because the vote was split evenly down the middle.

He left cynical of his country but optimistic about his personal prospects. He was owed hefty commissions for the Hortalez shipments and looked forward to organizing his accounts to support his claim. And he was buoyed to know that after the motion to keep him in Philadelphia had failed, a vote "directing Mr. A. Lee to repair forthwith to America" had passed by a whisker.

Lee's recall was a rebuke—his diplomatic career was finished. But two years later he would stage a comeback of sorts, getting elected to Congress for a three-year term. His membership on the Foreign Affairs Committee and Treasury Board was vigorous but frustrating. He would write Samuel Adams in 1782, "I can only lament what I cannot prevent, and make vain efforts to redeem an infatuated majority from the bondage of folly and private interest."

He was being modest, however. Not all those efforts were vain.

PORTSMOUTH, ENGLAND

After Gustavus Conyngham's appearance before the Marine Committee in February 1779, Chairman Richard Henry Lee washed his hands of the "complicated affairs of the cutter *Revenge*" and sold the vessel at public auction.

The buyers immediately leased it to the state of Pennsylvania for a two-week cruise with Conyngham at the helm. While chasing a pair of British privateers, he carelessly sailed "into the very teeth of *Galatea*," an enemy frigate. "I made every effort to escape," he wrote, "but her teeth were too many."

He was brought to New York, where, his identity established, he was charged with piracy by the station commander, Sir George Collier, who'd captured John Manley and *Hancock* almost two years earlier. To prove to "that monster" he was a legitimate combatant, Conyngham produced his Continental commission. The document had been drawn up in May 1777 to replace the original lost during his stint in the Dunkirk jail. By an oversight, it didn't cover the period when he'd captured *Prince of Orange*, the Harwich packet. The technicality gave Collier his pirate.

Conyngham was clapped in irons, "weight 55 pounds." Transferring him from jail to the vessel that would take him to Britain, the guards stood him "in the hangman's cart" used for hauling "deserters and others to the gallows and often executed before us close to the prison." Soldiers looking on grinned, "You will go next."

This psychological torture was followed by physical abuse ("in the black hole as usual") once he arrived at Mill Prison. Back in New York, Collier deemed "uncivil" a letter of humanitarian protest sent him from Congress. Due to "this predicament" of his own doing, Collier responded, Conyngham "is therefore sent to England to receive that punishment from his injured country which his crimes shall be found to deserve."

In Paris, where he now served as America's diplomatic plenipotentiary, Franklin took up Conyngham's cause. He praised Congress's decision to place, as a deterrent to the captain's execution, three captive British officers "in close confinement to abide his fate." Through written appeals to friends in Britain ("Your king will not reward you for taking this trouble, but God will") he secured Conyngham's transfer from the black hole into Mill's general prison population. From there, Franklin hoped, the captain might be freed via exchange.

A year earlier, the British government had agreed to begin exchanging captive American seamen for Britons held in France. Nothing had been done since, however. The admiralty wanted men exchanged in blocks of a hundred. Having released those brought in by Lambert Wickes in 1777, Franklin didn't have that many to offer. He tried to finesse the problem by pledging on his "solemn engagement" that if the prisoners at Forton and Mill were freed, "the surplus" would be made up in the release of British prisoners held in America.

The proposal was rejected on grounds that it would "be prejudicial to His Majesty's service to exchange prisoners upon account of debtor and creditor." Franklin scoffed at this reasoning. The admiralty "cannot give up the pleasant idea of having at the end of the war one thousand Americans to hang for high treason," he wrote.

John Paul Jones hadn't yet begun his fabled voyage aboard *Bonhomme Richard*; that expedition's many prizes together with the victory over HMS *Serapis* in September 1779 would net five hundred prisoners for exchange. To fatten the pot in the meantime, Franklin was obliged, despite old age, gout, and his aversion to financial wrangling and disagreeable personalities, to take up Deane's specialty of outfitting privateers.

He would happily have let French privateers gather the needed enemy prisoners—Louis XVI had authorized his subjects openly to "make reprisals and act hostilely against England" in the summer of 1778—but under the rules of exchange, that would only have benefited Frenchmen held in Britain. Reluctantly, Franklin set about commissioning three American warships to be based in Europe.

Black Prince, *Black Princess*, and *Fearnot* made multiple cruises around the British Isles between 1779 and 1780. They captured, burned, or ransomed almost two hundred prizes. Yet despite agreeing to make captives a priority, they brought in only ninety-five eligible for exchange. The reason was simple. Captives took up space, ate food, and required men to guard them or sail them back to port, reducing the privateer's ability to remain at sea in quest of loot.

The captains, Edward Macatter and Luke Ryan (who commanded both *Black Prince* and *Fearnot*), preferred to give Franklin signed "paroles" certifying that captives had been taken and subsequently released. Franklin, in no little exasperation, told them there was no way Britain would exchange live prisoners for bits of paper. "I think it right that you should trust no more to the honor of that nation, which has refused to return us a single man on account of those paroles."

He was further put out by his obligation, dumped on him by French officials who were disinclined to bother with prizes seized by foreigners, to adjudicate the legality, value, and share distribution of his vessels' many captures. Documents relating to American prizes carried into France languished on his crowded desk. Vergennes finally decided to commission Franklin's privateers under French auspices in July 1780. Given their disappointing prisoner-return, it was a move "most welcome" to Franklin.

It turned out badly for his two captains, however. As Irishmen sailing under a French flag, Ryan and Macatter were tried and convicted for "Felony and Piracy on the High Seas" after their capture by the Royal Navy a year later. Scheduled to hang

Gustavus Conyngham, feared in Britain as "the Dunkirk pirate," shifted between privateering and service in the Continental Navy. His full due of prize money and fame eluded him as a result. He captured or destroyed dozens of enemy vessels, yet after the war Congress repeatedly ignored his applications for payment and recognition.

at Portsmouth in May 1782, they were pardoned at the last moment.

Macatter's subsequent fate is unknown. Ryan died in debtor's prison in 1789. While sailing for Franklin he'd captured dozens of prizes worth thousands of pounds. The unpaid bill for which he was incarcerated at the end of his life was in the amount of £100 "for the inoculation of three of his children."

As for Gustavus Conyngham, after two failed escape attempts he "committed treason through his majesty's earth" and dug his way out of Mill Prison in November 1779. Sympathizers in London smuggled him to Amsterdam, from where he wrote Franklin of his desire, once he recovered from the effects of "irons, dungeons, hunger," to get to sea again. "I shall always be ready to serve my country, and happy should I be able to come alongside some of those petty tyrants."

He briefly sailed with John Paul Jones before hopping a

merchant ship bound for America in March 1780. It was captured, and Conyngham wound up in Mill again. After more
than a year of "severe and cruel treatment; dogs, cats, rats,
even the grass eaten by prisoners," he again escaped. In company with his wife, who'd journeyed to Europe to be near
him, he returned to Philadelphia with a letter from Franklin
certifying that he'd received a Continental commission dated
March 1, 1777.

He used the letter as the basis for an appeal for reinstatement
as a navy officer; once obtained, it would help his claim for
back pay and prize money. But in 1784 the Navy Board ruled
that the commission had been "intended for temporary expeditions only and not to give rank in the navy." In the Board's
view, in other words, he was merely a privateer.

Seven years later Conyngham presented Congress with an
account of his Revolutionary activity that included a request
for "compensation" in the amount of £2,381. Not even the support of Alexander Hamilton, Secretary of the Treasury, could
expedite the claim, which languished without a verdict.

Writing "your honorable body" in 1797, he bewailed his
"state of doubt and uncertainty, no investigation or report having yet been made." He continued to submit an "earnest and
solemn prayer" for a settlement every year until his death in
1819.

In 1828 a letter from one of Conyngham's former officers
found its way to Timothy Pickering, former judge of the Salem
Prize Court and a member of Congress at the time of Conyngham's first petition. The elderly writer had suffered "ruinous
losses" that now compelled him to seek "reward" from the government for his wartime service. "The name of Conyngham in
our little navy," he wrote hopefully, "at the commencement of
our Revolutionary War was very conspicuous."

Pickering, in his mid-eighties, composed a reply in his own
hand. "I know nothing of the subject of the inquiry," he wrote.

Ten

656 frowned on us 6121y until this 1179 and 56 ruined our 1200 in 1284. We 913 a 919 in two fine 916s 905 a brig 211'd 1254 Deane of 18 six-pounders and 1254 other a Bermudan sloop 211'd 2154 17 of ten four-pounders.

[Fortune frowned on us extremely until this spring and almost ruined our stock in trade. We own a part in two fine privateers, one a brig called the *Deane* of 18 six-pounders and the other a Bermudan sloop called the *Active* of ten four-pounders.]

    —Barnabas Deane to Nathanael Greene, September 5, 1781

1254 1150 17 was 201'd by 1254 191 in N London 730. 1254 *Deane* and other vessels we 913 came near 1117ing 1254 1081 627. Our 841 is about £800.

[The sloop *Active* was burned by the British in New London harbor. The *Deane* and other vessels we own came near sharing the same fate. Our loss is about £800.]

    —Barnabas Deane to Nathanael Greene, ten days later

W hat I have been dreading has come to pass," Nathanael Greene wrote his wife in October 1780. "George Washington has appointed me to the command of the Southern Army, General Gates being recalled to an examination into his conduct."

Greene's chagrin reflected the many setbacks to the rebellion that had followed France's entry into the war. More than two years after securing the alliance, America still was far from victory. Some of the war's bloodiest fighting lay ahead, and the thirty-eight-year-old general would be in the thick of it.

The North American operations of the French fleet had been the first disappointment. Admiral d'Estaing's arrival in 1778, bringing four thousand troops along with his eminent passengers Silas Deane and Conrad Gerard, compelled British forces to abandon Philadelphia for New York, a triumph for Americans still celebrating Burgoyne's defeat and William Howe's resignation from enemy command (he was replaced by Henry Clinton, who'd taken Newport in 1776).

But d'Estaing, after a feeble brush with the Royal Navy off New Jersey, failed in a joint assault with Continental forces to liberate Newport in August. A year later he unsuccessfully laid siege to Savannah, under British occupation since late 1778, in another joint expedition. The defeat, termed "the greatest event that has happened in the whole war" by an ebullient General Clinton, drove a wedge of distrust between American and French forces.

The British rode the momentum of the Savannah victory to the successful capture of Charleston in May 1780, inflicting on the rebels their single greatest toll of casualties and prisoners. After crushing Continental resistance in Georgia that same month, Clinton handed over his southern command to Charles Cornwallis and returned to New York.

Cornwallis's march through the Carolinas caused the region's loyalist-patriot tensions to erupt in what historians have called "the first American civil war." Fighting among partisan militia reached new levels of atrocity and civilian suffering. Fearing the colonies would splinter as a result, Congress, without consulting Washington, dispatched an army under Horatio Gates to repel the enemy's northward advance.

Against Burgoyne at Saratoga, Gates had been more lucky than good. Against Cornwallis at Camden, South Carolina, in August 1780, his most memorable feat was to flee the battlefield faster and farther than anyone had done before. "One hundred and eighty miles in three days and a half!" Alexander Hamilton wrote in dismay.

News of the Camden rout, which cost more than a thousand

American dead, reached Congress ten days after the treachery of Benedict Arnold was discovered. Arnold had solicited a £20,000 bribe to provide the enemy with the defensive plans of the key American stronghold at West Point. He was foiled only through the chance capture of Major John Andre, his British liaison to Clinton. The betrayal by one of its most brilliant officers ("Who can we trust now?" Washington wondered) stunned the nation. Pushed to the edge of panic by subsequent news of the fiasco at Camden, members of Congress—even those who, in the afterglow of Saratoga, had wanted him to replace the seemingly ineffective Washington—demanded that Gates be relieved of command of the Southern Army.

Typically, General Greene ("how wretched this state, to always be at war with one's inclinations") was of two minds about seeking the job. He was tired of running the quartermaster department. Though profitable thanks to personal commissions on government transactions, his logistical duties created the dispiriting circumstance of a public that "refuses me that degree of reputation due to my services" while also deeming "my merit less than my reward."

Beyond unavoidable whispers of graft, Greene caught blame for the country's larger fiscal woes. Now that four thousand Continental dollars bought only one dollar in gold, "certain members of Congress are endeavoring to spread among the people that the avarice and extravagance of the quartermaster staff are the principal cause of all the depreciation of the money." In fact the opposite was true. Measured in hard money rather than Continental paper, the per capita cost of supporting troops in the field had decreased under his stewardship as quartermaster general.

Yet as anxious as he was for a new assignment, he'd lost much of his belief in the glory of serving in battle. The failed Franco-American campaign at Newport in 1780 had brought scorn on the military. Greene, temporarily detached from his department to lead one of the American divisions, had performed well; the defeat resulted mainly from miscommunication between his volatile superior, General John Sullivan, and d'Estaing's offshore fleet. Rhode

Islanders, angry that the British hadn't been expelled, called the operation "ill planned and worse conducted." The loudest critics were John and Nicholas Brown.

When Greene heard the Providence brothers were saying that Continental commanders lacked audacity, he responded with uncharacteristic venom, firing off a letter to John Brown that opened with a shot at John's rearguard bravado. "Men often feel courageous at a distance from danger that faint through fear when they come to be exposed."

Venting a lifetime's resentment toward the man who'd financially bullied his family for decades, Green suggested that Rhode Island's scandalous heritage disqualified its citizens from making moral judgments. "However," he concluded, "I cannot help feeling mortified that those that have been at home making their fortunes and living in the lap of luxury and enjoying all the pleasures of domestic life should be the first to sport with the feelings of officers who have stood as a barrier between them and ruin."

Nicholas Brown came to his brother's defense, explaining with careful deference to Greene's rank that John's supposed "ungenerous insinuations" about the army's performance had been misrepresented. Mollified, the general wrote back (more politely than honestly) that perhaps he'd overreacted. "Your family is one of the first in this state and one whose good opinion and friendship I have always endeavored to cultivate. Therefore the least reproach would be more sensibly felt."

Greene's sensitivity to criticism finally drove him to resign as quartermaster general in July. Congress's recent reorganization of the department had resulted in the dismissal of his top aides (and business partners), Charles Pettit and John Cox. The implication of corruption was obvious and, to Greene, unacceptable. Congress answered his demand for a vote of confidence with silence. When Greene then submitted his resignation, only Washington's intercession prevented a vote to cashier him from the service for seeming to defy the republican principle of civilian control of the military.

Back in the field, Greene's first notable assignment was "tragical"—

he presided over the espionage trial of Benedict Arnold's cohort, John Andre. The twenty-nine-year-old British major was impossible to dislike; during the occupation of Philadelphia he'd impressed the townspeople with his fairness, dignity, and charm. Upon capture, had he been wearing his uniform plainly rather than under a topcoat he might have been exchanged as a prisoner of war. But as a spy attempting to pass as a civilian, his execution was certain and its means mandatory: hanging.

Andre requested a firing squad. Greene was inclined to allow it, but Washington, who admitted the major was "more unfortunate than criminal," insisted on hanging and left it to Greene to justify the decision to Andre's many American sympathizers. "He is either a spy or an innocent man," Greene told them. Permitting the more humane execution by firing squad "will awaken public compassion, and the belief will become general that there were exculpatory circumstances entitling him to lenity beyond which he received—perhaps entitling him to pardon. Hang him therefore, or set him free."

Andre was hanged on October 2, 1780. An observer of the major's demeanor before the scaffold described "some degree of trepidation, placing his foot on a stone and rolling it over and choking in his throat, as if attempting to swallow." After adjusting the noose about his neck, Andre asked those in attendance to bear witness "that I meet my fate like a brave man." Buried on the spot, his remains were later moved to London's Westminster Abbey, where a monument to his memory was erected by George III.

Greene's spirits hit bottom that fall. "I am such an unfortunate dog," he wrote Jeremiah Wadsworth. Wadsworth, the army's commissary general, was the primary investor along with Greene in the deceptively named Barnabas Deane & Company.

The partnership was the only money-loser in Wadsworth's vast portfolio; after the war he emerged as a leading banker and entrepreneur. But Barnabas Deane & Company had a larger stake in privateers than did Wadsworth's other ventures—and it seemed that any privateers to which Greene was connected failed. Though the general took no part in choosing vessels and captains, he was apologetic about the company's poor record. "We have been very unfortunate in our navigation," he wrote Wadsworth. "There is no help for these things. It is true I can ill afford it, but what is that to the purpose?"

His privateer exposure was even greater in the family-run Jacob Greene & Company. The capture of two of its warships the previous spring, worth $7,000 in hard silver, "destroyed all our plans for this season," Jacob lamented. "If we had never been concerned in navigation we should have been possessed of a much larger property than we now are."

Four months later, Jacob had more bad news. "We purchased a small part of a new privateer at Salem and the very first cruise she was taken, so let us turn to the right or left we are unfortunate." Lest Nathanael think Jacob was careless with his brother's money, Jacob assured him, "I am vexed and mortified at our ill success more on your account than my own. My connection is small compared with yours."

Named by Washington to command the Southern Army on October 14, Greene broke the news to his wife with regret, knowing it meant they wouldn't see each other until his return. Resolving his money woes would likewise have to wait, he sent his wife a summary of his holdings in case he was killed. In addition to their Rhode Island home, he owned a New Jersey farm and three thousand acres along the Hudson River. He had £2,500 invested in Barnabas Deane & Company and in deals with Pettit and Cox. But of the cash tied up with his brothers, "I know not nor will they give me any account. I suppose it is owing to their not knowing the state of their own affairs."

Greene reached Charlotte, North Carolina, in December. The army he inherited from Gates numbered 2,400 "naked and dispirited" men. Most belonged to "six weeks militia" and fought out of greed (Greene likened their pillaging to "the locusts of Egypt") or to settle personal scores and generational feuds. That the Quaker-born

Rhode Islander was able to persuade them that their "partisan strokes" were pointless "unless you have a good army to take advantage of your success" was the first of his many notable feats of command.

Almost two hundred years later, General George S. Patton would answer a reporter's question, "What makes a great general?" with a simple reply: "Not to be beaten." The definition particularly applies to Greene because throughout his campaign he never gained a single victory. Rather, he maneuvered his troops to inflict maximum damage with minimum casualties, withdrawing from each field of battle with his army's spirit and fighting ability intact and the enemy's depleted and shaken.

Greene combined the small-unit, guerrilla style of the militia with a nimbler version of the traditional practice of lining up armies in opposing ranks and smashing one another to pieces. His first deployment was his most famous. Against military principle, he divided his army in the face of Cornwallis's larger force, at times separating the two commands by more than a hundred miles yet periodically uniting them for battle.

It's been called "the most audacious and ingenious piece of military strategy in the war." Revealingly, Henry Clinton noted the instant confidence it gave British officers. "Thus separated," he wrote in his memoirs, Greene's army seemed "certainly not in a situation to encourage any hopes of success from its operations." The move prompted the aggressive Cornwallis likewise to split his army in order to pursue both American units. This further strained his supply lines and, thanks to Greene's hard-won appreciation of logistics and advance scouting, let the Americans dictate when and where to fight.

The portion of Greene's army led by Daniel Morgan defeated the cavalry of Colonel Banastre Tarleton at Cowpens in January 1781. Morgan then rejoined Greene, who nipped at the British in a series of skirmishes that drew Cornwallis northward away from his supply bases. In March Greene abruptly pivoted and confronted the enemy. His popularity and success had swelled his ranks to more than four thousand men, though 80 percent were raw recruits. Meanwhile casualties, disease, hunger, and desertion had reduced the redcoats to half that number. Cornwallis was desperate for conventional battle, however, and attacked the waiting Americans at Guilford Courthouse.

After a day of ferocious fighting, Greene broke contact first. He gathered his men and headed south, where he continued "not to be beaten" in engagements in Georgia and South Carolina. It had been six years since his first combat outside Boston. The enemy likewise had won that battle, but at a cost. "A few such victories would ruin them," he'd written. The lessons of that experience still applied, for similar "victories" over Greene in the second half of 1781 ultimately forced the British back to Savannah and Charleston to recover. Within a year both towns were evacuated.

As for Cornwallis, his army was so battered after Guilford Courthouse he'd limped to the coast to await reinforcements. From there he headed north to Yorktown, Virginia.

Greene's finances deteriorated all the while. Reluctant to trouble him with bad tidings, his business partners sent only sketchy reports. These were increasingly glum, the chronic "losing by sea" made more vexing by reports of "the amazing success of privateering to the eastward" in Massachusetts. Businessmen there "seem as secure as if the war was already determined in their favor," marveled Wadsworth. "They are building houses and barns and living in ease and plenty. They pay more ready money for foreign goods, especially the luxuries, in a month than they ever did in three before the war."

Understandably given his immersion in combat operations, the scope of Greene's financial decline took time to sink in. His replies to his partners' morose letters were almost jaunty about being "jilted" by capricious fate. Clinging to faith in "the smiles of fortune," his optimism carried a wistful awareness "that so much is left in the order of things to time and chance." As the unpleasant facts poured in, however, Greene turned philosophical. "If we are not rich we will be honest, and if we are not respected for our wealth we will be for our industry."

He took pains to lighten his partners' remorse for losing so much of his money. In response to Griffin Greene's confession that it was easier to gauge "how much we have lost than what we have left," he assured his cousin of his "grateful sentiments for the particular manner in which you seem to be engaged to promote my interest."

In August 1781, Charles Pettit informed Greene that their joint investment in a blast furnace "has sunk." Their "mercantile transactions" were faring even worse. Pettit was dumping their privateer shares at a loss even though, he said, "I am persuaded we will suffer deeply by it."

John Cox's note came next. "I take this opportunity to inform you that all our naval concerns are now reduced to the ship *Congress* which has been out a considerable time and done little or nothing."

Then Pettit again: "Confiding in your friendship and confidence," he explained to the general that he'd invested their last funds in several more privateers but had paid the insurance premiums only on some of them. The ones he'd insured had returned safe to port. The others had been captured, leaving him and Greene "all at risk" for their loss. Ultimately Pettit made good use of the experience; after the war he founded the Insurance Company of North America and became one of the richest men in Pennsylvania. But in 1782 it left him severely straitened, compelling him to end his letter with a sheepish reference to money he owed the general on a personal debt. "I venture to lean on your friendship to spare calling on me."

Greene subsequently learned from Barnabas Deane, in one of Deane's letters encrypted, at the general's nervous insistence, in an "alphabet of figures," that their company had "lost a fortune in a few months." In a rare expression of raw distress, he lamented to their co-partner Wadsworth, "I have gone through sufficient hardships and done business enough to entitle me to a decent fortune; and the wreck of my constitution requires repose, but alas fate will have it otherwise."

In 1782 the state of Georgia, in appreciation for his patriotic service, gave Greene a rice plantation called Mulberry Grove fourteen miles north of Savannah. "It's not like money in hand," he told Wadsworth, who loaned Greene £1,500 to get the place, which had been neglected during the war, up and running.

Their fortunes had greatly diverged. "I am told you are burdened with wealth," Greene wrote. "I am glad of it. There is no man who deserves it more or who I wish to possess the good things of this world in greater plenty than you." In 1784 he would sell his former partner his remaining stake in Barnabas Deane & Company for £123, one-tenth its value three years earlier.

Meanwhile the bad news out of Jacob Greene & Company kept coming. Jacob wrote that he and their family co-partners "are in a state of perplexity to know what to do." He put at £10,000 "our losses since the partnership commenced. We have tried all sizes of vessels from a frigate down to a small coasting sloop and found none of them to answer."

Griffin grumbled that the family's losses were unfair in light of "four or five years of pushing business in the most prudent and diligent manner." But everyone trusted that Nathanael wouldn't blame them. "When you see our state of losses and gain you will be satisfied and say men cannot get rich when fortune frowns."

Their excuses out of the way, Jacob and Griffin asked Nathanael to use his influence to "open some plan of business" for the company. The hope, Griffin proposed delicately, was that the general would "look upon us as deserving of being your partners. You shall plan and we will execute. The world looks upon men generally that are unfortunate as undeserving, but I hope you will judge us as we deserve."

Greene declined without giving a reason. "My disappointment is considerable, but I feel more for you than for myself. Thus my friendship will never forsake you nor shall the family want anything in my power to procure them."

He was more candid in a letter to his wife. "To have a decent income is much to be wished; but to be free from debt more so. I never owned so much property as now, and yet never felt so poor."

It was 1784. Three years earlier, Cornwallis had been cornered at Yorktown by ground forces under Washington and a French fleet under Admiral François de Grasse bombarding the British from Chesapeake Bay. Cornwallis's surrender had ended Britain's will to keep fighting, though violence continued sporadically in the south and more seriously in the West Indies, where European navies jockeyed for advantage prior to their governments sitting down to sign a peace treaty in September 1783.

By that time, Greene had sold his Rhode Island home to his brother Jacob and moved with his wife and four children to Mulberry Grove. He was bankrupt—hit with bills he hadn't expected, debts he couldn't pay. Creditors hounded him, but it was Congress that broke his back.

The last months of the war had left Greene's troops without sufficient food or clothing, "naked as the day they were born," he wrote. Robert Morris, now superintendent of finance, was in the process of instituting a policy to supply the military through fixed contracts rather than through private agents working on commission. With his men on the verge of mutiny, however, Greene retained a South Carolina businessman named John Banks to procure supplies in the expectation, once the new procedures were in place, that the bills would fall "upon Mr. Morris the financier or upon any state in the southern department, whichever may be the most agreeable."

He knew Banks to be a "suspicious character long engaged in contraband trade." But he was also, Greene wrote, "the only person who have the will and the means" to obtain what was needed amid the war's devastation. With no illusions about Banks's integrity, he implored him to keep prices "as low and moderate as the nature of the business will admit." And he appealed to Bank's heart, reminding him that such abject neglect "is hard upon troops who have bled so freely for this oppressed country."

But Banks was an inveterate speculator. Armed with government drafts that Greene had provided, he launched a scheme whereby they would actually go for buying tobacco, which then could be traded—and with British suppliers if need be, either the ones still in Charleston or others in the West Indies—for larger quantities of supplies than Greene had contracted for, leaving some left over to sell at a profit.

Greene guessed what Banks was up to ("it had an odd appearance to me"), but desperate to provide for his men, he gave little objection beyond "that he seemed to be prosecuting trade on principles not admissible." But, Greene testified later, "He had the example and practice of all the principal merchants in trade for his justification, and merchants will devise more ways and means for the preservation of their property than any other order of men."

Rumors arose that the former quartermaster general was also secretly profiting. The taint of associating with Banks led Greene to consider voiding their deal altogether. Realizing it would mean no supplies for his troops, he instead took a fateful step of pledging his remaining personal assets as collateral to complete the whopping £30,000 purchase—expecting, again, that Congress would pay it off once everything was explained.

He was wrong. Congress disavowed the transaction, a decision underpinned by the common presumption that Greene was rich; his obsessive discretion about his business activities had concealed his losses as well as his profits. Banks had no money to help pay the debt but did provide a statement in court that Greene "neither has, or ever had, any commercial connection with me of a private nature, or intimated a wish or desire of the kind."

Banks regretted "that I took an improper liberty with General Greene's name," but was confident that his partner had nothing to worry about. "I cannot suppose an idle surmise can affect a reputation so permanently established." But the general knew the ways of Congress. "How different in their conduct from the Romans who honored their officers even in adversity."

Greene implored Congress to reconsider its verdict against him. Colleagues and subordinates sent petitions expressing outrage that he should "have his conduct made a subject of public discussion, from a transaction which had the public good and the relief of the suffering soldiers for its objects." Congress refused.

By 1785 Greene's continuing woes had brewed pure hatred for Banks. "I verily believe if I was to meet him I should put him to death." He went to Virginia in a last attempt to squeeze money out the man. His fortunes were nothing if not consistent, however, for he found that Banks had died suddenly, leaving no assets and no documents of their erstwhile collaboration. Near to breakdown, Greene wrote his wife, "I tremble when I think of the enormous sums I owe. I seem to be doomed to a life of slavery and anxiety."

The following spring, the forty-four-year-old general collapsed from heatstroke while walking the grounds of Mulberry Grove. His friend, General Anthony Wayne, sent word around the army. "I have just seen a great and good man die."

Modern historians have assessed Greene's legacy this way: "The general who could not win a battle had brilliantly forced the enemy out of the southland in less than a year. As a strategist among the Patriots, he was second only to Washington; some would place him first."

His assessment of himself was humble. Fate, Greene wrote, "has never been much my friend. If she has granted me one favor, she has commonly brought on me two misfortunes to balance it."

Five years after his death, Caty Greene presented her husband's case for restitution to Treasury Secretary Alexander Hamilton. After noting Greene's error in not notifying Congress beforehand of his emergency deal with Banks, Hamilton supported the appeal.

On April 27, 1792, President Washington, on Congress's recommendation, "this day approved and signed an act for indemnifying the estate of the late General Nathanael Greene." The award was for $47,000, equal to well over $1 million today.

GUADELOUPE, WEST INDIES

Prime Minister Frederick North, architect of the infamous Pirate Act of 1777, fell from power in March 1782. Weeks later, John Manley was exchanged out of Mill Prison after a two-year stint during which he'd failed at three escape attempts, each of them followed with increasingly harsher penalties of reduced rations and confinement in the "black hole." He'd won admiration by challenging a bullying inmate to a duel with pistols probably acquired from prison officials who hoped both would be killed. The other prisoner backed down, converting his reputation for toughness into that of "a great coward," Manley wrote.

Back in America, he took command of *Deane*, a Continental frigate originally outfitted in France by Silas Deane and John Ross. Who exactly had chosen that name isn't clear, but in June 1782 Congress retracted the honor ("the person after whom she was called has by his perfidy and defection forfeited all title to every mark of honor or respect") and rechristened the vessel *Hague*.

In the West Indies Manley captured several prizes, including a transport armed with twenty guns, before engaging four British warships off Guadeloupe. Sailing inside a reef out of range of their fire, he blasted a thirteen-gun salute "in defiance" once safely away. The island governor commended him. "You have perfectly fulfilled the duty of a brave officer, and it is with utmost satisfaction that I pay the tribute to your honor." On his return voyage to Boston in 1783, Manley took the last great prize of the war, the 340-ton *Baille*, a fitting bookend to the ordnance ship *Nancy* whose capture in 1775 had made his name.

Hague was decommissioned in May, one of only two Continental warships to survive the war. The navy had logged 198 captures all told, 12 of them Royal Navy ships. Most were tallied by John Paul Jones, a full-time navy man, and Gustavus Conyngham, whose ambiguous combination of public and private service confounded Congress and obscured his posthumous renown.

Privateers, no doubt only because forced to it, captured or destroyed sixteen Royal Navy warships. At least six hundred of their prizes were settled in American courts; countless others were tried in foreign courts, retaken by the British, or lost somewhere at sea. Edward Stanton Maclay, the first serious chronicler of Revolutionary privateering, wrote in 1898, "It is very much to be regretted that many of the cruises and actions of these craft have not been recorded."

Maclay was an unabashed cheerleader for his subject. "Had it not been for our privateers, the Stars and Stripes would have been completely swept from the seas." His counterparts among historians of the Continental Navy have been compelled to be more circumspect. William M. Fowler, Jr., ends his book, *Rebels Under Sail*, with something like an apology for taking up so much of the reader's time. "If the Continental Navy had never existed, it is hard to see how the outcome of the Revolution could have been any different." And in his 2003 biography of John Paul Jones, Evan Thomas demythologizes Jones and the strategic significance of the navy in which he served while still giving full due to the character, valor, and sacrifice of Jones and his fellow sailors.

Jones died in France in 1792 full of resentment at the ingratitude of his country. More than a century later his remains were brought with an escort of warships to the U.S. Naval Academy at Annapolis, where his grave today is a national shrine. Manley, loathed by Jones but certainly his equal in furthering the American cause, died in Boston in 1793. The location of his grave is unknown.

Eleven

It's such a busy road. Everyone fighting to get ahead, pushing, shoving, using their elbows and feet, every man for himself and anyone who gets in the way is trampled in the crush. That's what you have to do. Personally, I've given up on it.
—*Beaumarchais,* The Marriage of Figaro, *1784*

After four years of excelling at what he called "the art of uniting war and commerce," William Bingham was anxious to leave Martinique and return home to Philadelphia. The signing of the Franco-American alliance had wrecked the island's status as a haven for arms dealers and privateers. Its cloak of neutrality had fallen away. No longer were French bills of lading or the tricolor flag a defense against Royal Navy attack.

The autonomy with which Bingham had operated to such success made the twenty-eight-year-old coolly self-certain in communications with his superiors. When Benjamin Franklin was slow in sending him details of the French alliance, he scolded the elderly diplomat. "I humbly think I should be made acquainted with its contents. As agent for the United States of America in the West Indies, every circumstance that regards the country I represent and that forms a subject of controversy immediately falls under my notice and attention."

His letters to Congress were likewise sharp with pique over its outstanding debt to him of more than $50,000 in hard currency for public advances he'd made out of pocket. In frustration, he tried to bill the Paris commissioners instead. Franklin's pointed silence brought an icy note from the young man. "I am unhappy to find that I am deprived of any answers to the numerous letters I have done myself the honor of writing you."

The brief stopover at Martinique of John Jay, on his way to Spain in 1779, persuaded the new ambassador that "our agent here is in high estimation and has done his duty faithfully." Jay convinced Congress to appropriate £5,000 "to discharge in part the debt due to the said William Bingham." Even so, with the island's business squelched by British–French clashes outside its harbor, Bingham didn't wait for an official release from Congress. Claiming "the state of my health absolutely requires it," he declared his duties "happily completed" and sailed for America at the turn of the year.

Before departing he composed a long report to Congress summarizing his activities. He confidently listed "critical" achievements in buying arms and outfitting privateers. Not only did they aggravate the British, they gave Martinique's military governor a perception of "reciprocal injuries" committed by Britain against French sovereignty. This provoked, Bingham wrote, "the ardent desire with which military men pant after war, and frequently inclined him to wink at my schemes."

He noted the money owed him ("a very large sum") and appealed for "justice towards a person who has been faithfully devoted to the public service." Knowing Congress's poor record of remunerating its agents, he closed with a resigned, almost cynical comment. "If I have undertaken a task beyond my abilities to accomplish I cannot expect to be honored with public approbation, which invariable in its decisions never consults anything but its own advantage. In that case, I shall be more afflicted than surprised."

He left at the right time. Dutch-owned St. Eustatius soon became, in a perfect reprise of Parliament's earlier denunciations of Martinique, the region's premier "nest of outlaws selling provisions, clothing, and all naval and warlike stores to the rebels and enemies of Britain." Some 235 American vessels had visited Martinique in 1777. In 1779, seven to ten arrived every day at St. Eustatius along with regular convoys of French merchant ships unable to approach the blockaded Martinique. The number of privateers launched from the American mainland more than doubled in the same period, with St. Eustatius now the handiest place in the West Indies to sell their prizes and refit.

In a vengeful rage, a British assault fleet under Admiral Rodney struck the island in February 1781, plundering its wealth and brutalizing its people, especially its established community of Jewish merchants and their families. Reports of the atrocities drew condemnation from British residents at nearby St. Kitts, sparked violent riots in Amsterdam, and fueled humanitarian protests in London. Petitions against Rodney circulated in Parliament and legal claims in excess of £300,000 were lodged against him by British merchants, whose goods his men had indiscriminately seized along with those belonging to other nations friendly and hostile.

Later in 1781, the incident had a profound strategic effect on the ongoing war in America. Preoccupied with protecting a huge convoy carrying to Britain the loot from St. Eustatius, much of it belonging to him, Rodney was derelict in intercepting the fleet of Admiral de Grasse on its way from the West Indies to Virginia, "where," Rodney himself predicted, "I am persuaded the French intend making their grand effort." That effort was at Yorktown, of course.

Bingham had been home for more than a year by then. Immediately on arrival he'd begun pressuring the person most in position to get Congress to pay up. Robert Morris had invested with him in privateers and trade ships throughout Bingham's stint on Martinique, a mutually profitable partnership that nonetheless had concluded with an unresolved debt from Morris to Bingham of £13,000. Bingham's habit of often bringing it up in his letters from Martinique had contributed to the testiness that entered their mentor–protégé relationship as the younger man grew in financial stature.

Engaged in myriad private deals on both sides of the Atlantic, Morris often committed his personal assets to expedite needed government purchases. This tangled overextension had been partly responsible for his difficulty in paying Bingham. There was also the practical challenge of slipping remittances past Royal Navy patrols. "You recollect," he wrote the agent at one point, "that I sent the schooner *Hope* to your address for the purpose of discharging part of this debt out of her cargo, but she was unluckily taken. There are accidents I could neither foresee nor prevent. I do not, however, plead this as a reason why you should not be paid nor in excuse for delay of payment as you may suppose."

United in Philadelphia, the men settled their accounts. Bingham next pushed Morris to back his claim against Congress. "You may well remember that the Committee of Secret Correspondence engaged the payment of my expenses and left any further compensation for my services to be settled at a future day." Of the government funds due him, if he'd had use of them on Martinique, "I might have derived ten times the advantage that the advances to Congress will procure me."

The argument was sound—but what most grabbed Morris's attention was Bingham's suggestion that only "a scrupulous attention to motives of delicacy" prevented him from enumerating still further monies owed. "Profitable private business," he hinted, "enabled me to support a part of them." Much of that business had been done in secret partnership with Morris. And given the climate of suspicion that now hung over all of Congress's financial deliberations, airing it in public wouldn't be good.

So Morris lobbied his colleagues on Bingham's behalf, pressing arguments ranging from the high cost of living on Martinique to the shabby appearance that refusing to pay would give a government trying to bolster its credit after years of fiscal irresponsibility. In fitful installments each contentiously debated, Bingham received most of his money by mid-1783, during which time he'd married the daughter of Morris's longtime partner Thomas Willing and parlayed his profits into a fortune in banking and land speculation that would become the largest in America.

He did endure one lingering irritation from the war years. The owners of *Pilgrim*, a Newburyport privateer whose capture of a cargo of flour he'd settled at Martinique in 1779, filed a lawsuit against him for $30,000 in unpaid prize money.

The legality of the capture had been in dispute at the time, and Bingham had credited the sale proceeds to Congress pending a proper ruling. By the time the vessel was proven to be British, the money had vanished in the thicket of wartime accounting. He was wealthy enough to fear the embarrassment of the lawsuit more than its cost, yet out of annoyance that Congress had reneged on an earlier promise to pay the owners, he fought it for more than twenty years, relenting only because he'd bought four million acres of land in New England and wanted no trouble with the Massachusetts court.

It was 1802 when Bingham's lawyers finally settled the case with a compromise payment. He was abroad in Europe at the time, and two years later would die there at age fifty-two. He'd had little contact with Morris since 1798, when the former superintendent of finance had been imprisoned for defaulting on millions of dollars of debt.

Still driven to speculate at more than sixty years old, Morris had bet his fortune on massive land purchases across six states only to see it shrink to notes worth 15 cents on the dollar when the nation's postwar economy stalled. Though Bingham had diversified his investments enough to withstand the recession, Morris's collapse brought down many other of Philadelphia's wealthiest men who'd been in partnership with him, a consequence as distressing to Morris as his own ruin.

Driven to near madness, the old man hid from gun-wielding creditors in the top floor of his mansion. "If ever I could have had a previous idea of such things happening to me, I would sooner have wheeled oysters all my days." Going to jail was almost a relief, though he felt, he said, "like an intruder" in the crowded cell to which he was initially assigned, "sleeping in other people's beds and sitting in other people's rooms." Always calculating, he clucked at the irony of his situation. "If my creditors were wise for their own sakes, they would not keep me idle here, when if I had my liberty I might work efficiently for their benefit." He was released three-and-a-half years later.

In the Revolution's immediate aftermath there were some commentators who ranked Morris at a level with Washington and Franklin. Beyond his efforts to finance the war, he'd led the way in persuading Congress to repay people and institutions for debts incurred in the cause. "That the payments of debts may be expensive, it is infinitely more expensive to withhold the payment," he argued. "The former is the expense of money, but the latter involves the destruction of that source from which money can be derived when all other sources fail. That source is public credit. The country in which it may with greatest ease be established and preserved is America, and America is the country which most stands in need of it."

Congress's determination to pay its bills led to its demand of the often recalcitrant colonies to pay federal taxes. As Morris understood (and as Hamilton, his philosophical heir, put into practice in creating the Bank of the United States in 1791), nationalizing the debt and insisting on its payment would help unify the country behind a central government. "A public debt, supported by public revenue, will prove the strongest cement to keep the confederacy together," Morris wrote.

One of Morris's biographers suggested "fame looks acidly on financial failure" to explain the irony of a former titan living out his last days so obscure and downtrodden. Morris would have concurred. "Large fortunes do not always bring happiness," he cautioned his daughter shortly before his death in 1806. "Misery to the possessor is frequently the result."

Words he'd earlier written to Franklin summarize his legacy best. "There is a period in the progress of things, a crisis between the ardor of enthusiasm and the authority of law, when much skill and management are necessary to those who are charged with administering the affairs of a nation."

Such a crisis had gripped America during the years of violent chaos that followed the Declaration of Independence. In that period Morris's pecuniary improvisations helped his nation triumph. Though not for want of trying, they didn't do the same for him.

Silas Deane died in Britain in 1789. Like Morris, he was broke—but unlike Morris he wasn't so much forgotten as willfully purged from the Revolution's honor roll of contributors.

After his bitter grilling before Congress in 1779–80, he'd returned to France in the naïve hope that he could organize his accounts sufficiently to persuade his antagonists in the Lee–Adams camp of the integrity of his public service and the justice of his claims for compensation. Rumored in America to have amassed a fortune (Nathanael Greene heard he'd founded "the greatest commercial house in Europe"), Deane learned on arriving in Paris of the total loss of his last $50,000 left with Edward Bancroft and others to invest in his absence. On the heels of this blow came the slow realization that Congress had no intention of paying him any money. "I can neither think nor write without dwelling on it. It lies down with me at night. It rises with me in the morning. I take up my pen and resolve not to write about it, but before a page is written I have referred to it."

Disillusioned and vulnerable, Deane was tempted by promises, proffered through Bancroft, of a favored business relationship with the British government if the colonies rejoined the empire. He agreed to his friend's request for a series of letters expressing his "private judgment" of the benefits of reconciliation. Pleased by Deane's assessment that independence would prove "a curse instead of a blessing," Bancroft's spymasters in London arranged for the letters to fall into American hands in hopes their publication might soften the resistance.

The timing couldn't have been worse. The letters appeared in a New York newspaper just as the nation was celebrating its monumental victory at Yorktown. Deane was vilified throughout the colonies with "the same infamy," wrote James Madison, "as that of his friend Arnold." His few remaining friends had no choice but to denounce him, though some privately conceded that he "writes many serious truths however unwilling we may be to admit them."

The reaction stunned Deane. "Have I asserted anything for fact which is not such? I have said that it was not friendship for us, or regard for the liberties of mankind, which induced France to declare in favor of our independency, but solely to improve the favorable moment for humbling an ancient rival and enemy."

But puncturing the image of French generosity was less offensive to his countrymen than the suggestion that they ought to reconcile with Britain. "Is it become treason in 1781," he wondered in dismay, "to recommend such terms of peace and accommodations as are infinitely preferable to those unanimously proposed by Congress in 1774, before the war began, and repeated in 1775, after the sword was drawn?" The answer to that question, after Yorktown especially, was yes.

The one man who might have stemmed the tide of condemnation was Franklin. He'd always expressed "an exceeding good opinion" of his former colleague. But at seventy-five, never without ailments, and riding a crest of national acclaim, Franklin declined public comment "lest he should be led into a controversy he wished to avoid."

The elusiveness that had served Franklin so well in the negotiations with France was no help to Deane now. Frustrated by his silence, Deane wrote him a long letter alleging "similar and greater concessions" to Britain that Franklin had advocated in the past. Deane, who'd once told Congress that he could endure any public scorn "if at the same time it be known that Franklin was my guide, philosopher, and friend," knew he'd lost him as an ally when Franklin sent back a rebuke that, in a twist on the routine decorum with which gentlemen usually ended their letters, closed with a gratuitous jab that Deane's revisionist views "make it impossible to say with the same truth and cordiality that I am your affectionate friend and humble servant."

Yet even as he snubbed Deane, behind the scenes Franklin urged Congress to finish its investigation into his accounts. "Even between enemies," he told Robert Morris, it was proper to pay a man his full due. When Deane learned of this gesture, he wrote Franklin a final reflection in May 1782:

"If America shall, on experiment, find herself happier and more free under the present system than she ever was under the other, I shall rejoice to find that I have judged erroneously. I will trespass no further on your time," he went on, "than to assure you that, however greatly your sentiments may have changed, I retain the same respect and esteem for you as when I had the honor to be numbered among your friends."

A year later Franklin went on record as having "never known or suspected any cause to charge Silas Deane with any want in probity." This incensed Arthur Lee, still rabidly trying to bring down his imagined rivals. "I am strongly inclined to believe that Silas Deane receives a pension from Dr. Franklin and Robert Morris, as hush money. The evidence which he must have of the frauds and wickedness of these two men is such as would ruin them."

Deane, now penniless and living alone in Britain, where he'd fled after his anti-French opinions became known in Paris, did indeed have a secret benefactor: Edward Bancroft. His friend's generosity was, in Bancroft's typically two-edged way, both a lifeline and a prison sentence. The "charitable subscription" and small flat "a little way out of town" that he provided were useful in keeping Deane under watchful control.

The former spy had much to lose these days—wife, children, a large pension for his wartime betrayals, and a good probability that Parliament would grant him lucrative "monopoly rights" stemming from his laboratory studies in the chemistry of color, his area of expertise before he'd taken up spying and speculating. He didn't need Deane resurfacing to blab about their pursuits during the war, particularly their encouragement of James "John the Painter" Aitken's bid to torch the Portsmouth shipyard. Deane had supported the act as a legitimate attack on the enemy's navy. Bancroft had supported it, after placing his bet with his broker, to drive down the British stock market—not exactly something to commend him to the London society to which he aspired.

Thus Bancroft wasn't pleased when Deane began slowly to rehabilitate his image. He published essays in America that recast his support for reconciliation in commercial rather than political terms; even as an independent nation America's most compatible trading partner was its former adversary, he argued. He then contributed to an influential British pamphlet, *Observations on the Commerce of the American States*, suggesting that the loss of its colonies might actually benefit Britain, leaving it the advantages of American trade without "the burdens of colonial administration."

Some British lords presented to the king Deane's plan for a canal between Quebec's Lake Champlain and New York's St. Lawrence River; called "practicable and useful both in a commercial and political view," the canal was built fifty years later. And in America, businessmen showed interest in partnering with him to build steam-powered grain mills based on British models Deane had studied.

Bancroft responded to his friend's resurgence by moving him still farther from London and monitoring his mail. But encouraged by Robert Morris's observation that "resentments toward our disaffected daily subside," Deane prepared to return to America in 1789. In June he sent George Washington a letter via Jeremiah Wadsworth saying that in his ten-year quest for respect and recompense, "my hopes are revived that I shall no longer solicit in vain."

Three months later, hours before departure on a homebound vessel booked by Bancroft, he ate "a hearty breakfast," took ill at midmorning, and died at two that afternoon. Bancroft arranged an immediate burial near the town of Dover. ("There is no gravestone but interment is believed to have been in St. George's Churchyard," was the notation in the parish's Register of Burials). He then anonymously composed an obituary suggesting Deane had committed suicide. The act was understandable to British officials who knew Deane had suffered "the most abject poverty in the capital of England, and has for the last few months been almost in danger of starving." And it made sense to those Americans who believed him "unconscious of rectitude yet not uncallous to remorse" and therefore, by killing himself, inclined to "expiate a treacherous desertion of the cause of his country." But it was less understandable in light of the rise in spirits evident in his last letters.

The possibility that Bancroft killed him is strong. He had a motive: fearing to lose control and influence over the unstable, indiscreet American who knew so many damning details of Bancroft's past. And he had the know-how, for the specialty of his medical studies in South America as a young man had been natural poisons—their chemistry, symptoms, and use.

Curare, made from a jungle vine and which causes death by slow asphyxiation (Deane was said to have gasped "inarticulate sounds" as he died), was his favorite. In a scientific paper written on the subject in 1769, Bancroft had admitted to bringing a quantity of curare powder back with him to Britain. He explained that natives in Surinam, where he'd studied, usually administered the poison in a drink "to revenge past injuries that have long been neglected and are thought forgotten. On these occasions they always feign an insensibility of the injury which they intend to revenge, and even repay it with services and acts of friendship until they have destroyed all distrust and apprehension of danger in the destined victim."

The facility to be both cynical and sincere that Bancroft displayed as a double agent and as a friend constitutes the last piece of circumstantial evidence in the case for thinking he murdered Deane. He once observed that news of Deane's sudden passing may have caused "his best friends to rejoice most at the event." The reason would have been their concern that Deane's rejuvenation was doomed and all that really awaited him in America was disappointment to himself and discomfiture, to put it mildly, to his family and friends.

Princeton historian Julian P. Boyd, in his 1959 dissection of their relationship, "Silas Deane: Death by a Kindly Teacher of Treason?" articulates Bancroft's rationale: "Self-preservation as well as compassion might serve to justify an act that would deprive the world of nothing and Deane of little except time to experience further pain and humiliation."

In other words, a mercy killing.

Deane's partner Beaumarchais never got his money either. The Frenchman calculated that Congress owed him more than 2 million livres (about £80,000) for the military supplies, integral to the victory at Saratoga, that Hortalez & Company had sent to America in 1777; the sum made him Congress's largest individual creditor. But Arthur Lee's groundless assertion that the supplies had been a gift from the French government had created a nagging sense of what Robert Morris called "a mysteriousness in this transaction."

P. A. CARON DE BEAUMARCHAIS.

The French courtier, Pierre-Augustin Caron de Beaumarchais, shared his partner Silas Deane's combination of idealism and incorrigibleness in the quest to promote American liberty while getting rich through privateering and gunrunning. Unlike Deane, the collapse of his financial ambitions didn't diminish his faith in the Patriot cause.

Beaumarchais's case wasn't helped by his past ties with the now despised Deane. But rather than renounce their friendship, Beaumarchais expressed "compassionate feeling for a man worthy of a better lot." The sentiment held even after Deane's criticisms of France were published. "I will always do him the justice that he is one of those men who has contributed most to the alliance of France with the United States."

In 1784 Congress was on the verge of approving Beaumarchais's claim when a review committee led by Arthur Lee ruled that its entire basis was invalid because "Mr. Silas Deane was not authorized to settle the accounts" with Hortalez.

In 1788 Beaumarchais tried again. This time rather than reject the claim, Lee's committee worked the numbers to show that, instead of deserving a payoff, Beaumarchais in fact owed Congress almost a million livres. And so it went, back and forth, for twenty years.

In the interim, France reaped consequences of supporting American liberty that were as contrary to its expectations as those that befell Beaumarchais. Debt incurred in the war broke the French treasury. Meanwhile Britain remained America's main trading partner and so retained its prewar power. Vergennes died knowing his machinations had bankrupted his country, while Louis XVI died on the guillotine knowing that the citizens howling for his head were inspired by the distant revolution he'd financed.

Beaumarchais's postwar plays are full of political cynicism whose source isn't hard to guess. "Playing a role well or badly," he wrote in *The Marriage of Figaro* (1784), "sending spies everywhere and rewarding the traitors; tampering with seals, intercepting letters, and trying to dignify your sordid means by stressing your glorious ends. That's all there is to politics, and you can have me shot if it's not."

In the play's sequel, *The Guilty Mother*, his skepticism extended beyond the hypocrisies of government. "Chance, the hidden god! The Ancients used to call you destiny. Nowadays, we've got another name for you."

Beaumarchais's family renewed his claim against Congress after his death in 1799. Even the absence of Arthur Lee, dead since 1792, didn't hasten the process, which took until 1818 before a report was delivered. In an indication of how times had changed, Robert Morris, who'd died in penniless obscurity, was cited in the report as the "great revolutionary financier" whose insistence on the sanctity of a nation's fiscal integrity was the basis of its opinion "that the heirs of Mr. Beaumarchais are creditors of the United States." Still, almost twenty more years passed before the money was paid—800,000 francs, about a quarter of Beaumarchais's original claim.

Silas Deane got a similar reprieve of a sort when Congress reopened his case in 1841. Determining that previous audits of his Revolutionary accounts were "erroneous, and a gross injustice," Congress awarded Deane's heirs $37,000—about $1 million today.

1782

BROOKLYN, NEW YORK

In the spring of 1781, Christopher Vail had set sail aboard a privateer only two days after returning home from voyages, sea battles, and British imprisonment that had kept him away from his Connecticut home for more than two years. "We were out 25 days," he wrote of the subsequent expedition, "took nothing." Undeterred, he promptly joined the sixteen-gun *Jay* in a venture that bagged eight small prizes "all of which we got safe into New London."

While refitting the sloop as a more powerful brig, Vail was present when "the notorious Benedict Arnold," a British commander now, led a raid against New London in September to destroy the port's privateering capability. Dozens of Americans were massacred in cold blood. The commander of the local fort was fatally run through with his sword as he gave it over in surrender. "I know of one man," Vail wrote, "who told me they put the muzzle of a musket to his mouth and fired down his throat. The ball came out about three inches below his jaw."

The attackers sailed away the next morning. Vail was right behind them, crewing again on a privateer. Captured days out of port, he wound up on the prison hulk *Jersey* in Brooklyn's Wallabout Bay. Eleven hundred Americans festered there amid disease and filth ("for 12 feet around the hatches was nothing but excrement"). The death rate averaged eight per day. "They were carried on shore in heaps, then carried to the edge of the bank where a hole was dug one or two feet deep and all hove in together."

One day in October 1781 the sound of cannon echoed over the East River's opposite shore from where the dead of the prison ships lay buried. News of Cornwallis's surrender at Yorktown had reached the patriots in New Jersey; they were shooting off volleys in celebration. Vail's anxious hope that things now might change for the better was fulfilled when, "in a few days after this, a cartel arrived from New London and I was exchanged."

He caught a fever on his way home and "lost my senses for 27 days." When he revived, someone asked whether, after so much hard luck, he would venture to sea again. "I told the person that I never would if I begged my bread from door to door." Yet with the fighting dragging on, and with loyalist transports still plying to and from New York, he couldn't stay away. "I shipped myself out on board the sloop *Randolph* of 16 guns and 70 men."

He cruised unsuccessfully on several more vessels until late in the summer of 1782. While serving aboard *John*, "with but one gun and 24 men," he hailed a transport whose papers indicated a nondescript cargo of flour and flax bound for Providence. Suspicious, Vail cracked opened a barrel and was amazed to find that "by some means or other the flour had turned into inkstands." Its cargo was a trove of loyalist "conveniences" worth £4,000 sterling.

Of the tens of thousands of patriot privateersmen, a huge proportion died; of the survivors, only a fraction wound up with money in hand. Vail was one of the lucky ones, and after collecting his earnings he retired from sea roving and looked ahead to life in a new America. He also did what young men throughout history have done upon gaining their fortunes. "I got married," he wrote, "and remained at home until the next spring, when peace took place."

At the time Vail was making his score on *John*, a contemporary he never knew, Andrew Sherburne of Portsmouth, New Hampshire, was cruising the West Indies on an American letter of marque called *Scorpion*.

Having found in 1781 that prize money he'd earned earlier in the war had been spent by his mother while he was in prison in Britain, Sherburne had been forced to sign up for another sea venture despite his lingering ill health. "Some ambition" figured in the decision, he admitted, "and probably no small share of pride."

Off the island of Montserrat, *Scorpion* had just welcomed aboard a French pilot crew to steer it into the harbor when the British warship *Bee* closed to within one hundred yards. There was a strange moment of calm as the heavily armed brig, "ports up and guns out," held its fire. *Scorpion*'s French sailors "jumped below," Sherburne later wrote, "and others fell upon their faces, crying out *'foutre d'Anglais'*."

The broadside didn't come. *Bee* wheeled seaward "under all the sail she could set" as the Montserrat fort opened fire. Cannonballs splashed behind the fleeing brig. For the rest of his life Sherburne would marvel, "She had opportunity to do us considerable injury by raking us, but her commander had the humanity and generosity to refrain."

Ashore on the island, Sherburne got drunk for the first time. "I was not a little mortified at the thought of having been intoxicated, and resolved to guard against this destructive practice." He also got his first glimpse of slavery. "I was appalled to see the hungry and almost naked slaves suffering the cruel scourges of their drivers, some of them having iron collars about their necks with a chain suspended from it; others with a heavy chain fastened to the leg, and in other instances two chained together."

Scorpion exchanged its cargo of Virginia tobacco for limes, sugar, and rum. Though the homeward journey featured several narrow escapes from British pursuers, "within two days' sail of our port we fancied ourselves almost safe." Suddenly they were run down by the frigate *Amphion*. After surrendering, *Scorpion*'s 13 crewmembers were brought aboard the warship and placed "under two decks, where we found near a hundred of our countrymen who had fallen into their hands."

The prisoners knew where they were bound. "Our hopes of a prosperous voyage were now blasted; our property gone, and no other prospect than that of taking up quarters on board the old *Jersey* prison ship in New York harbor."

It was November 1782, more than a year after Yorktown and more than four years after France and America had signed their treaty of alliance—milestones that meant little now. "I had just entered the eighteenth year of my age and had now to commence a scene of suffering almost without parallel."

Aboard *Jersey*, anchored 120 miles from where Christopher Vail was settling down with his bride in Connecticut, the worst of Sherburne's war was about to begin.

Twelve

There were many persons in Salem dejected on the return of peace, but a greater spirit of industry arises among the inhabitants than I had expected to see after the idleness and dissipation introduced by the business and success of privateering.

—*Timothy Pickering, December 1783*

Wartime entrepreneurialism, privateering especially, was a testament to individual initiative. Yet in his comprehensive study, *Business Enterprise in the American Revolutionary Era*, Robert A. East downplays the significance of those "giants of enterprise who molded the opinions of their fellows." The greater legacy of the era's business boom was that "social forces of the generation had taught many persons to think alike." The common thought they'd learned was of making money.

Before the war, this would have been viewed as undermining the virtues of a proper republic. "Like Puritanism," writes Gordon S. Wood, "of which it was a more relaxed, secularized version, republicanism was essentially anti-capitalistic, a final attempt to come to terms with the emergent individualistic society that threatened to destroy once and for all the communion and benevolence that civilized men had always considered to be the ideal of human behavior."

The question of whether rampant capitalism benefited America or endangered it was at the heart of the Deane–Lee division in Congress, with the Virginia Lees, along with Henry Laurens of South Carolina, uniting with the Adamses of Massachusetts to condemn "the joint combination of political and commercial men" exemplified by Deane, Robert Morris, and their ilk.

The Lees, though infected with jealousy and personal feuds, based their position on "the principles and manners of New England, wise, attentive, sober, diligent, and frugal." But during the 1780s they realized that the Puritan egalitarianism they idealized ran counter to their preference for a permanent aristocracy founded on bloodlines and landed wealth. As a result, their belief that New England most fully embodied "that spirit which finally has established the Independence of America" devolved into one more point of resentment.

John and Samuel Adams were more genuine in praising their fellow New Englanders' "generous feeling for the public and for each other." Consequently they were shocked when their home state succumbed to "a spirit of avarice" as the war progressed. John in particular—he'd been one of the first to call for unleashing privateers, after all— lamented that his vision of Boston as a "Christian Sparta" had been overwhelmed by a tide of speculation, materialism, and self-interest.

"Rich and numerous prizes," wrote one Bostonian of his town's roaring economy late in the war, "are the grand engines." Sea captains, waterfront agents and lawyers, and the "new race of merchants" from Essex County (the so-called "meaner people" in 1775), were now Boston's financial elite, dwelling in mansions unaffordable to "those who are not in business."

Samuel Warren was dismayed by the change. "Fellows who would have cleaned my shoes five years ago have amassed fortunes and are riding in chariots." And Samuel Adams decried "the expensive living of too many, the pride and vanity of dress which pervades through every class." These newly rich seemed "almost the only men of power, riches, and influence." Their migration to Boston would ultimately hurt the commercial status of Essex County, though for now it seemed a logical move of upward mobility.

Portsmouth, New Hampshire, where John Langdon had done so well bankrolling privateers he'd built a bridge for the town, also flourished, as did coastal communities in Connecticut and Delaware. Philadelphia and Providence were thriving, though Newport, Savannah, and Charleston still struggled after their lengthy British occupations.

All in all, East summarizes, "the country was not left in the deplorable economic state frequently attributed to it." The demographics had shifted, however. In addition to established merchants who'd successfully exploited the war's freewheeling commercial environment, America's wealthy now included the entrepreneurs of Revolutionary trade and privateering, "a small but vigorous set of newcomers, invariably young in years but national in viewpoint, who were prepared to take the business bit in their teeth and set a faster pace for the future."

Franklin, returning to America in 1785, noted the new construction and abundance of goods seemingly indicative of a healthy economy. But shipping tonnage was in decline. While exports continued to sell, imports plummeted after a brief, postwar inundation from European merchants backlogged with surplus from the long conflict. Euphoric in the first months after victory, Americans welcomed the glut with a consuming spree; the resulting debt showed up in increased bankruptcies two years later. The military was no longer the insatiable customer for equipment and food it had been. When European economies faltered under the weight of their war debt, demand fell for American lumber, flour, and tobacco, further hurting farmers and merchants.

American privateer commissions were revoked by a Marine Committee decree signed by Robert Morris in March 1783. Yet in Boston, even with privateers no longer delivering prizes laden with desirable cargoes, there was enough supply to last for seven years sitting in local warehouses. Inventory was sold at a loss. Ships sat empty, crews idle.

The scene was repeated all along the coast. But lacking the agricultural hinterlands of New York, Philadelphia, and the south, ports in Massachusetts and Rhode Island felt the slowdown more acutely. Their situation worsened after Britain, through its navigation act of 1783, vindictively tried to restrict American trade with its West Indian colonies. The same businessmen who'd leaped into privateering again took innovative steps in response. They undercut European prices by as much as 20 percent to tempt island merchants to defy the law and accept American bargains. And with traditional markets in Britain, France, and Spain drying up, they used expertise gained in running privateers to promote commerce with Russia and Scandinavia and, most importantly, to open trade with China.

In the last years of Revolutionary privateering, the trend had been for larger vessels that could stay at sea longer, carry extensive armaments and prize crews, and yet still sail fast. Refitting these for transport was only part of the immense cost of sending them on distant trade expeditions, which could run as high as $100,000. But the war's many privateer partnerships, formed to share expenses and distribute risk, found a perfect application in these global ventures. Legal firms and insurance consortiums were on hand to facilitate arrangements as they'd done with countless privateer ventures just a few years earlier. Most of these were based in Boston, so Boston soon became the center of America's Far East trade.

Some of the wealthiest privateer investors launched expeditions on their own. Elias Hasket Derby refitted his large warship *Grand Turk* and dispatched it, with one of his privateer skippers at the helm, to Canton, China, in 1785. The venture must have done well, for five years later he laid out half his fortune to mount another that returned profits four times the original cost. His Salem neighbors, the Cabots, similarly had the means, the vessels, and the captains, to mount expeditions themselves. So did the Browns in Providence.

But the Revolution's greatest effect on business practices had been to accustom individualist Americans to financial partnerships and institutions. Thus national, state, and eventually private banks proliferated as the new century progressed, and speculation and trade became driven as much by syndicates as by separate merchants. These syndicates sprang up in towns throughout America and became the preferred business mechanism not only for aggressive newcomers but for the "conservative element" that in the past had operated either alone or strictly with family members.

Privateering—daunting in its risks, irresistible in its potential rewards—had stimulated this collective capitalism. The postwar depression fixed it in the American landscape as a way to share the pain of slowdown and the fruits of recovery. As for other consequences, East puts it plainly. "The tendency of hard times was to weed out the smaller businessmen to the eventual benefit of the larger; and to evolve more highly organized business communities, all of which cleared the way for greater business activity in the later years."

Slavers, by contrast, rarely worked in partnerships. How many there were—that is, how many New England maritime magnates kept their slave ship investments separate from other ventures in their portfolios—will never fully be known. Various penalties and proscriptions relating to the African slave trade were adopted around New England between 1780 and 1788. Aside from its illicitness, slavery's disrepute induced most men to hush up their involvement. "After the ban of 1788," the historian James A. Rawley observes, "Bostonians concealed their clandestine activities." He adds, "Their heirs have not been disposed to place the family records in public repositories."

The south had slavery's buyers and brokers; Virginia and South Carolina were the main receiving points. New England had the expertise to outfit and insure the transport ships. The main towns from which voyages launched had been leaders in privateering: Boston and Salem; Newport, Providence, and Bristol in Rhode Island; and to a much lesser extent, Portsmouth, New York, and Philadelphia. But to call it a similar social phenomenon misses the point that privateering's preference for cooperative ventures was almost entirely absent from New England slaving.

Instead of partnerships, businessmen and families usually put up the money alone. That their names are few in number is deceptive, since most, "working through middlemen and correspondents," hid their participation from public scrutiny. The major known participants in the postwar slave trade—the Graftons of Salem, the

Perkinses of Boston, the Champlins of Newport, and the D'Wolfs of Bristol—had been active in privateering but not on the level of the Cabots, Derbys, and Tracys. Only rarely does one of those top-tier names appear in the records as an owner of a ship bound for Africa. With more money in hand and more reputation to lose, they were perhaps less tempted by the profits of slaving; perhaps they concealed their activities better; or perhaps they were repulsed by the business.

A database of vessels launched between 1783 and 1810 compiled by James A. McMillin in *The Final Victims* shows that many were former privateers or converted prizes. Privateering's larger vessels presented obvious advantages for slave transport. And since slave ships, even large ones, required as few as nine crewmen, there was plenty of room for human cargo. Skippers were often former privateer masters. Some were young members of the same few clans that funded the ventures, apprenticing in the family trade.

Roughly a hundred slave voyages, with a capacity of ten thousand Africans, are known to have sailed from North America in the 1780s. The actual number is certainly greater; there are many examples of ships registering as whalers and cargo ships to disguise their purpose. The majority originated in New England. In 1783 a news item from Africa reported that many, "mostly from Boston," were bringing in rum to exchange for slaves. Two years later a British visitor counted six ships, "from Boston and its vicinity," waiting offshore "to take slaves only, and more are daily expected."

Three-fifths of all North American slave ships came from Rhode Island, a statistic in keeping with its obdurate iconoclasm. In 1781, calling it "a yoke of tyranny," Rhode Island had rejected a national impost tax proposed by Robert Morris to help settle Congress's debts; suspicions of centralized government likewise made it the last of the original colonies to ratify the Constitution, and only then after asserting that federal taxes be levied "in such way and manner as the legislature of this state shall judge best." Similarly, antislavery laws that were unassailable in most northern states were subject to hot debate and frequent violation in Rhode Island. Moses Brown led the push for anti-slave trade legislation. His brother John led the resistance, often diluting the fines and restrictions down to a point of inconsequence.

John funded several slave voyages but not nearly as many as others in the state, especially James and Henry D'Wolf, who funded dozens. Rather, his main contribution to the trade was as an unabashed advocate for its perpetuation on competitive grounds. He argued that businessmen had a right "to enjoy the benefits of a trade permitted by all the European nations." It supported rum distillers and put revenues in the treasury, and as for its alleged inhumanity, the slave trade benefited Africans since it "much bettered their condition," he said.

Harassed and shamed by his brother, (and in fact sued several times by Moses's abolitionist group), John was privately uneasy about slaving and claimed to be forced into it "from necessity, seeing no other way to pay the revenue of the United State to whom I owed near 100,000 dollars." Though he indeed had sunk much of his manufacturing and privateer wealth into postwar investments that the economy's downturn sharply reduced, his whining drew no sympathy from Moses.

On the contrary, Moses pointed out that John had "found means" to influence jurors to lower fines levied against him for trafficking in slaves, and he charged that John's complaint of persecution by Rhode Island leaders was disingenuous, since in truth he would have been "prosecuted more severely had it not been for the influence of those he calls his enemies."

Yet even while condemning his brother, Moses seemed to understand that John was helplessly addicted to slaving's high profits. John promised him several times, "I shall not be any more concerned in the guinea trade," only to relapse. In 1787 he vowed that henceforth Moses could "do what you think right respecting the proposed prohibition." A year later, needing funds to support the expansion of his fishing fleet and the construction of a gin distillery, he mounted two quick expeditions to Africa.

As late as 1800, the addiction still held. Moses wrote a friend that

John "has now a ship he has been refitting which if he does not sell I fear he would, again, be tempted to send on a slave voyage." The only reason that voyage never materialized was that John found a more profitable venture, dispatching his refitted privateer, *General Washington*, on a two-year expedition to China.

John's lust for speculation was matched by other appetites. When he died in 1803 his nickname, "the Providence Colossus," was as much a tribute to his girth as to his commercial stature. In the last years of his life he devoted much energy to Rhode Island College; he'd served as its treasurer for twenty-five years. He was a fierce advocate for public education, scolding wealthy citizens who educated their children privately when "hundreds there is in this town who is not able to build a house to school their children in."

A year after John's death, his nephew endowed a professorship of English oratory in his uncle's name. The college subsequently changed its name to Brown University in honor of its benefactors. In 2003 it sponsored a multiyear study of the controversial issue of government reparations for slavery. University president Ruth J. Simmons termed the inquiry "a special obligation" due, she wrote, to "Brown's history."

In his biography of the clan, *The Browns of Providence Plantations*, James B. Hedges illuminates John's moral obstinacy while crediting him at least with a lack of hypocrisy. And while acknowledging his contributions to the Revolution and to higher education, Hedges ultimately highlights the one objective John sought above all others: "A record such as this can hold its own with that of the best businessmen of the period."

A truer epitaph never was written.

PROVIDENCE, RHODE ISLAND

Andrew Sherburne was one of the last men released from the Brooklyn prison ships, remaining until after George III declared an end to hostilities in the spring of 1783. In five months of confinement on *Jersey*, "I had some trying scenes to pass through," he later recalled. It was an understatement.

Sherburne's memoir, written forty years after the war, grimly details *Jersey*'s omnipresent hardship, despair, and death. Yet one of its strongest passages carries no physical descriptions. Of rumors that ran among the prisoners that so much death could only result from jailers poisoning their food, he simply shakes his head. "No—there was no such mercy there. Nothing was employed which could blunt the susceptibility to anguish, or which, by hastening death, could rob its agonies of a single pang."

Penniless and lame from frostbite suffered the past winter (he'd often awoke covered in snow that blew in through the seams of *Jersey*'s decrepit planking), Sherburne was ferried to Newport with a boatload of other ex-prisoners. From there, he traveled by horse and foot to Portsmouth, arriving home just before his nineteenth birthday.

Five years later, he returned to New York seeking back pay for his service on the Continental sloop *Ranger*. It amounted to "about seventy-three dollars, worth at this time between twelve and thirteen cents on the dollar." From town he walked to the East River and gazed across to Wallabout Bay, "where yet lay that wretched old prison ship where I had suffered almost everything but death." On the far shore, the sand embankment "under which a large majority of my shipmates had left their bones" lay barren and unmarked. "I shall not undertake to describe the sensations of my soul on this occasion."

Never fully healthy again, Sherburne had trouble finding work. Eventually he established himself as a schoolteacher, got married and had children, then became a Baptist minister and military chaplain in the War of 1812. He published his memoir in 1828 for two reasons. Regarding his children's welfare, he was "not ashamed to confess that the avails which may arise from the sale of this humble performance must be almost their only inheritance." And he believed that through reading of his travails, "Americans may properly appreciate the freedom which they enjoy while they learn the price of its purchase."

At a dollar per copy, the book sold well. Some people bought it out of charity "to relieve the declining years" of its author. Others wanted to understand "the sufferings and deliverances of our naval prisoners during the Revolutionary conflict."

Sherburne's gratitude for their patronage is best captured in his expression of lifelong debt to the citizens of Rhode Island, who, in a welcome revision of the colony's reputation for rank self-interest, had generously opened their homes and pocketbooks to the emaciated, traumatized, lice-ridden mariners after their release from *Jersey*.

Ashamed of their haggard appearance, the privateersmen initially had declined what was the first of many offers of food and lodging from local families. "We are not fit to be where clean people are."

Their hosts would have none of it. "Come, sit down and make yourselves as comfortable as you can. You must have had a hard time of it. You have been sick. But now you have got among your friends again." Sherburne saw tears in their eyes as they spoke. "I scarcely know of any one circumstance in my life that has more frequently occurred to my mind than this."

Resuming their northward trek the next morning, he and his

companions walked through Providence and saw its bustle of new construction. It was spring, the war was over, and they were going home. The power of the moment overwhelmed them. "We could not help but exalt that we had once more set our feet in the land of liberty."

Notes

Abbreviations

NDAR   *Naval Documents of the American Revolution*
Naval Historical Center, Washington, DC
NGP   *Papers of General Nathanael Greene*
Rhode Island Historical Society, Providence, RI
SDP   *Silas Deane Papers*
New-York Historical Society, New York, NY

Prologue

xiii   *"very much torn"*: William Bartlett to George Washington, April 11, 1775, NDAR, vol. 2, p. 881.
"'Tis luck": Captain John Collins to Vice Admiral Samuel Graves, Oct. 12, 1775, NDAR, vol. 2, p. 417.
"very badly" and *"blowed off"*: Almanacs of John White and William Wetmore, Oct. 10, 1775, NDAR, vol. 2, p. 386.
xiv   *"burn, sink, and destroy"*: Admiral Samuel Graves to Captain James Wallace, Sept. 17, 1775, NDAR, vol. 2, p. 129.
"Graves and his harpies": William Tudor to John Adams, Sept. 30, 1775, NDAR, vol. 2, p. 248.
"a thief": Comments of a New York Tory, NDAR, vol. 1, p. 1269.
"their loose discipline": Journal of Ambrose Serle, July 13, 1776, NDAR, vol. 5, p. 1062.
"bold enough to dare": "Extract of a Letter from one of the fleet at Boston, Dated Nov. 30, 1775," NDAR, vol. 3, p. 1203.

Introduction

xvi   *"in the land way"*: George Washington to Benedict Arnold, Dec. 5, 1775, NDAR, vol. 2, p. 1283.

xvii   *righteous zeal:* Robert A. East, *Business Enterprise in the American Revolutionary Era*, p. 27.

xviii *the lowest taxed:* Robert Harvey, *A Few Bloody Noses*, p. 4.

       "This corrupt age": Nathanael Greene to Griffin Greene, May 25, 1778, NGP, vol. 2, p. 405.

       "a gamester's hope": Nathanael Greene to Jacob Greene, May 6, 1778, NGP, vol. 2, p. 381.

       "doing something constantly": Robert C. Alberts, *The Golden Voyage*, p. 36.

       "to sink Britain": George Washington to John Augustine Washington, July 7, 1775, NDAR, vol. 1, p. 983.

xix   *"this country likewise":* Sheldon S. Cohen, *Yankee Sailors in British Gaols*, p. 28.

xx   *"some accident":* Helen Augur, *The Secret War of Independence*, p. 234.

       "insult": Lord Stormont to Lord Weymouth, April 16, 1777, NDAR, vol. 8, p. 772.

xxi   *"No kind of business":* Gardner Weld Allen, *Massachusetts Privateers of the Revolution*, p. 15.

xxii *The date is interesting:* Mack Thompson, *Moses Brown*, p. 15.

ONE

3   *"disturbed our navigation":* William R. Staples, *The Documentary Description of the Destruction of the Gaspee*, p. 3.

      "stormy petrel": East, p. 71.

      "lose the whole": James B. Hedges, *The Browns of Providence Plantations*, p. 16.

      "reputation for contraband": Harvey, p. 12.

4   *"out of my line":* Samuel Adams to James Warren, Feb. 1, 1777, *Samuel Adams Papers.*

      "gentlemen of this town": Staples, p. 3.

      "hogstealer": Merrill Jensen, *The Founding of a Nation*, p. 425.

      "conveniences": Gordon S. Wood, *The American Revolution*, p. 13.

5   *"salutary neglect":* Ibid., p. 18.

      "I have devoted": Nathanael Greene to Samuel Ward, Jr., April, 1772, NGP, vol. 1, p. 26.

6   *"my duty"* and *"unwarrantable":* Staples, p. 5.

      "a pirate himself": Ibid., p. 6.

      "as bait": Ibid., p. 8.

      "violent infringement": Samuel Adams, *The Rights of the Colonists, A List of the Violations of Rights and a Letter of Correspondence*, Nov. 20, 1772, *Samuel Adams Papers.*

7   *"brutal, hoggish":* John Adams diary 19, 16 Dec. 1772–18 Dec. 1773, *Adams Family Papers.*

      "you have no business" and *"ridiculous errands":* Staples, p. 6.

7   *"the opposite point"*: The Saturday Evening Post, vol. VIII, no. 421.
    Philadelphia, Aug. 22, 1829.
8   *"I am the sheriff"*: Staples, p. 14.
    "penalty" and *"gold laced beaver"*: Ibid., p. 108.
    "daring insult": Ibid., p. 25.
9   *"take an advantage"*: Hedges, p. 206.
    "the self-denial of their neighbors": Ibid., 204.
    "Star Chamber Court": John Adams diary 19, 16 Dec. 1772–18 Dec. 1773,
    Adams Family Papers.
    "such provocation": Samuel Adams to Darius Sessions, Jan. 2, 1773, *Samuel
    Adams Papers.*
    "We were all sensible": Thomas Jefferson, July 27, 1821, *Thomas Jefferson Papers.*
    "bears no resemblance": Charles Dudley to Admiral Montagu, July 23, 1772,
    Gaspee Papers, Manuscripts Collection of the Rhode Island Historical Society.
10 *"public emolument"*: Thompson, p. 57.
    "zeal": Ibid., p. 62.
    "ruffled shirts": Staples, p. 87.
    "principal inhabitants": Ibid., p. 105.
    "general bad character" through *"could not possibly be guilty of"*: Ibid., p. 35.
11 *"no intimation"*: Ibid., p. 87.
    "no probability": Ibid., p. 105.
    "whatever reparation": Editor's note, NGP, vol. 1, p. 34
    "exceeding tempestious": Ibid., p. 35.
12 *"drunken sailors"*: Susan Danforth. "No New Taxes! Conflicts that led up to
    the burning of the *Gaspee.*" The Bridge, *Newspaper of the Pawtuxet Village
    Association,* Spring 2003, p. 3.
    "the holding of Negroes in slavery": Thompson, p. 83.
13 *"unrighteous traffic"*: Hedges, p. 82.
    "love of money": Ibid., p. 341.
    "the arch individualist": Ibid., p. 84.
    "mad fits": Nicholas Cooke to Samuel Ward, July 7, 1775, NDAR, vol. 2,
    p. 972.
14 *"a more moderate and conciliatory attitude"*: Thompson, p. 112.
    "binding" and *"in the power of this colony"*: Hedges, p. 213.
15 *"sincerity"* and *"so clear in opinion"*: Ibid., p. 214.
    "Divine providence": Nicholas Brown to Nathanael Greene, Feb. 2, 1776,
    NGP, vol. 1, p. 191.
    "for want of them": George Washington to Philip J. Schuyler, November 16,
    1775, *The George Washington Papers at the Library of Congress, 1741–1799.*
    "a generous price": Journal of the Continental Congress, July 15, 1775, NDAR,
    vol. 1, p. 892.
    "undue advantage": George Washington to Nicholas Cooke, Aug. 31, 1775,
    The George Washington Papers at the Library of Congress, 1741–1799.

16 *"give them the preference":* John Brown to George Washington, Nov. 3, 1775, NDAR, vol. 1, p. 871.

"entirely failed": Hedges, p. 219.

"run in by night": Nicholas Brown to Captain Sylvanus Jenckes, Jan. 19, 1776, NDAR, vol. 3, p. 859.

17 *"It unfortunately happened":* Narrative of Willing, Morris & Co. to the Secret Committee of the Continental Congress, Sept. 19, 1775, NDAR, vol. 2, p. 329.

"good Florence oil": Nicholas Brown to Captain James Westcott, Feb. 14, 1776, NDAR, vol. 3, p. 1278.

18 *"Powder expected to fall":* William Spear to John Spear, Jan. 1, 1776, NDAR, vol. 3, p. 659.

"vitriolic" exchanges: East, p. 130.

19 *"many accusations"* and *"as deeply engaged":* Hedges, p. 271.

1775 MACHIAS, MAINE

20 *"fouling pieces":* Edgar Stanton Maclay, *A History of American Privateers,* p. 56.
21 *"the special malice":* Ibid., p. 61.
22 *"not pay any regard":* Petition of Boston Committee to the Massachusetts General Court, July 13, 1776, NDAR, vol. 5. p. 1055.

"unjustly received": Journal of the Massachusetts Council, Nov. 16, 1776, NDAR, vol. 7, p. 184.

"glad they've got rid of him": John Bradford to John Hancock, March 6, 1777, NDAR, vol. 8, p. 36.

Two

23 *"gradual and therefore incurable":* Edmund Burke to Lord Rockingham, Sept. 14, 1775, NDAR, vol. 2, p. 716.

a tentative approach to warfare: Wood, p. 79.

24 *"Where is the boasted navy":* "Intelligence from London," Sept. 25, 1775, NDAR, vol. 2, p.733.

"power to plunder anything": Governor James Wright to Admiral Samuel Graves, NDAR, vol 1, June 27, 1775. p. 764.

"continually popping out": Narrative of Vice Admiral Graves, Sept. 1, 1775, NDAR, vol. 1, p. 1282.

"put on the appearance": Admiral Samuel Graves to Captain George Vandeput, July 18, 1775, NDAR, vol. 1, p. 913.

"the most ungracious duty": Mark M. Boatner III, *Encyclopedia of the American Revolution,* p. 446.

24 *"more hated and despised"*: "Extract of a letter from Boston, Aug. 19, 1775,"
NDAR, vol. 1, p. 1183.
"in every way more harassed": Admiral Samuel Graves to Philip Stephens,
Sept. 12, 1775, NDAR, vol. 2, p. 83.

25 *"all the calamities"*: George Washington to the inhabitants of Bermuda, Sept.
6, 1775, NDAR, vol. 2, p. 28.
"care of Mr. Hugh James": Anonymous letter to New York Committee of
Safety, Nov. 4, 1775, NDAR, vol. 2, p. 885.
"under the sole guidance": James Thomas Flexner, *George Washington in the
American Revolution*, p. 50.

26 *"deliberated at intervals"*: Douglas Southall Freeman, *George Washington*, vol. 3,
p. 529.
"A fortunate capture": Chester G. Hearn, *George Washington's Schooners*, p. 7.
"a great means of protecting": Nicholas Cooke to the Massachusetts
Committee of Safety, June 27, 1775, NDAR, vol. 1, p. 762.
"at the yard arm" and *"always catch a man"*: Sally D. Wilson, "Who Was
Whipple?" *Revolutionary Portraits: People, Places and Events from Rhode
Island's Historic Past*, Providence: Rhode Island Bicentennial Foundation,
1976, p. 6.
"a speedy reconciliation": Benjamin Franklin to Silas Deane, Aug. 27, 1775,
NDAR, vol. 1, p. 1243.

27 *"quixoticism indeed"*: Donald W. Beattie and J. Richard Collins, *Washington's
New England Fleet*, p. vi.
"pecuniary zeal": E. James Ferguson, *The Power of the Purse*, p. 10.
"The delicacy is absurd": William Tudor to John Adams, Sept. 30, 1775,
NDAR, vol. 2, p. 248.
"equip any vessel": Massachusetts Act Authorizing Privateers and Creating
Courts of Admiralty, Nov. 1, 1775, NDAR, vol. 3, p. 834.

28 *"can we doubt the propriety"*: Elbridge Gerry to Samuel Adams, Oct. 9, 1775,
NDAR, vol. 2, p. 369.
"not less than one hundred": Elias Hasket Derby to Nathaniel Silsbee, Feb. 23,
1776, NDAR, vol. 3, p. 1245.
"intercept transports daily": "Letter from the Camp at Cambridge," Oct. 1,
1775, NDAR, vol. 2, p. 262.

29 *"so basely sordid"*: George Washington to the New York Provincial Congress,
Aug. 8, 1775, NDAR, vol. 1, p. 1093.
"The price you mention" through *"the General is much dissatisfied"*: Joseph Reed
to John Glover, Oct. 16 and 17, 1775, NDAR, vol. 2, pp. 472, 474.

30 *"the idlest scoundrels"*: Stephen Moylan to Joseph Reed, Oct. 21, 1775, NDAR,
vol. 2, p. 598.
"all prizes": Agreement between Jonathan Glover and William Bartlett, Nov.
14, 1775, NDAR, vol. 2, p. 1019.
"too polite": Beattie and Collins, p. 5.

30 *"rules which take place"*: Hearn, p. 12.
31 *"He met us on the steps"*: Ibid., p. 46.
32 *"not a competent judge"*: Ibid, p. 44.
  "sectional balancing": Charles Royster, *A Revolutionary People at War*, p. 108.
  "attacked by a twenty gun ship": Diary of Ezekiel Price, Dec. 12, 1775, NDAR, vol. 3, p. 96.
33 *"totally unserviceable"*: Carpenters' Survey of the Armed Brig *Washington*, Dec. 8, 1775, NDAR, vol. 3, p. 9.
  "hanged as traitors": "Extract of a Letter from Portsmouth," Jan. 21, 1776, NDAR, vol. 3, p. 522.
  "voluntarily, which was false": Hearn, p. 75.
  "Uncertainty about the fate": Beattie and Collins, p. 14.
34 *"to secure and detain"*: Cohen, p. 27.
  "and never fired since": Captain William Coit to Major Samuel Blachley Webb, Nov. 11, 1775, NDAR, vol. 2, p. 914.
  "stripping the prizes": Beattie and Collins, p. 39.
  "plague, trouble, and vexation": George Washington to the Continental Congress, Dec. 4, 1775, *The George Washington Papers at the Library of Congress, 1741–1799.*
35 *"deficiency of public spirit"*: Hearn, p. 68.
  "the most fortunate circumstance": Stephen Moylan to William Bartlett, Nov. 26, 1775, NDAR, vol. 2, p. 1160.
  "universal joy": Caspar F. Goodrich, "Washington's Attitude Toward the Navy," *The Washington Association of New Jersey Archive* (1907).
  "opened with a tragedy": Brigadier General Horatio Gates to Benjamin Franklin, Dec. 5, 1775, NDAR, vol., 2, p. 1283.
  Jefferson's giddy estimate: Thomas Jefferson to John Page, Dec. 10, 1775, NDAR, vol. 3, p. 39.
  "made their fortunes": Edward Green to Joshua Green, Dec. 3, 1775, NDAR, vol. 2, p. 1247.
36 *digging graves*: Account submitted in connection with the capture of the British schooner, *Margaretta*, Oct. 14, 1775, NDAR, vol. 2, p. 448.
  "with regard to such vessels": William Bartlett to George Washington, Nov. 9, 1775, NDAR, vol. 2, p. 944.
37 *"make out abstracts"*: Beattie and Collins, p. 39.
  "having received no instruction": Hearn, p. 154.
  "They will have cash" through *"it will be impossible"*: Beattie and Collins, p. 38.
38 *"nothing but enmity"*: Hearn, p. 100.
  "we must have them": Beattie and Collins, p. 17.
  "any goods, wares, or merchandize": Ibid., p. 18.
  "libeled in the courts": Ibid., p. 38.
39 *"the uncertainty"*: Will of John Earnest Kessler, Aug. 3, 1776, NDAR, vol. 6, p. 28.

39 *"I am informed":* Jonathan Glover to Samuel Tucker, Feb. 3, 1776, NDAR, vol. 3, p. 1108.

"Providence militates": Morning Post and Daily Advertiser, Jan. 8, 1776, NDAR, vol. 3, p. 488.

"tamely and supinely": Hearn, p. 108.

"laid upon the admiral": Ibid., p. 107.

"good for nothing": Ibid., p. 106.

40 *"during the continuance":* London Gazette, Tuesday, Dec. 19, to Saturday, Dec. 23, 1775, NDAR, vol. 3, p. 440.

"not one in ten": A Loyalist Captain to Abraham Van Alstyne, Feb. 4, 1776, NDAR, vol. 3, p. 1129.

"expect many more losses": Robert Morris to John Langdon, April 4, 1776, NDAR, vol. 4, p. 664.

"for the good of the country": Andrew Brown to the Massachusetts General Court, Mar. 28, 1776, NDAR, vol. 4, p. 546.

41 *"old prejudices":* Joseph Reed to George Washington, March 7, 1776, NDAR, vol. 4, p. 219.

"however numerous our cruisers": Vice Admiral Molyneux Shuldham to Philip Stevens, Feb. 26, 1776, NDAR, vol. 4, p. 83.

"I cannot suppose": Vice Admiral James Young to Count de Nozieres, March 9, 1776, NDAR, vol. 4, p. 279.

42 *"astonished":* Count de Nozieres to Vice Admiral James Young, March 14, 1776, NDAR, vol. 4, p. 346.

"my heart was much engaged": John Adams to Abigail Adams, April 28, 1776, NDAR, vol. 4, p. 1296.

"intelligence from America": James Young to Philip Stephens, April 7, 1776, NDAR, vol. 4, p. 703.

"reinforce your squadron": Philip Stephens to James Young, May 20, 1776, NDAR, vol. 4, p. 1130.

43 *"precarious and defenseless":* John Brown to Vice Admiral Clark Gayton, March 22, 1776, NDAR, vol. 4, p. 461.

"surveys and attestations": "Intelligence from a London Newspaper," Jan. 10, 1776, NDAR, vol. 3, p. 498.

"Time is drawing fast": Captain Charles Pope to Thomas Rodney, Aug. 1, 1776, NDAR, vol. 6, p. 8.

1776 BOSTON, MASSACHUSETTS

44 *"many towns contend":* Ronald N. Tagney, *The World Turned Upside Down*, p. 201.

"wind being easterly": Richard Devens to John Adams, May 17, 1776, NDAR, vol. 5, p. 133.

45 *"Don't give up the vessel"*: Tagney, p. 209.
    "ferocity rather than bravery": Hearn, p. 221.

THREE

47 *"brilliant marriages"*: Kalman Goldstein. "Silas Deane: Preparation for Rascality," pp. 75–97.

48 *"a peculiar fatality"*: Silas Deane to Elizabeth Deane, March 1, 1776, SDP, vol. 1, p. 119.
    "How tedious": Robert Morris to Silas Deane, March 10, 1776, NDAR, vol. 4, p. 284.
    "circumstances by no means favorable": Ferguson, p. 25.
    "a leading young merchant": East, p. 126.
    "vast designs": Boatner, p. 742.
    "some deep design": East, p. 197.

50 *"If my services had been more conspicuous"*: Alberts, p. 463.
    "I have known very honest men": Goldstein, p. 77.

51 *"connive at certain things"*: Augur, p. 130.
    "we have been so unfortunate": Brian N. Morton and Donald C. Spinelli, *Beaumarchais and the American Revolution*, p. 58.

52 *"beneficial commercial intercourse"*: Memoir of the Commerce of America and Its Importance to Europe, Aug. 15, 1776, SDP, vol. 1, p. 184.
    "Look upon my house": Morton and Spinelli, p. 64.

53 *"The want of instructions"*: Silas Deane to the Secret Committee, SDP, vol. 1, p. 342.
    "extremely uneasy": Silas Deane to the Secret Committee, Oct. 1, 1776, SDP, vol. 1, p. 287.
    "considerable quantities of stuff": Secret Committee to Silas Dean, Oct. 1, 1776, SDP, vol. 1, p. 294.
    "Politics and my business": Silas Deane to the Secret Committee, Nov. 1776, SDP, vol. 1, p. 343.

54 *"especially soldiers of fortune"*: Beaumarchais to Silas Deane, July 26, 1776, SDP, vol. 1, p. 166.
    "unable to say nay": Morton and Spinelli, p. 80.
    "give character and credit": Augur, p. 144.
    "Harassed to death": Silas Deane to the Secret Committee, Nov. 28, 1776, SDP, vol. 1, p. 371.
    "I hope the terms": Silas Deane to the Secret Committee, Nov. 6, 1776, SDP, vol. 1, p. 340.
    "of the first property": Silas Deane to the Secret Committee, Oct. 1, 1776, SDP, vol. 1, p. 291.

55 *"skirmish rather than battle"*: Silas Deane to Vergennes, Oct. 17, 1776, SDP, vol. 1, p. 322.

55 *"what is certain":* Giambattista Pizzoni to her government in Venice, July 12, 1776, NDAR, vol. 6, p. 474.

56 *"fond of parade":* Silas Deane to the Secret Committee, Nov. 28, 1776, SDP, vol. 1, p. 371.

"any number of recruits": Silas Deane to the Secret Committee, Nov. 2, 1776, SDP, vol. 1, p. 339.

"United Independent States": Silas Deane to the Secret Committee, Oct. 17, 1776, SDP, vol. 1, p. 324.

"If the reverse": Silas Deane to the Secret Committee, Oct 17, 1776, SDP, vol. 1, p. 327.

57 *"the order issued by Congress":* Vergennes to Garnier, June 21, 1776, NDAR, vol. 6, p. 431.

"striking proof": Silas Deane to the Secret Committee, Dec. 1, 1776, SDP, vol. 1, p. 389.

"capital stroke": Silas Deane to John Jay, Dec. 3, 1776, SDP, vol. 1, p. 396.

58 *"unless some powerful aid":* Augur, p. 152.

"I rise at six": Silas Deane to Elizabeth Deane, July 9, 1776, SDP, vol. 1, p. 71.

"very charitable": Silas Deane to Jonathan Williams, Jan. 13, 1778, SDP, vol. 2, p. 327.

59 *"they belong to Willing & Morris":* Maryland Council of Safety to the Maryland Delegates in the Continental Congress, June 1, 1776, NDAR, vol. 5, p. 341.

60 *"extensive connections":* Robert Morris to Silas Deane, Sept. 12, 1776, NDAR, vol. 6, p. 793.

"linens": Willing & Morris to William Bingham, June 3, 1776, NDAR, vol. 5, p. 361.

61 *"solicit in your behalf":* Silas Deane to the Committee of Secret Correspondence, Nov. 6, 1776, NDAR, vol. 7, p. 728.

"2/3ds on account": Robert Morris to Silas Deane, Aug. 11, 1776, NDAR, vol. 6, p. 147.

62 *"be ever mindful":* Robert Morris to Silas Deane, Oct. 2, 1776, SDP, vol. 1, p. 305.

"at least twenty-two hours": Frederick Wagner, *Robert Morris*, p. 44.

"the lowest reptiles": Augur, p. 229.

64 *"entirely an American":* Ibid., p. 259.

"an indissoluble partnership": Julian P. Boyd, "Silas Deane: Death by a Kindly Teacher of Treason?" I, p. 187.

"it costs something": Silas Deane to John Jay, Dec. 3, 1776, NDAR, vol. 1, p. 396.

65 *"If I was sure":* Evan Thomas, *John Paul Jones*, p. 101.

66 *"soon boarded her"* through *"know not how to replace":* Captain Lambert Wickes to Samuel Wickes, July 2, 1776, NDAR, vol. 5, p. 883.

67 *"a stop be put":* Margaret Brown, "William Bingham," p. 76.

"with as much respect": London Chronicle, April 29, 1777, NDAR, vol. 8, p. 478.

"the risk may be divided": Brown, p. 59.

68 *"fast sailing"*: Ibid., p. 57.
"persons on the spot": Willing & Morris to William Bingham, Dec. 6, 1776, NDAR, vol. 7, p. 387.
"If Congress means": Wagner, p. 35.
69 *"we want to throw funds"*: Ferguson, p. 80.
"an officer in Morris's position": Ferguson, p. 77.
70 *"If the American cruisers"*: Alberts, p. 30.
"hitherto only attempted": Brown, p. 67.
"harmony and exchange": Alberts, p. 58.
71 *"Whoever can pay the most"*: Vergennes to M. Garnier, June 21, 1776, NDAR, vol. 6, p. 430.
72 *"unholy spectacle"*: Allen, p. 18.
"all the French pirates": "News from St. Christopher," April 12, 1777, NDAR, vol. 8, p. 333.
"rather too young": Committee of Secret Correspondence to the Commissioners in France, Dec. 30, 1776, NDAR, vol. 7, p. 631.
"having had several vessels taken": Robert Morris to William Bingham, Dec. 4, 1776, NDAR, vol. 7, p. 368.
73 *"to increase the number"*: Robert Morris to William Bingham, April 25, 1777, vol. 8, p. 429.
"It is not necessary": Alberts, p. 55.
"experience could cure him": Robert Morris to Silas Deane, Sept . 12, 1776, NDAR, vol. 6, p. 793.
74 *"the real state of affairs"*: Count D'Argout to Gabriel de Sartine, December 23, 1776, NDAR, vol. 7, p. 588.
75 *"those who were foremost in noise"*: Wagner, p. 35.
"I shall remain here": Robert Morris to Silas Deane, Dec. 20, 1776, NDAR, vol. 7, p. 528.
76 *"Stocks are beginning to sink"*: Edward Bancroft to Silas Deane, February 1777, SDP, vol. 2, p. 5.
"three sets of the papers": The American Commissioners in France to the Secret Committee of the Continental Congress, Feb. 6, 1777, NDAR, vol. 8, p. 570.
77 *"a new and extensive world"*: Memoir of Silas Deane, Dec. 31, 1776, SDP, vol. 1, p. 442.

1776 PROVIDENCE, RHODE ISLAND

78 *"The common class of mankind"*: John Paul Jones to Robert Morris, Oct. 17, 1776, NDAR, vol. 6, p. 1302.
"divine service": "Rules for the Regulation of the Navy of the United Colonies," Nov. 28, 1775, NDAR, vol. 2, p. 1174.

80 *"Indian":* Assignment of Prize Money by Daniel Cocarry, Oct. 24, 1776, NDAR, vol. 6, p. 1399.

"Division, confusion": Owners of Privateer *Eagle* to William Ellery. Dec. 3, 1776, NDAR, vol. 7, p. 357.

Four

81 *"unheard-of":* Editor's note, NGP, vol. 1, p. 6.

"merchants in general": Nathanael Greene to Samuel Ward, Sr., Oct. 10, 1775, NGP, vol. 1, p. 138.

82 *more religious diversity:* "A Memorial to the Trustees and Fellows of Rhode Island College," NGP, vol. 1, p. 11.

"very early": Nathanael Greene to Samuel Ward, Jr., Oct. 9, 1772, NGP, vol. 1, p. 46.

"I am at variance": Nathanael Greene to Samuel Ward, Jr., Aug. 29, 1772, NGP, vol. 1, p. 38.

"tumult and uproars": Nathanael Greene to Samuel Ward, Jr., Sept. 24, 1770, NGP, vol. 1, p. 14.

"She confesses": John Buchanan, *The Road to Guilford Courthouse,* p. 10.

"Venus's War": Nathanael Greene to Elihue Greene, Sept. 6, 1776, NGP, vol. 1, p. 296.

83 *"Nothing but the affection":* John F. Stegeman and Janet A. Stegeman, *Caty,* p. 46.

"perpetually falling out": Nathanael Greene to Samuel Ward, Jr., Aug. 29, 1772, NGP, vol. 1, p. 44.

"a place in Connecticut": Buchanan, p. 262.

"the subject of ridicule": Ibid., p. 264.

84 *"spent lavishly":* Stegeman, p. 47.

"black pages": Ibid., p. 65.

85 *"great defects":* Nathanael Greene to Jacob Greene, June 28, 1775, NGP, vol. 1, p. 92.

"too dear a rate": Nathanael Greene to Nicholas Cooke, June 22, 1775, NGP, vol. 1, p.89.

"the cause of our bleeding country": Nicholas Brown to Nathanael Greene, Feb. 2, 1776, NGP, vol. 1, p. 191.

86 *"Were I at liberty":* Nathanael Greene to Jacob Greene, Oct. 3, 1775, NGP, vol. 1, p. 305.

87 *"a few zealous officers":* Nathanael Greene to Jacob Greene, March 17, 1778, NGP, vol. 2, p. 317.

88 *"necessary additional works":* Hedges, p. 270.

89 *Washington advised Congress to scuttle them:* William M. Fowler, Jr., *Rebels Under Sail,* p. 215.

89   *"wrong or unjust things"*: John Langdon to Josiah Bartlett, July 28, 1776, NDAR, vol. 5, p. 1259.

"*extortioners*": John Langdon to Josiah Bartlett, Sept. 14, 1776, NDAR, vol. 6, p. 815.

"*against the public good*": Continental Marine Committee to Rhode Island Frigate Committee, Oct. 9, 1776, NDAR, vol. 6, p. 1187.

"*to the prejudice*": Hedges, p. 271.

"*bear hard on the characters*": Journal of the Rhode Island Frigate Committee, Oct. 21, 1776, NDAR, vol. 6, p. 1348.

90   *"the two worst"*: Robert Morris to Silas Deane, Dec. 20, 1776, NDAR, vol. 7, p. 528.

"*My blood now boils*": John Langdon to William Whipple, Jan. 15, 1777, NDAR, vol. 7, p. 957.

"*a considerable number*": John Langdon to Josiah Bartlett, Sept. 14, 1776, NDAR, vol. 6, p. 815.

"*jealousy of one state*": Continental Marine Committee to Rhode Island Frigate Committee, Oct. 9, 1776, NDAR, vol. 6, p. 1187.

"*very fine ship*": Robert Morris to Silas Deane, Dec. 20, 1776, NDAR, vol. 7, p. 528

"*they want to be out after prize money*": John Langdon to Josiah Bartlett, Aug. 19, 1776, NDAR, vol. 6, p. 229.

"*worthy friends at Providence*": John Langdon to John Hancock, Jan. 22, 1777, NDAR, vol. 7, p. 1011

"*come all you young fellows*": Application for Letter of Marque and Reprisal for sloop *Montgomery*, Aug. 8, 1776, NDAR, vol. 6, p. 117.

91   *"six soldiers killed"*: Lieutenant Colonel Archibald Campbell to Major General William Howe, June 19, 1776, NDAR, vol. 5, p. 619.

"*cannot be well avoided*": Owners of the Rhode Island privateer sloop *Diamond* to Captain Thomas Stacy, Aug. 21, 1776, NDAR, vol. 6, p. 252.

"*appurtenances and cargo*": *Providence Gazette*, Saturday, Oct. 12, 1776, NDAR, vol. 6, p. 1232.

"*the price affixed by law*": Hedges, p. 262.

"*double the property*": East, p. 78.

92   *"division of the plunder"*: Commodore Esek Hopkins to Stephen Hopkins, June 8, 1776, NDAR, vol. 5, p. 424.

"*not greatly superior*": Richard Buel, Jr., *In Irons*, p. 84.

"*after a dreadful slaughter*": *London Chronicle*, July 29, 1776, NDAR, vol. 6, p. 428.

93   *his reputation slid*: Thomas, p. 52.

"*owing to a number of members*": Commodore Esek Hopkins to John Hancock, Nov. 2, 1776, NDAR, vol. 7, p. 17.

"*favored their operation*": Esek Hopkins to the Continental Marine Committee, Dec. 10, 1776, NDAR, vol. 7, p. 435.

"*aid of our sister states*": Proclamation of Governor Nicholas Cooke, Dec. 7, 1776, NDAR, vol. 7, p. 395.

94 *"he does not improve":* John Bradford to Leonard Jarvis, June 18, 1777, NDAR, vol. 9, p. 135.

95 *"who was bred in a shop":* Thomas, p. 90.

"not that I've the least doubt": John Langdon to Robert Morris, Nov. 6, 1776, NDAR, vol. 7, p. 59.

"to the greatest advantage": William Bingham to John Langdon, July 14, 1777, NDAR, vol. 9, p. 288.

"to make their fortunes": Thomas, p. 88.

"Under the guise": John Bradford to Leonard Jarvis, June 18, 1777, NDAR, vol. 9, p. 135.

96 *"I must rely on you":* Captain John Paul Jones to Robert Morris, July 28, 1777, NDAR, vol. 9, p. 345.

1776 BROOKLYN, NEW YORK

97 *"crowded promiscuously together":* Timothy Parker to Governor Jonathan Trumbull, Dec. 9, 1776, NDAR, vol. 7, p. 421.

98 *"the greatest humanity":* South Carolina Navy Board to Captain Edward Allen, Jan. 16, 1777, NDAR, vol. 7, p. 977.

"they must starve": Observations by the Late Master of the British Ship *Spiers*, Sept. 1776, NDAR, vol. 7, p. 300.

"a man had better": Deposition of William Barry, June 11, 1776, NDAR, vol. 5, p. 481.

99 *"starving and dying each meal":* Deposition of Thomas Warner, Aug. 19, 1777, NDAR, vol. 9, p. 771.

"The prisoners to exchange": William Bell Clark, *Ben Franklin's Privateers*, p. v.

"panting, sweating, and fainting": "Humanitas" to the Lord Mayor of London, Aug. 5, 1776, NDAR, vol. 6, p. 529.

FIVE

101 *"'Tis our business to study":* David McCullough, *1776*, p. 206.

102 *"our troops are naked":* Nathanael Greene to General Alexander McDougall, Jan. 28, 1778, NGP, vol. 2, p. 259.

103 *"His Excellency presses it":* Nathanael Greene to General Henry Knox, Feb. 26, 1778, NGP, vol. 2, p. 294.

104 *"consistent with your honor":* Griffin Greene to Nathanael Greene, May 24, 1778, NGP, vol. 2, p. 401.

"You must not let people see": Nathanael Greene to Jacob Greene, May 24, 1778, NGP, vol. 2, p. 404.

"I have given extensive orders": Nathanael Greene to George Washington, May 3, 1778, NGP, vol. 2, p. 372.

104 *"partiality that His Excellency"*: Nathanael Greene to Griffin Greene, May 25, 1778, NGP, vol. 2, p. 405.

"how the public views me": Nathanael Greene to Jacob Greene, May 24, 1778, NGP, vol. 2, p. 404.

"Neither must you lend": Nathanael Greene to James Calhoun, Sept. 30, 1778, NGP, vol. 2, p. 528.

105 *"a thousand opportunities"*: Editor's note, NGP, vol. 2, p. 309–312.

"Let it be valued": Nathanael Greene to Jacob Greene, June 4, 1777, NGP, vol. 2, p. 104.

"while it rains upon us": Nathanael Greene to Jacob Greene, Aug. 11, 1777, NGP, vol. 2, p. 137.

"with so many losses": Jacob Greene to Nathanael Greene, May 7, 1777, NGP, vol. 2, p. 73.

"Great things may yet be done": Nathanael Greene to Griffin Greene, May 25, 1778, NGP, vol. 2, p. 405.

106 *"the finest circle of ladies"*: Stegeman, p. 61.

107 *"However just and upright"*: East, p. 87.

"the valuable prizes": George Washington to Major General William Heath, Sept. 30, 1777, NDAR, vol. 9, p. 982.

"The case is very different": Isaac Smith, Sr., to John Adams, Aug. 13, 1777, NDAR, vol. 9, p. 739.

108 *"no objection to sporting"*: Nathanael Greene to Samuel A. Otis, July 4, 1779, NGP, vol. 4, p. 203.

"I don't wish to become an adventurer": Nathanael Greene to Samuel A. Otis, Sept. 17, 1779, NGP, vol. 4, p. 394.

"ruined the place": Hedges, p. 282.

"play them like a trick": John B. Livingston to Robert R. Livingston, Oct. 11, 1776, NDAR, vol. 6, p. 1213.

109 *"This harbor"*: James Warren to Samuel Adams, Nov. 18, 1776, NDAR, vol. 7, p. 195.

"money crazy": East, p. 73.

"exorbitant sum": Ibid., p. 74.

1778 Barbados, West Indies

110 *"I fear nothing"*: Captain Nicholas Biddle to Charles Biddle, June 16, 1775, NDAR, vol. 5, p. 564.

"avoid two-deckers": Robert Morris to Captain Nicholas Biddle, Jan. 30, 1777, NDAR, vol. 7, p. 1064.

"strike a stroke": Marine Committee to Captain Nicholas Biddle, April 26, 1777, NDAR, vol. 8, p. 441.

112 *"missing at sea"* through *"long absent"*: Tagney, p. 396.

SIX

113   *"their chief maritime strength"*: Vice Admiral Richard Lord Howe to Commodore Sir Peter Parker, Dec. 22, 1776, NDAR, vol. 7, p. 552.
"Our people may as well fight": John Adams to Major Joseph Ward, July 17, 1776, NDAR, vol. 5, p. 1118.
"At Providence, I fear": John Adams to James Warren, April 6, 1777, NDAR, vol. 8, p. 281.

114   *"low ebb"*: East, p. 51.
suppressed the county's fishing and sea trade: Tagney, p. 238.
"what they dig up on wharfs": David Cobb to Robert Treat Paine, Sept. 9, 1776, NDAR, vol. 6, p. 754.
"assimilate with the brains": New York Journal, July 11, 1776, NDAR, vol. 5, p. 1028.
"privateering mad": James Warren to Samuel Adams, Aug. 15, 1776, NDAR, vol. 6, p. 191.
"Dutch cap, check shirt": Tagney, p. 235.

117   *"certain men"*: Boatner, p. 99.
"all the Continental prizes": Marine Committee to John Bradford, Aug. 6, 1776, *Letters of Delegates to Congress, 1774–1789*, Library of Congress.
"now are an ornament": John Bradford to John Hancock, June 20, 1776, NDAR, vol. 5, p. 635.
"superintend over the whole": Hearn, p. 170.

118   *"all at variance"* through *"not the least probability"*: John Bradford to John Hancock, July 1, 1776, NDAR, vol. 5, p. 849.
"so important a station": John Bradford to Robert Morris, May 30, 1776, NDAR, vol. 5, p. 304.
"The powder ship was taken": John Bradford to Robert Morris, July 14, 1776, NDAR, vol. 5, p. 1071.

119   *"men too little impressed"*: John Bradford to George Washington, July 29, 1776, NDAR, vol. 5, p. 1269.
"great complaints are made": John Bradford to George Washington, Aug. 12, 1776, NDAR, vol. 6, p. 153.
"the smallest inclination": George Washington to John Hancock, Aug. 7, 1776, NDAR, vol. 6, p. 98.
"the pivot": Introduction, NDAR, vol. 3, p. xiii.
"our first great admiral:" Dudley W. Knox, *The Naval Genius of George Washington*, p. 1.

120   *"for my account"*: John Bradford to John Daniel Schweighauser, Nantes Merchant, Nov. 1, 1776, NDAR, vol. 7, p. 4.
"a notorious fact": John Bradford to Robert Morris, Sept. 4, 1776, NDAR, vol. 6, p. 690.

120 *"there are schemes on foot":* John Langdon to William Whipple, Aug. 5, 1776, NDAR, vol. 6, p. 55.

"the exigency of the army": John Bradford to the Continental Marine Committee, April 9, 1777, NDAR, vol. 8, p. 302.

121 *"great bickering and uneasiness":* John Bradford to the Secret Committee, Jan. 17, 1777, NDAR, vol. 7, p. 980.

"could not be trusted": Hearn, p. 204.

"We find complaints are made": Ibid., p. 235.

"this growing evil" through *"like pirates":* John Bradford to George Washington, Aug. 12, 1776, NDAR, vol. 6, p. 153.

122 *"That such despicable characters":* John Paul Jones to Joseph Hewes, Jan. 12, 1777, NDAR, vol 7, p. 937.

"blunt, honest": Philip Chadwick Foster Smith, *Fired By Manley Zeal,* p. 43.

"with a cutlass": Joshua Davis, *A Narrative of Joshua Davis,* p. 5.

123 *"a ship and a wheelbarrow":* James Warren to John Adams, Feb. 22, 1777, NDAR, vol. 7, p. 1257.

"therefore exerted himself": Smith, p. 41.

"such creatures as himself": Ibid., p. 43.

"as the jackal does the lion": Ibid., p. 47.

"impudent": Ibid., p. 41.

"drones": Ibid., p. 51.

124 *"like the Jews and Samaritans":* Ibid., p. 47.

"not less than 10,000": Benjamin Rush to Richard Henry Lee, Dec. 21, 1776, NDAR, vol. 76, p. 543.

"The government has been forward": Petition of the Agents for the Privateer Ship *American Tartar* to the Massachusetts General Court, March 22, 1777, NDAR, vol. 8, p. 179.

"if the terms suit me": Elias Hasket Derby to the Massachusetts Board of War, March 3, 1777, NDAR, vol. 8, p. 17.

"execrate the policy": James Warren to John Adams, April 23, 1777, NDAR, vol. 8, p. 405.

"I am sorry the embargo": John Adams to James Warren, April 6, 1777, NDAR, vol. 8, p. 282.

"foremast men": *Williamson's Liverpool Advertiser and Mercantile Chronicle,* Dec. 27, 1776, NDAR, vol. 7, p. 808.

125 *"a rope in the night":* Captain Thomas Thompson to John Langdon, Sept. 8, 1777, NDAR, vol. 9, p. 895.

"16 killed": Acting Lieutenant Charles Jordan to Vice Admiral Clark Gayton, Oct. 19, 1777, NDAR, vol. 10, p. 217.

126 *"We are endeavoring":* James Warren to John Adams, April 23, 1777, NDAR, vol. 8, p. 282.

"This has roused the indignation" through *"life or limbs":* James Warren to John Adams, April 27, 1777, NDAR, vol. 8, p. 452.

126 *"take off the restrictions"*: Owners of Massachusetts Privateers to the Massachusetts General Court, April 19, 1777, NDAR, vol. 8, p. 375.

127 *"stinking New England rum"*: Officers of the Continental Navy Frigate *Boston* to Captain Hector McNeill, April 24, 1777, NDAR, vol. 8, p. 419.
"The owners are willing": Report to the Massachusetts General Court of the Committee appointed to confer with Captain John Manley, April 21, 1777, NDAR, vol. 8, p. 390.
"The profit to you": John Adams to James Warren, May 6, 1777, NDAR, vol. 8, p. 920.
"If we should fall in": Smith, p. 52.
"swinging a great cutlass": Ibid., p. 59.

128 *"irresolute and undecided"*: Ibid., p. 87.
"with many oaths": Ibid., p. 85.
"poured a number of shot": Captain Sir George Collier to Philip Stephens, July 12, 1777, NDAR, vol. 9, p. 272.
"sad reverse": James Warren to John Adams, Aug. 19, 1777, NDAR, vol. 9, p. 730.
"redeem poor Manley": John Bradford to Robert Morris, Sept. 17, 1777, NDAR, vol. 9, p. 934.
"overbearing haughtiness": James Warren to John Adams, Oct. 12, 1777, NDAR, vol. 10, p. 124.

129 *"good fortune seems to stick"*: Stephen Moylan to William Watson, Dec. 13, 1775, NDAR, vol. 3, p. 81.

130 *"wish to God it had been my head"*: Smith, p. 87.
"the only man of real courage": Ibid., p. 87.

1779 PENOBSCOT, MAINE

131 *"no general sense of urgency"*: Tagney, p. 369.

132 *"a reinforcement of heavy ships"*: Ibid., p. 367.
claimed the lives of hundreds: Ibid., p. 378.
"Our irregular troops": George E. Buker, *The Penobscot Expedition*, p. 109.
"brave experienced good officers": Tagney, p. 380.

133 *"since deceased"*: Buker, p. 123.
"that you may regain the character": Ibid., p. 163.

SEVEN

134 *"utmost bad consequence"*: Smith, p. 87.
"very successful against the Americans": "Extract of a letter from Antigua, April 2," NDAR, vol. 8, p. 260.

135 *"dying apace"*: Ambrose Serle to Lord Dartmouth, April 3, 1777, NDAR, vol. 8, p. 266.

"Put no confidence": "Extract of a Letter from a Gentleman on board the *Roebuck*," *The General Advertiser, Liverpool*, NDAR, vol. 8, p. 61.

"we shall all die with hunger": "Extract of a Letter from Grenada," April 18, 1777, NDAR, vol. 8, p. 372.

that number increased fivefold: M. Garnier to Vergennes, Sept. 10, 1776, NDAR, vol. 6, p. 597.

"all the advantages of war": "Extract of a letter from an English gentleman at Martinico, dated March 21," NDAR, vol. 8, p. 176.

"No step the Ministry could take": "Extract of a letter from St. Vincent's to a merchant in Liverpool, dated May 5," NDAR, vol. 8, p. 917.

"An open enemy": "News from St. Christopher," April 16, 1777, NDAR, vol. 8, p. 355.

136 *"these Dutch browse"*: M. Garnier to Vergennes, Aug. 16, 1776, NDAR, vol. 7, p. 549.

"so far debased": Admiral James Young to Governor Johannes de Graaf, Dec. 14, 1776, NDAR, vol. 7, p. 86.

"guarding a coast 1500 miles long": Marquis de Noailles to Vergennes, April 4, 1776, NDAR, vol. 8, p. 741.

"petitioning for an accommodation": *Boston Gazette*, Dec. 30, 1776, NDAR, vol. 7, p. 625.

"much is risked and nothing gained": The Committee of Secret Correspondence to Silas Deane, Aug. 7, 1776, NDAR, vol. 6, p. 102.

137 *"All reports to the contrary"*: *Public Advertiser*, Jan. 30, 1777, NDAR, vol. 8, p. 554.

"They have no idea": "Extract of a letter from an officer on board the *Eagle*, off New York, June 9," NDAR, vol. 9, p. 78.

"manifesting their real weakness": Estienne Cathalan to Willing, Morris, & Company, June 6, 1776, NDAR, vol. 6, p. 406.

"unmanly way of fighting": Narrative of Colonel Ethan Allen, May 3–20, 1776, NDAR, vol. 5, p. 175.

"against the laws of God": Commodore Sir Peter Parker to Vice Admiral Richard Lord Howe, Dec. 12, 1776, NDAR, vol. 7, p. 457.

"all the horrors of rebellion": Captain John Macartney, R.N., to Commodore Sir Peter Parker, Dec. 12, 1776, NDAR, vol. 7, p. 456.

138 *"piratical"*: Captain Andrew Snape Hamond to Hans Stanley, Sept. 24, 1776, NDAR, vol. 6, p. 973.

so few American captives opted to switch sides: Narrative of Captain Andrew Snape Hamond, Sept. 2–30, 1776, NDAR, vol. 6, p. 1065.

"coming in for them by hundreds": Ambrose Serle to the Earl of Dartmouth, Jan. 1, 1777, NDAR, vol. 7, p. 832.

"to prosecute this diabolical war": Major Charles Stuart to his father, the Earl of Bute, Jan. 1, 1777, NDAR, vol. 7, p. 827.

138   *"the great superiority of the English navy":* M. Garnier to Vergennes, June 24, 1776, NDAR, vol. 6, p. 444.
"defensive kind of war" through *"favorable moment":* Narrative of Captain Andrew Snape Hamond, Nov.–Dec., 1776, NDAR, vol. 7, p. 665.

139   *"of very little consequence":* Narrative of Captain Andrew Snape Hamond, Jan.–March, 1777, NDAR, vol. 8, p. 149.

140   *"Upon casting up accounts":* William Bingham to Silas Deane, Sept. 29, 1776, NDAR, vol. 6, p. 1046.
"insufficient resources": M. Garnier to Vergennes, June 24, 1776, NDAR, vol. 6, p. 444.
"disturbances in several places": Mercure de France, December 1766, NDAR, vol. 7, p. 722.
"public opinion and the law": N.A.M. Rodger, *The Wooden World*, p. 164.
"about thirty men drowned or wounded": Marquis de Noailles to Vergennes, Nov. 1, 1776, NDAR, vol. 7, p. 722.

141   *"the present barbarous war":* "Extracts from Parliamentary Debates," NDAR, vol. 7, p. 719.
"It is unnecessary to say" through *"disagreeable appearance":* "Extracts from Parliamentary Debates," NDAR, vol. 7, p. 720.
"It is beginning to snatch away": Marquis de Noailles to Vergennes, Nov. 22, 1776, NDAR, vol. 7, p. 754.
"most of the men withdrew": Marquis de Noailles to Vergennes, Nov. 1, 1776, NDAR, vol. 7, p. 723.

142   *"the first example of resistance":* Marquis de Noailles to Vergennes, Dec. 17, 1776, NDAR, vol. 7, p. 794.
"cruel, persecuting" through *"every part of the realm":* Cohen, p. 28.
"the precarious tenure": Journal of Samuel Curwen, Feb. 20, 1777, NDAR, vol. 8, p. 599.
"ineffectually petitioned against it": Jonathan Williams, Jr., to the Secret Committee, March 11, 1777, NDAR, vol. 8, p. 665.
"A shocking place" through *"into paradise":* Cohen, p. 55.

143   *"negligence or connivance":* Ibid., p. 68.
"than Turkish enemies": John Porter to Benjamin Franklin, June 6, 1777, NDAR, vol. 9, p. 381.
"gallows will be our destiny": Cohen, p. 92.

144   *"little short of civil war":* Ibid., p. 94.
"cruising for northward vessels": Connecticut Gazette, Nov. 1, 1776, NDAR, vol. 7, p. 7.
"the needs of merchant shipping": Marquis de Noailles to Vergennes, Dec. 27, 1776, NDAR, vol. 7, p. 809.

145   *"our very heavy losses":* Owners instructions to Captain William Bell, Jan. 31, 1777, NDAR, vol 7, p. 1074.
"all manner of assistance": James Young to Governor Johannes de Graaf, Dec. 14, 1776, NDAR, vol. 7, p. 486.

145 *not only tolerated privateers, but invested in them:* Vice Admiral James Young to Governor Johannes de Graaf, Dec. 14, 1776, NDAR, vol. 7, p. 486.

146 *"these seas now swarm":* Vice Admiral James Young to Philip Stephens, March 9, 1777, NDAR, vol. 8, p. 70.

"upward of fifty sail": "Extract of a letter from Philadelphia," Jan. 26, 1776, NDAR, vol. 7, p. 1046.

"the acts of violence": Count d'Argout to Vice Admiral James Young, Feb. 2, 1777, NDAR, vol. 7, p. 1088.

"not only illegal": Vice Admiral James Young to Governor Craister Greathead, Jan. 16, 1777, NDAR, vol. 7, p. 976.

147 *"seizing and sending into port":* Vice Admiral James Young to Philip Stephens, March 8, 1777, NDAR, vol. 8, p. 62.

"support and protection": Vice Admiral James Young to Philip Stephens, March 8, 1777, NDAR, vol. 8, p. 64.

"Three years in this climate": Vice Admiral James Young to the Earl of Sandwich, Oct. 28, 1777, NDAR, vol. 10, p. 335.

"They have many pirates out": *Pennsylvania Journal*, April 23, 1777, NDAR, vol. 8, p. 411.

148 *"hostility toward neutral flags":* Marquis de Noailles to Vergennes, April 4, 1777, vol. 8, p. 741.

"One son of a bitch": Captain Cornelius White to T.J. & W. Cochran, Halifax, May 15, 1777, NDAR, vol. 8, p. 971.

"349 slaves": "Extract of a letter from a Mate of the *Derby*, to his brother in Liverpool, dated Dominica, Oct. 28, 1777," *London Packet*, Jan. 19–21, 1777, NDAR, vol. 10, p. 337.

"dissatisfied at their taking": "Extract of a Letter from Capt. Cook, Commander of the *Black Prince*, from Senegal, to Dominica with 215 Slaves, lately taken by an American Privateer, to his owners," *Daily Advertiser,* Jan. 2, 1778, NDAR, vol. 10, p. 173.

"At present we are in some danger": Marquis de Lafayette to Adrienne de Noailles de Lafayette, May 30, 1777, NDAR, vol. 6, p. 1046.

149 *"Shall we say they are pirates":* M. Garnier to Vergennes, July 26, 1776, NDAR, vol. 6, p. 505.

"We may venture to assure you": Lords Commissioners, Admiralty, to Lord Weymouth., Sept. 27, 1777, NDAR, vol. 9, p. 663.

"put things aright": Vergennes to the Marquis de Noailles, Sept. 27, 1777, NDAR, vol. 9, p. 666.

1779 New London, Connecticut

150 *"with drawn swords"* through *"exchange of prisoners":* Christopher Vail, *Christopher Vail's Journal (1775–1782)*.

151 *"ship to ship slogging match"*: Robert Gardiner, ed., *Navies and the American Revolution 1775–1783*. p.109.
"an accident" through *"two years, four months"*: Vail, *Journal*.

EIGHT

155 *"not to live"*: Silas Deane to Beaumarchais, March 24, 1777, NDAR, vol. 8, p. 705.
"covetous": Augur, p. 196.
"all the committees": Committee of Secret Correspondence Memorandum, Oct. 11, 1776, NDAR, vol. 6, p. 1086.
156 *"faithless principles"* through *"witch brew"*: Augur, p. 217.
157 *"I have been a servant"*: Ibid., p. 291.
"haughty": Stacy Schiff, *A Great Improvisation*, p. 217.
"His tricks": Augur, p. 294.
"little, hissing": Schiff, p. 204.
158 *"quicken the resentments"*: William Bingham to Continental Congress Secret Committee, Dec. 28, 1777, NDAR, vol. 10, p. 821.
"with a little encouragement": Augur, p. 234.
"insidious subtlety": Lord Stormont to Lord Weymouth, Oct. 3, 1776, NDAR, vol. 6, p. 629.
"gratitude and affection": American Commissioners in France to Vergennes, July 17, 1777, NDAR, vol. 9, p. 510.
159 *"pushed with vigor"*: Augur, p. 168.
"The latter appears": "Statement concerning the employment of Lieut. Col. Edward Smith with regard to Captain Hynson and a Sketch of the Information Obtained," March 31, 1777, NDAR, vol. 8, p. 725.
"of infinite prejudice": Silas Deane to Robert Morris, August 23, 1777, SDP, vol. 2, p. 106.
"He daily proves himself": Benjamin Franklin to the President of Congress, March 31, 1778, SDP, vol. 2, p. 445.
"he has enemies": Augur, p. 269.
160 *"over the sea captains"*: Ibid., p. 236.
"done with advantage": "Statement concerning the employment of Lieut. Col. Edward Smith with regard to Captain Hynson and a Sketch of the Information Obtained," March 31, 1777, NDAR, vol. 8, p. 729.
161 *"much addicted to lying"*: James Breck Perkins, *France in the American Revolution*, p. 55.
162 *"The great object"*: "Statement concerning the employment of Lieut. Col. Edward Smith with regard to Captain Hynson and a Sketch of the Information Obtained," March 31, 1777, NDAR, vol. 8, p. 728.
"from some quarter or other": Augur, p. 176.

162 *"When all are ready"*: Ibid., p. 177.

"distress caused by weather": E. Gordon Bowen-Hassell, *Sea Raiders of the American Revolution*, p. 10.

163 *"some convenient place"*: Augur, p. 221.

"Is this not acknowledging": *Public Advertiser*, Jan. 20, 1777, NDAR, vol. 8, p. 538.

164 *"Carmichael and myself"*: Augur, p. 224.

"as to the illegality": Bowen-Hassell, p. 7.

"intelligence that may arrive": Ruth Y. Johnstone, "American Privateers in French Ports," p. 357.

"the registers must not": Vergennes to M. de Clugny, Sept. 22, 1776, NDAR, vol. 6, p. 609.

165 *"if there had been fraud"*: Johnstone, p. 361.

"humane treatment": *The General Advertiser*, Liverpool, Friday, July 4, 1777, NDAR, vol. 9, p. 455.

"They pay very little regard": Captain Lambert Wickes to the American Commissioners, June 28, 1777, NDAR, vol. 9, p. 441.

166 *"The prizes are sold"*: Silas Deane to Robert Morris, Aug. 23, 1777, SDP, vol. 2, p. 107.

"sequestered and detained": Vergennes to Benjamin Franklin and Silas Deane, July 16, 1777, NDAR, vol. 9, p. 501.

"Vergennes insisted": Lord Stormont to Lord Weymouth, July 30, 1777, NDAR, vol. 9, p. 540.

"usual frivolous answer": Lord Stormont to Lord Weymouth, Nov. 5, 1777, NDAR, vol. 10, p. 973.

"This sort of war": Vergennes to the Marquis de Noailles, July 26, 1777, NDAR, vol. 9, p. 536.

"if you are taken": Captain Lambert Wickes to Captain Henry Johnson, Sept. 14, 1777, NDAR, vol. 10, p. 640.

"5 a.m. saw a sail": Journal of H.M. Cutter *Alert*, Lieutenant John Bazely, Sept. 19, 1777, NDAR, vol. 9, p. 651.

167 *"would not stand"*: Johnstone, p. 365.

"a very worthy man": Bowen-Hassell, p. 14.

"the distressed situation": Captains Lambert Wickes and Samuel Nicholson to the American Commissioners in France, Sept. 6, 1777, NDAR, vol. 9, p. 631.

"We received the enclosed": Augur, p. 244.

1780 NEWFOUNDLAND, CANADA

168 *"Ships were building"* through *"very unwell"*: Andrew Sherburne, *Memoirs of Andrew Sherburne*.

NINE

173 *"I always acted under orders"*: Robert Wilden Neeser, ed., *Letters and Papers Relating to the Cruises of Gustavus Conyngham, a Captain of the Continental Navy 1777–1779*, p. 218.
"this piratical enterprise": Perkins, p. 162.

174 *"The capture of the* Orange*" through "prize money"*: *Public Advertiser*, Thursday, May 15, 1777, NDAR, vol. 8, p. 847.

175 *"strong proof"*: George III to Lord North, May 14, 1777, NDAR, vol. 8, p. 844.
"It matters little": Vergennes to Marquis de Noailles, May 31, 1777, NDAR, vol. 8, p. 880.
"Whatever may be the strength": Vergennes to Marquis de Noailles, May 31, 1777, NDAR, vol. 8, p. 881.

176 *"to stumble on a war"*: Jonathan Williams, Jr., to the American Commissioners in France, Feb. 22, 1777, NDAR, vol. 8, p. 604.
"an act so notorious": Augur, p. 163.
"part owner": John Ross to Arthur Lee, Dec. 3, 1777, NDAR, vol. 10, p. 1064.
Deane bought his stake: East, p. 134.
"painted blue and yellow": Neeser, p. 46.
"desperadoes": "Extract of a letter from Havre de Grace, dated June 19," London Packet, June 25 to June 27, 1777, NDAR, vol. 9, p. 411.

177 *"reprisal for damages sustained"*: Neeser, p. 64.
"verbal explanations": Ibid., p. 2.
"no interest in diplomacy": Bowen-Hassell, p. 32.
"his bold expeditions": Neeser, p. 96.
"things too glaring": Ibid., p. 26.
"changing the ownership": Augur, p. 192.
"a very serious fault": Ibid., p. 193.
"done by Mr. Deane": Neeser, p. 111.

178 *"declaring them and their countrymen"*: Augur, p. 231.
"Hodge is set at liberty": Neeser, p. 110.
"Now it was Britain's enemies": Donald A. Petrie, *The Prize Game*, p. 21.

180 *"Individuals who may be concerned"*: Neeser, p. 131.
"artful and wicked": Ibid., p. 123.
"whether you understand it so": Arthur Lee to John Ross, Nov. 26, 1777, NDAR, vol. 10, p. 1040.
"misrepresented or misconstrued": John Ross to Silas Deane, Dec. 16, 1777, NDAR, vol. 10, p. 1106.
"all the money he will ask": Neeser, p. 131.
"a letter of credit": Ibid., p. 195.

181 *"turned to little account"*: Ibid., p. 145.

181 *"unsuccessful, expensive cruises"* through *"under private instructions"*: John Ross to Arthur Lee, Dec. 3, 1777, NDAR, vol. 10, p. 1064.
"prejudicial to our affairs": Silas Deane's Narrative, read before Congress, SDP, vol. 3, p. 144.

182 *"try her chance to America"*: Neeser, p. 133.
"bounty": Ibid., p. 151.

183 *"I admit that the command"*: Ibid., p. 220.
"financial accounts": Bowen-Hassell, p. 40.
"sacredly promised" through *"I was then possessed of"*: Neeser, p. 220.

184 *"Arthur Lee, Esquire"*: Ibid., p. 158.
"paid on public account": Ferguson, p. 88.
"eyes sparkling": Silas Deane to Edward Bancroft, Feb. 1777, SDP, vol. 2, p. 9.

185 *"about three pound"*: Jessica Warner, *The Incendiary*, p. 115.
"to destroy, at one blow": Silas Deane to Edward Bancroft, Feb. 1777, SDP, vol. 2, p. 6.
"I feel more": Warner, p. 232.
"gravity given to the matter": Ibid., p. 231.

186 *"a long indisposition"*: Silas Deane to Charles W. F. Dumas, Oct. 1, 1777, SDP, vol. 2, p. 164.
"as obnoxious to England": Silas Deane to Barnabas Deane, Oct. 7, 1777, SDP, vol. 2, p. 177.
"my only hope": Silas Deane to Barnabas Deane, April 20, 1780, SDP, vol. 4, p. 130.
"in high spirits": Silas Deane to Conrad A. Gerard, May 11, 1777, SDP, vol. 2, p. 52.
"The two ships": Lord Stormont to Lord Weymouth, July 2, 1777, NDAR, vol. 9, p. 452.
"a smile of heaven": John Bradford to John Hancock, March 20, 1777, NDAR, vol. 8, p. 155.

187 *"no return was expected"*: Arthur Lee to the Committee of Commerce, Aug. 16, 1777, NDAR, vol. 9, p. 572.
"The king furnished nothing": Morton and Spinelli, p. 201.
"everything he says": Augur, p. 137.
"This gentleman is not a merchant": Arthur Lee to the Committee of Commerce, Aug. 16, 1777, NDAR, vol. 9, p. 573.

188 *"You are sensible"*: Silas Deane to the Committee of Commerce, Sept. 3, 1777, NDAR, vol. 9, p. 625.
"as much general joy": Augur, p. 252.

189 *"all the fruits of this war"*: Ibid., p. 260.
"their borrowed plumes": Arthur Lee to Theodoric Bland, Dec. 13, 1778, SDP, vol. 3, p. 80.

190 *"complimentary to your abilities"*: Augur, p. 280.
"I have in my possession": Beaumarchais to Vergennes, March 13, 1778, SDP, vol. 2. p. 399.

190   *"retire with honor":* Silas Deane to Jonathan Williams, March 21, 1778, SDP, vol. 2, p. 421.

191   *"zeal, activity, and intelligence":* Vergennes to the president of Congress, March 25, 1778, SDP, vol. 2, p. 434.
      "It is hinted now": William Lee to Francis Lightfoot Lee, Nov. 11, 1777, SDP, vol. 2, p. 213.

192   *"Adams-Lee junto":* Ferguson, p. 94.
      "open dissensions": Augur, p. 274.
      "a man of integrity": Benjamin Franklin to James Lovell, Oct. 17, 1779, SDP, vol. 4, p. 109.

193   *"if America should be successful":* "Statement concerning the employment of Lieut. Col. Edward Smith with regard to Captain Hynson and a Sketch of the Information Obtained," March 31, 1777, NDAR, vol. 8, p. 728.
      "a few hours' notice": Silas Deane to William Carmichael, June 30, 1784, SDP, vol. 5, p. 318.
      "I thought it was likewise": Morton and Spinelli, p. 199.

194   *"this business with Conyngham":* Neeser, p. 149.
      "the localist and power-weakening emphasis": Wood, p. 146.
      "The rancor it left": Ferguson, p. 104.

195   *"I can only lament":* Arthur Lee to Samuel Adams, April 21, 1782, *Letters of Delegates to Congress: March 1, 1781–August 31, 1781.*

1782 Portsmouth, England

196   *"complicated affairs":* Neeser, p. 156.
      "her teeth were too many": Ibid., p. xlviii.
      "You will go next": Ibid., p. 159.

197   *"is therefore sent to England":* Ibid., p. 183.
      "in close confinement": Ibid., p. 186.
      "Your king will not reward you": William Bell Clark, p. 12.

198   *"upon account of debtor and creditor":* Ibid., p. 13.
      "hang for high treason": Ibid., p. 14.

199   *"I think it right":* Ibid., p. 120.
      "for the inoculation": Ibid., p. 175.
      "committed treason" through *"petty tyrants":* Neeser, p. 190.

Ten

201   *"What I have been dreading":* Stegeman, p. 81.

202   *"first American civil war":* Thomas E. Griess, ed., *Early American Wars and Military Institutions*, p. 28.
      "One hundred and eighty miles": Boatner, p. 415.

204 *"ill planned"* through *"between them and ruin"*: Nathanael Greene to John Brown, Sept. 6, 1778, NGP, vol. 2, p. 507.
"Your family": Nathanael Greene to John Brown, Oct. 4, 1778, NGP, vol. 2, p. 539.

205 *"He is either a spy"*: Harvey, p. 346.
"an unfortunate dog": Nathanael Greene to Jeremiah Wadsworth, Aug. 29, 1780, NGP, vol. 6, p. 245.

206 *"There is no help"*: Nathanael Greene to Jeremiah Wadsworth, May 8, 1780, NGP, vol. 5, p. 550.
"destroyed all our plans": Jacob Greene to Nathanael Greene, May 7, 1780, NGP, vol. 5, p. 549.
"We purchased a small part": Jacob Greene to Nathanael Greene, Sept. 7, 1780, NGP, vol. 6, p. 269.
"the locusts of Egypt": Harvey, p. 372.

207 *"unless you have a good army"*: Ibid., p. 373
"Thus separated": Editor's Introduction, NGP, vol. 6.

208 *"A few such victories"*: Nathanael Greene to Nicholas Cooke, June 22, 1775, NGP, vol. 1, p.89.
"the amazing success": Jeremiah Wadsworth to Nathanael Greene, July 10, 1782, NGP, vol. 11, p. 429.
"the smiles of fortune" through *"for our industry"*: Nathanael Greene to Griffin Greene, Oct. 22, 1780, NGP, vol. 6, p. 422.

209 *"we will suffer deeply"*: Charles Pettit to Nathanael Greene, Aug. 23, 1781, NGP, vol. 9, p. 227.
"I take this opportunity": John Cox to Nathanael Greene, Sept. 20, 1781, NGP, vol. 9, p. 338.
"I venture to lean": Charles Pettit to Nathanael Greene, June 14, 1782, NGP, vol. 11, p. 330.
"fate will have it otherwise": Nathanael Greene to Jeremiah Wadsworth, Feb. 9, 1782, NGP, vol. 10, p. 337.

210 *"I am glad of it"*: Nathanael Greene to Jeremiah Wadsworth, July 1, 1782, NGP, vol. 11, p. 389.
"a state of perplexity": Jacob Greene to Nathanael Greene, May 4, 1783, NGP, vol. 12, p. 640.
"judge us as we deserve": Griffin Greene to Nathanael Greene, May 21, 1783, NGP, vol. 12, p. 677.
"My disappointment is considerable": Griffin Greene to Nathanael Greene, June 10, 1783, NGP, vol. 12, p. 690.
"To have a decent income": Stegeman, p. 112.

211 *"Mr. Morris the financier"*: Nathanael Greene to John Banks, April 23, 1782, NGP, vol. 11, p. 105.
"this oppressed country": Nathanael Greene to John Banks, Dec. 25, 1782, NGP, vol. 12, p. 345.

212 *"He had the example":* Nathanael Greene to Benjamin Harrison, March 28, 1783, NGP, vol. 12, p. 543.

"I cannot suppose": Statement of John Banks, Feb. 15, 1783, NGP, vol. 12, p. 444.

"his conduct made a subject": Statement of General Anthony Wayne and Colonel Edward Carrington, Feb. 15, 1783, NGP, vol. 12, p. 446.

213 *"I verily believe":* Stegeman, p. 112.

"I tremble": Ibid., p. 115.

"good man die": Ibid., p. 124.

"some would place him first": Griess, p. 32.

"never been much my friend": Nathanael Greene to Barnabas Deane, Dec. 25, 1782, NGP, vol. 12, p. 8.

"this day approved": Stegeman, p. 154.

1782 GUADELOUPE, WEST INDIES

214 *"a great coward":* Cohen, p. 190.

"the person after whom she was called": Charles Thompson to Robert Morris, June 1, 1782, *Letters of Delegates to Congress.*

"tribute to your honor": Tagney, p. 387.

215 *"much to be regretted":* Maclay, p. 206.

ELEVEN

216 *"I humbly think":* Brown, p. 72.

"I am unhappy": Ibid., p. 76.

217 *"our agent here":* Ibid., p. 76.

"more afflicted than surprised": Alberts, p. 454.

"nest of outlaws": Andrew Jackson O'Shaughnessy, *An Empire Divided*, p. 216.

218 *"You recollect":* Robert Morris to William Bingham, Oct. 1, 1778, *Letters of Delegates to Congress: October 1, 1777–January 31, 1779.*

219 *"Profitable private business":* Brown, p. 81.

220 *"wheeled oysters":* Wagner, p. 130.

"That the payments of debts": Morton and Spinelli, p. 322.

221 *"Large fortunes":* Alberts, p. 371.

222 *"I can neither think":* George L. Clark, *Silas Deane, a Connecticut Leader in the American Revolution*, p. 189.

"curse instead of a blessing": "To the Free and Independent Citizens of the United States of North-America," Nov. 3, 1783, SDP, vol. 5, p. 237.

"the same infamy": Boyd, I, p. 168.

"many serious truths": Joseph Reed to Nathanael Greene, Feb. 9, 1782, NGP, vol. 10, p. 337.

223 *"Is it become treason"*: Boyd, I, p. 170.
"*an exceeding good opinion*": Augur, p. 333.
"lest he should be led": Boyd, I, p. 191.
"make it impossible" and *"Even between enemies"*: Augur, p. 334.
"If America shall": Silas Deane to Benjamin Franklin, May 13, 1782, SDP, vol. 5, p. 88.

224 *"any want in probity"*: Boyd, III, p. 532.
"I am strongly inclined": Ibid., p. 530.
"colonial administration": Boyd, I, p. 539.

225 *"practicable and useful"*: Lord Dorchester to Lord Sydney, Oct. 24, 1787, SDP, vol. 5, p. 481.
"resentments toward": Robert Morris to Silas Deane, Dec. 5, 1785, SDP, vol. 5, p. 471.
"my hopes are revived": Silas Deane to George Washington, June 25, 1789, SDP, vol. 5, p. 525.
"There is no gravestone": Clark, Silas Deane, p. 253.
"abject poverty": Reprinted from a London newspaper in the *American Mercury*, Dec. 28, 1789, SDP, vol. 5, p. 533.
"a treacherous desertion": Boyd, I, p. 173.

226 *"to revenge past injuries"* through *"rejoice most at the event"*: Ibid., p. 179.
"pain and humiliation": Boyd, III, p. 548.
"a mysteriousness": Morton and Spinelli, p. 284.

227 *"compassionate feeling"*: Ibid., p. 285.

228 *"the heirs of Mr. Beaumarchais"*: Ibid., p. 322.

1782 Brooklyn, New York

229 *"We were out 25 days"* through *"when peace took place"*: Vail, *Journal*.

231 *"Some ambition"* through *"almost without parallel"*: Sherburne, *Memoirs*.

Twelve

233 *"social forces of the generation"*: East, p. 323.
"Like Puritanism": Wood, *The Creation of the American Republic, 1776–1787*, p. 418.
"the joint combination": Ibid., p. 420.

234 *"the principles and manners"* through *"Christian Sparta"*: Ibid., p. 423.
"Rich and numerous prizes": East, p. 213.
a logical move of upward mobility: Ibid., p. 214.

235 *Americans welcomed the glut*: Buel, p. 247.
there was enough supply: East, p. 246.

237   *"working through middlemen"* through *"daily expected"*: James A. Rawley, *The Transatlantic Slave Trade*, p. 349.

239   *"bettered their condition"*: Hedges, p. 84.
       "from necessity" through *"prosecuted more severely"*: Ibid., p. 83.
       "not be any more concerned": Thompson, p. 191.

240   *"hundreds there is"*: Ibid., p. 53.

1783 PROVIDENCE, RHODE ISLAND

241   *"I had some trying scenes"* through *"in the land of liberty"*: Sherburne, *Memoirs*.

BIBLIOGRAPHY

Books

Alberts, Robert C. *The Golden Voyage: The Life and Times of William Bingham.* Boston: Houghton Mifflin, 1969.

Allen, Gardner Weld. *Massachusetts Privateers of the Revolution.* Boston: Massachusetts Historical Society, 1927.

Augur, Helen. *The Secret War of Independence.* New York: Duell, Sloan & Pierce, 1955.

Beattie, Donald W. and J. Richard Collins. *Washington's New England Fleet; Beverly's Role in Its Origins 1775–77.* Salem: Newcomb & Gauss, 1969.

Beaumarchais, Pierre-Augustin Caron de. *The Figaro Trilogy.* Oxford: Oxford University Press, 2003.

Boatner, Mark M., III. *Encyclopedia of the American Revolution.* New York: Van Rees, 1966.

Bowen-Hassell, E. Gordon, Dennis Michael Conrad, and Mark L. Hayes. *Sea Raiders of the American Revolution: The Continental Navy in European Waters.* Washington, D.C.: Naval History Center, 2003.

Buchanan, John. *The Road to Guilford Courthouse.* New York: John Wiley & Sons, 1998.

Buel, Richard Jr. *In Irons: Britain's Naval Supremacy and the American Revolutionary Economy.* New Haven: Yale University, 1998.

Buker, George E. *The Penobscot Expedition: Commodore Saltonstall and the Massachusetts Conspiracy of 1779.* Annapolis: Naval Institute Press, 2002.

Clark, George L. *Silas Deane, a Connecticut Leader in the American Revolution.* New York: G. P. Putnam's Sons, 1913.

Clark, William Bell. *Ben Franklin's Privateers: A Naval Epic of the American Revolution.* New York: Greenwood Press, 1956.

Coggins, Jack. *Ships and Seamen of the American Revolution.* Harrisburg, Pennsylvania: Stackpole, 1969.

Cohen, Sheldon S. *Yankee Sailors in British Gaols: Prisoners of War at Forton and Mill, 1777–1783.* London: Associated University Presses, 1995.

Davis, Joshua. *A Narrative of Joshua Davis, an American Citizen who was Pressed and Served On Board Six Ships of the British Navy.* Boston: B. True, 1811.

East, Robert A. *Business Enterprise in the American Revolutionary Era.* New York: Columbia University, 1938.

Ellis, Joseph. *Founding Brothers: The Revolutionary Generation.* New York: Vintage, 2002.

Ferguson, E. James. *The Power of the Purse.* Chapel Hill: University of North Carolina, 1961.

Flexner, James Thomas. *George Washington in the American Revolution.* Boston: Little, Brown, 1967.

Freeman, Douglas Southall. *George Washington.* New York: Scribner's, 1951.

Fowler, William M., Jr. *Rebels Under Sail: The American Navy during the Revolution.* New York: Charles Scribner's Sons, 1976.

Gardiner, Robert, ed. *The Line of Battle: The Sailing Warship 1650–1840.* London: Conway Maritime Press, 1992.

———. *Navies and the American Revolution 1775–1783.* London: Chatham Publishing, 1996.

Griess, Thomas E., ed. *The West Point Military History Series: Early American Wars and Military Institutions.* Wayne, N.J.: Avery Publishing, 1986.

Harvey, Robert. *A Few Bloody Noses: The Realities and Mythologies of the American Revolution.* New York: Overlook, 2003.

Hearn, Chester G. *George Washington's Schooners.* Annapolis: Naval Institute Press, 1995.

Hedges, James. B. *The Browns of Providence Plantations: Colonial Years.* Cambridge: Harvard University, 1952.

Hielscher, Udo. *Financing the American Revolution.* New York: Museum of American Financial History, 2003.

Hurst, Ronald. *The Golden Rock: An Episode of the American War of Independence.* Annapolis: Naval Institute Press, 1996.

Jensen, Merrill. *The Founding of a Nation: A History of the American Revolution, 1763–1776.* Oxford: Oxford University Press, 1968.

Knox, Dudley W. *The Naval Genius of George Washington.* Boston: Houghton Mifflin, 1932.

Konstam, Angus and Angus McBride. *Privateers and Pirates: 1730–1830.* Oxford: Osprey, 2001.

Maclay, Edward Stanton. *A History of American Privateers.* New York: Burt Franklin, 1899.

McCullough, David. *1776.* New York: Simon & Schuster, 2005.

McDowell, Bart. *The Revolutionary War: America's Fight for Freedom.* Washington, D.C.: National Geographic Society, 1967.

McMillin, James A. *The Final Victims: Foreign Slave Trade to North America, 1783–1810.* Columbia: University of South Carolina, 2004.

Morton, Brian N. and Donald C. Spinelli. *Beaumarchais and the American Revolution.* New York: Lexington, 2003.

Neeser, Robert Wilden, ed. *Letters and Papers Relating to the Cruises of Gustavus*

Conyngham, a Captain of the Continental Navy 1777–1779. London: Kennikat, 1970.

O'Shaughnessy, Andrew Jackson. *An Empire Divided: The American Revolution and the British Caribbean.* Philadelphia: University of Pennsylvania, 2000.

Perkins, James Breck. *France in the American Revolution.* Whitefish, Montana: Kessinger Publishing, 2006.

Petrie, Donald A. *The Prize Game: Lawful Looting on the High Seas in the Days of Fighting Sail.* New York: Berkeley, 1999.

Rawley, James A., *The Transatlantic Slave Trade.* New York: W. W. Norton, 1981.

Rodger, N.A.M. *The Wooden World: An Anatomy of the Georgian Navy.* New York: W. W. Norton, 1996.

Royster, Charles. *A Revolutionary People at War: The Continental Army and American Character, 1775–1783.* New York: Norton, 1981.

Schiff, Stacy. *A Great Improvisation: Franklin, France, and the Birth of America.* New York: Henry Holt, 2005.

Sherburne, Andrew. *Memoirs of Andrew Sherburne: A Pensioner of the Navy of the Revolution.* Providence: M. M. Brown, 1831.

Smith, Philip Chadwick Foster. *Fired By Manley Zeal: A Naval Fiasco of the American Revolution.* Salem: Peabody Museum, 1977.

Staples, William R. *The Documentary Description of the Destruction of the Gaspee.* Providence: Rhode Island Publications Society, 1990.

Stegeman, John F. and Janet A. Stegeman. *Caty: A Biography of Catharine Littlefield Greene.* Athens: University of Georgia, 1977.

Tagney, Ronald N. *The World Turned Upside Down: Essex County During America's Turbulent Years, 1763–1790.* West Newbury: Essex County History, 1989.

Thomas, Evan. *John Paul Jones: Sailor, Hero, Father of the American Navy.* New York: Simon & Schuster, 2003.

Thompson, Mack. *Moses Brown: Reluctant Reformer.* Chapel Hill: University of North Carolina, 1962.

Wagner, Frederick. *Robert Morris: Audacious Patriot.* New York: Dodd, Mead, 1976.

Warner, Jessica. *The Incendiary: The Misadventures of John the Painter, First Modern Terrorist.* New York: Thunder's Mouth, 2004.

Whitehill, Walter Muir. *Captain Joseph Peabody.* Salem: Peabody Museum, 1962.

Wilbur, C. Keith. *Pirates & Patriots of the Revolution.* Philadelphia: Chelsea House, 1973.

Wood, Gordon S. *The American Revolution: A History.* New York: The Modern Library, 2002.

———. *The Creation of the American Republic, 1776–1787.* Chapel Hill: The University of North Carolina Press, 1969.

———. *The Radicalism of the American Revolution.* New York: Vintage, 1993.

Articles

Baack, Ben. "The Economics of the American Revolutionary War," EH.Net Encyclopedia, edited by Robert Whaples, Nov. 14, 2001. Accessed Sept. 5, 2005. <http://www.eh.net/encyclopedia/contents/baack/war.revolutionary .us.php>

—————. "Forging a Nation State: The Continental Congress and the Financing of the War of American Independence," *Economic History Review*, LIV, 4 (2001).

Boyd, Julian. "Silas Deane: Death by a Kindly Teacher of Treason?" *William and Mary Quarterly*, 3rd Series, vol. 16, nos. I, III, IV, April, July, Oct. 1959.

Brown, Margaret L. "William Bingham, Agent of the Continental Congress in Martinique," *Pennsylvania Magazine of History and Biography*, issue 61, Jan. 1937.

Cohen, Sheldon S. "Samuel Peters Comments on the Death of Silas Deane," *The New England Quarterly*, vol. 40, Sept. 1967.

Cook, Frank Gaylord. "Robert Morris." *The Atlantic Monthly*. vol. 66, issue 397: Nov. 1890. pp. 607–618.

Danforth, Susan. "No New Taxes! Conflicts that Led up to the Burning of the Gaspee." *The Bridge, Newspaper of the Pawtuxet Village Association*, Spring 2003.

Goldstein, Kalman. "Silas Deane: Preparation for Rascality." *The Historian*, vol. 43, no. I, Nov. 1980.

Goodrich, Casper F. "Washington's Attitude Toward the Navy." *The Washington Association of New Jersey Archive*, 1907.

Johnstone, Ruth Y. "American Privateers in French Ports, 1776–1778." *Pennsylvania Magazine of History & Biography* LIII (Oct. 1929), p. 352.

Skaaren, Lorna. "Robert R. Livingston and the American Revolution." *The Livingston Legacy: Three Centuries of American History*. From the symposium, June 6–7, 1986. Accessed March 6, 2006. <http://www.hrmm.org/ steamboats/livingston/skaaren.html>

Storch, Neil T. "The Recall of Silas Deane." *The Connecticut Historical Society Bulletin*, vol. 38, no. I, Jan. 1973.

Vail, Christopher. *Christopher Vail's Journal (1775–1782)*. Newsday.com: 2006. Accessed Nov. 3, 2006. http://www.newsday.com/community/guide/ lihistory/ny-historyhs401av1,0 ,1855052,print.story

Wilson, Sally D. "Who Was Whipple?" *Revolutionary Portraits: People, Places and Events from Rhode Island's Historic Past*. Providence: Rhode Island Bicentennial Foundation, 1976.

Index

Page numbers in *italics* refer to illustrations.

A Note on the Type

This book was set in Garamond. Based on the sixteenth-century types of Claude Garamond, this version by G. G. Lange was drawn for the Berthold foundry after studying specimens in Paris and Antwerp.

Composed by North Market Street Graphics,
Lancaster, Pennsylvania
Printed and bound by Berryville Graphics,
Berryville, Pennsylvania

Designed by Anthea Lingeman